Music from the Heart

~ Music from the Heart

Compositions of a Folk Fiddler

COLIN QUIGLEY

The University of Georgia Press

ATHENS & LONDON

© 1995 by the University of Georgia Press

Athens, Georgia 30602

All rights reserved

Designed by Kathi L. Dailey

Set in Berkeley Old Style

by Tseng Information Systems, Inc.

Printed and bound by Thomson-Shore, Inc.

The paper in this book meets the guidelines for permanence
and durability of the Committee on Production Guidelines
for Book Longevity of the Council on Library Resources.

Printed in the United States of America

99 98 97 96 95 C 5 4 3 2 1

Library of Congress Cataloging in Publication Data

Quigley, Colin.

    Music from the heart : compositions of a folk fiddler / Colin Quigley.

      p. cm.

    Includes bibliographical references and index.

    ISBN 0-8203-1637-7 (alk. paper)

    1. Benoit, Emile, 1913– . 2. Fiddle tunes—Newfoundland—
Port-au-Port Peninsula—History and criticism. 3. Folk music—
Newfoundland—Port-au-Port Peninsula—History and criticism.
I. Title.

ML418.B4135   1995

787.2′162′0092—dc20   93-39721

British Library Cataloging in Publication Data available

∼ Contents

~ Preface

In late August of 1978 I drove across the island of Newfoundland from the city of St. John's near Cape Spear, the easternmost point in North America, to the Port-au-Port Peninsula, which extends into the Gulf of St. Lawrence at the far west of the island, a twelve-hour trip in my Volkswagen bug on the two-lane Trans-Canada Highway. I had been living in Newfoundland that year as a graduate student of folklore at Memorial University. I made the trip, not just to camp in the provincial park at Picadilly Head as I did the day of my arrival, but rather to visit a man I had recently met, a fiddler who had performed at the provincial folk festival earlier that summer, Emile Benoit, a Frenchman of sixty-odd years, who lived a few miles further on, past the end of the paved road and nearly at the end of any road at all. He'd said, sure, to come visit him at home anytime, and I'd taken him at his word. After all, this was why I had come to Newfoundland, to meet a folk musician and hear him play at home—a genuine folk fiddler playing traditional music for the people he had grown up with, the people who shared that tradition. I had already encountered and come to love such music at home in the United States, but within a mediated milieu of records, tapes, festivals, and coffee houses. I had slowly worked my way closer to some of its sources by traveling with others who knew the way: to an old-time dance in southern New Hampshire; to a dance in West Virginia; to the New England Old Time Fiddlers Association contest in Barre, Vermont; to the Bunratty bar in the Bronx and Irish fiddlers playing loudly through pickups and amps; to another bar in New York's Greenwich Village, where my friends gathered to play and a young woman mentioned she had studied folk song in Newfoundland. So I had gone there and was now at the fiddler's doorstep, armed with a tape recorder, a camera, my fiddle, and some ideas about fieldwork, when I got cold feet. I couldn't simply arrive at his door! But I couldn't allow myself to give up after coming so far; I simply had to go on, and, after all, M. Benoit had invited me. I arrived. He wasn't at home, but his wife said, come in, he's out making hay.

Two weeks later I had more than a few blisters, a new musical mentor, and a friend with whom I would come to work in a variety of ways over the next ten years, through many changes in both our lives. I went on for another degree and moved to California; he became increasingly well-known and continued to play, to compose, and to perform more and more widely. Emile died just as I finished this writing in August 1992. I am grateful for the time we spent together and grateful, too, for his encouragement of my work and his exhortation as I struggled to compose a piece myself: "But you'll do something out of that, what you're doing there. . . . You got to try. You got [a] tape recorder. You got tapes, everything like that. . . . You got good fingers, eh? You can play some god damn nice stuff. Compose some nice stuff. You're allowed too!" (Q-tape 20).

Music from the Heart emerged from this relationship. It is an investigation of musical creativity in an oral tradition carried out through the close examination of an exemplary fiddler from French Newfoundland. It is a detailed study of a particular musician and his social milieu, which addresses the broad topic of creativity in tradition. A fine-grained picture of a North American instrumental tradition emerges by following the odyssey of this French-Newfoundland fiddler, Emile Benoit, through a changing musical milieu that spans most of the twentieth century and moves from a small rural community to international festivals.

Although an outline of the musical and social features of fiddling tradition in Newfoundland can be discerned from published, archival, and commercially recorded sources, little is known about many of the fiddlers whose playing has been recorded in these sources.[1] This lack of biographical information necessarily limits our understanding of the function of the music in the lives of musicians and their communities as well as of its history. The detailed information available from a few informants such as Emile, however, can compensate for this lack and provide insight into the dynamic play of forces shaping their recorded musical production.

Major features of fiddling tradition in Newfoundland are clearly revealed through examination of the experiences of an individual such as Emile.[2] Born in 1913, Emile became the preeminent dance musician of

Newfoundland's Port-au-Port Peninsula, a role he actively maintained until the early 1960s, when local musical tastes for public performance began to change under the influence of mainstream mass-mediated North American culture. During the late 1960s a movement for Newfoundland cultural re-vitalization opened new opportunities for his musical expression, and he once again became a premier performer in what is now a musical community of international scope.

Emile, however, is not only an undisputed representative of tradition. He provides an excellent focus for a study of creativity because it is also vividly apparent that he served as far more than a conduit for traditions. Emile was a self-conscious creator and innovator whose music "comes from the heart," as he explains it, whose compositions carry rich personal associations, and whose performances of them were meant to convey strongly felt values to his audiences. An analysis of how he thought about his music and how these conceptions were shaped is central to an understanding of the meaning of his music. Emile's musical thought processes are not atypical of the tradition. Rather, the intensity of his commitment to self-expression in this medium transformed his knowledge and skills into powerful tools for compositional creativity, highlighting the generative underpinnings of this musical tradition. The formal constraints on this music, which stem from its use as dance accompaniment, its dependence on aural transmission, and its aural (and tactile) compositional processes, however, do not limit its potential as a medium of self-expression. In fact, its relative formal simplicity may allow for a clearer perception of fundamental musical generative principles than is often possible within traditions employing more complex structures. Its detailed examination from this perspective reveals the distinctive place such oral traditions hold among the world's diverse systems of music making.

It would be possible to represent Emile's music as resulting from a confluence of influences, including French, Scottish, Canadian, Irish, and American fiddling, by employing conventional models of analysis which examine music structure, variation, and performance practice, but a more dynamic picture of this expressive system emerges when attention is focused explicitly on its generative processes. The compositional practice of Emile Benoit is thus at the center of this investigation, which opens upon many worlds of folk music today, in Newfoundland, in Canada, in North America, and elsewhere, for Emile traversed all of these places as a major player in the folk music venues of the world. The particularity of this research strategy offers an incisive view of the construction of this tradition, achieved by countless individuals working both in concert and contention as they strive to shape their experience in meaningful ways through artful representations.

A research perspective focusing on Emile's compositions, the "sound object," alone would not serve well an investigation of this man's music. Nor would a methodology that focused primarily on the social contexts of musical behavior throughout his community. Rather, my research perspective places the musician, who is viewed as the active agent of tradition, at the center of investigation. I explore both social and cognitive dimensions of music making through ethnographic methods, examining in detail the particular circumstances of Emile Benoit's life and music-making experiences to answer the questions I have posed. This approach applies emerging research paradigms in cultural and humanistic anthropology, ethnomusicology, and folklore, which call for attention to the role of individuals in the production of expressive behavior. My research and its presentation are structured by asking what life experiences influenced the values and beliefs that affected Emile's music making; what aspirations motivated him to compose and perform; what conceptions of himself and his role as a musician influenced his performances; what shaping influence might his training in the musical tradition have had; and what musical concepts inform his performances and compositions.

Direct observation of Emile's compositional practice combined with extended periods of participant observation in music making and interviewing to elicit self-reflective commentary on the act of composing provides the central data for examination of these processes. This approach differs somewhat from those that have dominated the investigation of North American instrumental music in particular and Western folk music in general. It thus provides a complementary alternative to what has been until recently an overwhelming emphasis on regional and historical explanatory frameworks in folk music scholarship (Elschek 1981, 70). Composition remains one of the "least studied and least well understood of all musical processes" within the field of musicology generally (Sloboda 1985, 103). Although the "raw materials used by composers" in the West have been studied for several centuries, very few scholars have addressed the "actual processes by which composers conceive melodic material," an observation equally applicable to studies of folk musicians (Sparks 1984, 104).

Individual musicians are the active agents of the creative process (Hopkins 1976). The values musicians hold as a result of their experience in particular societies combine with their musical knowledge in performing situations to shape the act of musical creation and give it meaning. Study of such individuals, their ideas, and their practice is thus central to an understanding of musical creativity. Within the broader field of anthropology, moreover, this approach has been described as well suited to the investigation of the meaning systems that give significance to culturally produced messages (D'Andrade 1984, 109). Along with James Porter, I would suggest that the study of individual performers is essential if we are to discover the meaning systems not only of traditional singing but of any musical community (1986, 24).

Folklore research has demonstrated that to understand such expressive processes as narrating or music making, one needs to take account of the performer's life experience, values, and conceptions of self and others as well as the "text" and its performance context. In anthropology the "historically situated, meaning-searching and strategizing subject" is increasingly a center of attention (A. Seeger 1987, 492–93). In ethnomusicology emphasis on the individual is a recent and as yet relatively weak area of development.[3] Study of selected individuals in this manner can support generalizations about creative and expressive processes in particular. Indeed, comparisons of musical creativity, innovation, and individual freedom within different musical systems have been called for by Bruno Nettl (1983, 25–35, 278–89), and John Blacking stresses that studies of musical creativity are fundamental to our understanding of any music:

> If the value of music in society and culture is to be assessed, it must be described in terms of the attitudes and creative processes involved in its creation, and the functions and effects of the musical product in society. . . . The value of music is . . . to be found in terms of the human experiences involved in its creation . . . and music that enhances human consciousness . . . music that is for being . . . is art, no matter how simple or complex it sounds, and no matter under what circumstances it is produced. (Blacking 1973, 53, 50)

This book is an attempt to detail the musical thought processes of an outstanding creator in a traditional idiom. It is a response to the challenge to explore the nature of musicality and discover its salient characteristics, its human constants and cultural variability (Blacking 1973, 50). I refer throughout the text to work in folklore studies and ethnomusicology that impinges on these concerns. Precedents for this study in the general literature of folklore and ethnomusicology are discussed, and the major concerns, perspectives, and methodologies that inform earlier scholarship are illustrated, primarily in the notes to each chapter. Through detailed examination of a wide range of factors influencing the compositional practice of a particular musician I hope to further understanding of the complex cognitive processes of musical composition and illuminate the musical expression of a talented performer and composer, at the same time revealing something of the dynamic site of artistic production and cultural representation which is folk music today.

∼ A Note on Sources

Citations from the collections of the Memorial University of Newfoundland Folklore and Language Archive (MUNFLA), which include copies of much of my own fieldwork materials, appear in the text as M-tape or M-MS together with an archival accession and shelf list numbers. Working copies of many of these tape recordings and manuscripts as well as other documents are held in the collections of the Centre d'Etudes Franco-terreneuviens (CEFT) and are so cited when appropriate. Some field recordings that remain in my possession alone at present are cited as Q-tapes.

1 ∼ My Son, I Had a Hard Life Story

Emile Benoit, the Man and the Musician

How can one achieve the insight into an artist's personality that will allow understanding of his creative life? I knew and worked with Emile Benoit over a period of almost ten years, sharing a variety of experiences, watching and noting his behavior, asking innumerable questions, and listening closely as he spoke of his life to me and others. A simple presentation of biographical facts, as I have been able to piece them together, however, provides merely the framework of lived experience. Examination of the changing character of my relationship with Emile is an essential part of this study, providing the framework within which to consider his personality, as our perceptions of one another necessarily determined the nature of much of the data I was able to gather.[1]

Emile Benoit was born on March 24, 1913, in Black Duck Brook (l'Anse-à-Canards), one of several francophone communities on the Port-au-Port Peninsula of western Newfoundland. His family has a long history in the community, and his genealogy unites the two groups of French settlement in this region: Breton fishermen and Acadians from Nova Scotia (Thomas 1983, 28–35). Emile's grandfather Henri was born in Black Duck Brook, and so was his father, Amédée. Family tradition has it that Emile's great-grandfather came to the "French shore" in Newfoundland as a fisherman from Saint-Malo in Brittany. He may have deserted from a ship, as did many others early in the nineteenth century, and settled near the family's present home, or more likely, he may have stayed to supervise work in

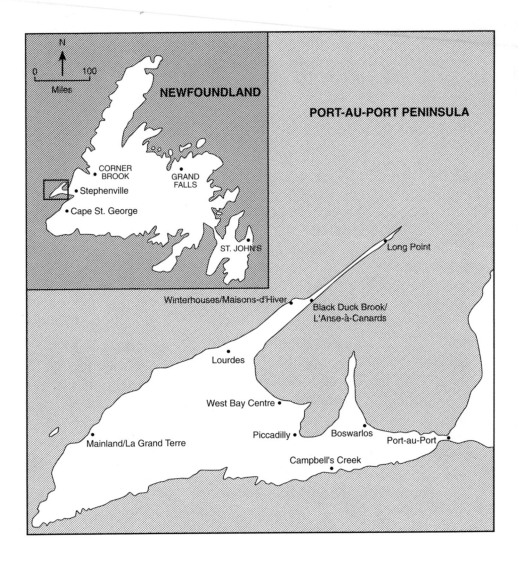

the fishing industry's shore installations and remained permanently. The ruined foundations of the French "factory" at which he may have worked are still visible not far from Emile's home (Thomas 1983, 124–25).[2]

Emile's mother, Adeline Duffenais, was Acadian, originally from Cheticamp, Cape Breton. Although some Acadians arrived in Newfoundland following the *grand derangement* of 1755, most of the Acadian immigration came from Cape Breton after 1830. More Acadian French settled around Bay St. George than on the Port-au-Port proper and were considered distinct from the French population there. Eventually intermarriage mixed the two groups, and today the name Duffenais, along with others more common among Acadians, is well-known throughout the peninsula (Thomas 1982, 2; 1983, 30–31, 125).

Emile was the first surviving child and was followed by two brothers and three sisters. He attended school in Black Duck Brook through the third grade, and there at age twelve he first began to speak English. French remained the primary language of these communities until the building of the U.S. air force base in Stephenville in 1940. The economic incentive of employment encouraged many to learn English, and the process of assimilation into the dominant anglophone population continued steadily during the next twenty years (Thomas 1982, 3).

During Emile's childhood most children stopped attending school by the time they were fourteen or fifteen years old, the boys going to fish and the girls to find other work, although, like Emile, many left even earlier. Emile explains that as the eldest son he had many responsibilities at home, especially because his father was away several days a week delivering the mail.

Like most men in this region, Emile made a living working at a variety of trades. He was only nine years old when he first went to fish with his father. Emile recalled this event, describing how he had tried and tried to hook a codfish. His father, who had caught quite a few, reassured him that God would provide, when he called out, "garde-la!" at the sight of a fish near the surface. Emile, in boyish excitement, leaped over the side to grab it. His father pulled him back by the seat of his pants, and Emile, soaking wet, came up with the fish. There you see, his father said, I told you the good Lord would provide! (Thomas 1983, 127).[3]

His father's early death left Emile as the family breadwinner; by the time he was fifteen Emile was fishing alone with his then thirteen-year-old brother Joachim. He fished throughout his life, giving up this activity only in 1980. He continued the small-scale mixed farming that was once more common, keeping a few sheep and cows and growing the hay to feed them through the winter. Unlike most men of the region, however, Emile did not spend his winters working "in the woods" logging. He went only once, working as "cookee" and saved most of his pay for the five-month period (Thomas 1983, 128). Emile also worked as a blacksmith and a carpenter and always provided these services for himself.

First wed at twenty-one years of age, Emile was widowed at thirty. He had four children, and the youngest was only four years old when his wife died, leaving him to care for the children with the help of his sisters. He remained single for seven years and worked "in the woods" during this period. With his second wife, Rita, nineteen years younger than he, Emile has a second family of nine children, the youngest of whom, Roberta, was still living at home during the time of my fieldwork.

Emile played other roles in the community, including that of veterinarian and doctor (Thomas 1983, 129–40). He established a reputation for his skill doctoring animals that led to his caring for people when the need arose. In his youth the community was virtually isolated for much of the year, and even with today's improved road system it remains relatively remote. In winter, the community could be cut off by heavy snows; the nearest doctor, forty miles away, was generally unavailable for emergencies.

Emile often relied on traditional folk medicine, his experience, and intuition in providing veterinary and medical care. Cows were helped through difficult calvings. Fractured bones were set and infections prevented. As Emile tells it, he cured himself of tuberculosis by drinking cod-liver oil until it literally came out of his pores. His first wife, however, could not stomach this remedy and died of the disease. He once even acted as a midwife (Thomas 1983, 129–40), turning his sister's child in the womb. When I first visited his home, Emile proudly showed me the set of tools given him by a visiting dentist to pull teeth. Until he received them, he had used a pair of pliers of his own fashioning. Emile believed that under different circumstances he could have become a doctor (Thomas 1983, 140).

He also played a significant role in his community as a fiddler and entertainer. In 1973, at sixty years of age, just when his working life might have been expected to draw to a close, Emile's lifelong pastime of playing the violin blossomed into a new career. He came to the attention of many people involved in the promotion of traditional Newfoundland cultural expressions and quickly established himself as a well-known performer at

Emile and his daughter Roberta on stage.

"folk"-oriented events and venues throughout the province. It was through participation in such activities that we first met.

Emile often recounted the story of how he learned to play, no doubt in part because he was so often asked about it, developing a standard narration about how he acquired his first instrument and learned his first tune.[4] The story's outlines remain constant, although the details with which he embellished it and through which he brought the events to life varied with each telling.[5] Although each musician's experience is unique, many parallels are found in reports of the learning experiences of other fiddlers.[6] Emile absorbed many features of the fiddling tradition as a child before learning to play the instrument. He practiced the framework of performance by first pretending to play on a toy fiddle. He tapped his feet, he sang, he sat and moved in the appropriate ways. He thus internalized an image of the performance model.[7] Emile also became familiar with fundamental musical features such as rhythmic patterns, tempo, form, and tonality of a basic repertoire by singing before attempting to master the muscular coordination required for their realization on the instrument. By building on this foundation he was able to achieve a basic level of competence as a player during a short and intense period of independent practice after being shown only the barest essentials of technique.[8] He then practiced performing within the social confines of his family and finally emerged into a more public sphere, where he soon received the recognition and stature accorded to acknowledged public performers.[9]

Emile grew up with a family heritage of musicianship, although he was not surrounded by musical relatives as seems to be the case in some other families well-known to students of traditional music such as the Doughertys of Northern Ireland (Feldman and O'Doherty 1979, 33–112). Nevertheless, there was music in the Benoit family, and everyone knew it. The concept of musicianship as an inherited gift is common on the Port-au-Port, as elsewhere in Newfoundland (Ashton 1981). When seeking other musicians on the Port-au-Port, for example, I was consistently referred to families rather than individuals. "Oh yes," I would be told, "the Cornects [of Mainland] all play." Or it might be the Tourots from Three Rock Cove, the Formangers of Long Point, the Felix brothers of Cape St. George, or other families. Musical networks are primarily family based, and by extension, because most families reside in the same place, community based as well. The publicly performing members of families thus identified usually include several brothers. Sometimes they play the same instrument and perform independently. Emile and his brothers, for example, all played violin and

Emile and his brother Joachim at home recording.

seldom performed together. In such a case, though all are fully competent in the range of performing skills, each brother may adopt a specialized role. Emile's younger brother Joachim, for example, often identified himself as more of a dancer than a fiddler. Other families perform in cooperative ensembles. The Tourot brothers have public roles as dancer, accordionist, and guitar player. The Cornects have played a variety of instruments in several combinations, including violin, accordion, guitar, mandolin, bass, and drums.

Emile's family traces their musical heritage to his grandfather, who was apparently an accomplished musician and public performer.

> [Joachim] was telling me that your grandfather played, right?
> Oh he was a violin player. . . . He learnt from the Scotch you know. . . . Now I'm gonna tell you, when he died my father was only four year old. . . . [Grandfather] was thirty-two years old when he died.
> That's young.
> Yes he got pneumonia.

So you didn't know him then.

No he only lived seven days. Galloping consumption they call it. Blood turn [to] water you know. Only live seven days. Too darn bad. If he could've lived, you know, [to] seventy-five or eighty, you know, something like that, well . . . I would have seen my grandfather. I would have heard him playing. And I would have catch his playing see. But he went too quick, so.

That's too bad.

Well now there's a story. There's a story that happened, a true story. Sometime eh, a fiddler like . . . he was—they told me, the old people, you know, eh—he could make you cry. He could play and make you cry. And then he'd turn it [to] the other side, [and] you had to go [to move, to dance]. Sick or not, you had to go. It'd go right through you [the sound, that is]. It was never known on the west coast here a fiddler like him. Them Scotch and all that from the highland, nah, they couldn't touch him. But, [what] he got, he got from . . . here. Used to be [like that], but when I was born, me, they was all gone them fellas. It was like another world.

So there was nobody around.

Oh no, all gone. There was Frenchmen fishing the lobsters here and all that [then]. That was all gone that. The [place] was left naked. It was all gone. Irish and Scotch and all that, it was all gone. (M-tape 81-502/C5311)

Although Emile's father did not learn to play the violin, he passed on the family tradition to Emile and his two brothers, Joachim and Ben, who saw themselves as inheritors of their grandfather's gift for music.

How come all three of you chose to play the fiddle?

Joachim Benoit: I don't know. Now my grandfather he, he was a real violin player him. He was the best around.

What was his name?

Henri Benoit. Now, his son, my poor father, he couldn't play at all. Couldn't play at all?

Not one jig. Used to play this [demonstrates the opening bars of the same tune Emile plays as his "First Tune"]. Couldn't play a jig. And Emile now, when he came, he's next to his grandfather, so it must run in the blood I suppose eh? (M-tape 81-502/C5311)

Thus it was his father's rudimentary musical efforts that first inspired Emile.

I was about eight years old, something like that, eight and a half years old. But my father used to—he had no violin—he'd take two little kindling and then he'd put that [together] and sing. But he used to sing funny. Yeah. Say he sing this one now, like say Irish Wash Woman, well he'd sing it . . . and rub the two sticks [sings "Irish Wash Woman" at slow tempo]. So good enough, by the jeez. Listening to that and jeez I liked that. So, well and good, he was telling me about his father. His father was a fiddler, my grandfather. . . . Well he growed up and he got married. . . . His mother give him the violin. So he had the violin. He tried to learn but he couldn't learn at all, at all, at all. So he give it up. (M-tape 81-502/C5319)

I'm gonna tell you the way I done it. I was eight years old and my [father] used to take two little kindlin' eh? Two little stick, then he rub, he do like a violin, you know eh? Then we'd dance eh? My brothers, my sister, we'd get together and we'd dance and him, he'd sing. (Q-tape 8)

I can easily imagine this scene, having seen Emile's twelve-year-old daughter Roberta dancing in their kitchen while he played and friends and relatives encouraged and rewarded her with an occasional quarter.

Emile's first musical experiences were of his father pretending to play the violin and Emile's first attempts at producing music were much like his father's, on a toy violin made for him when he was about eight years old.

Yes but, when I got around eight years, eight years old . . . I said, "Dad, why you don't make me *violon*? Why you don't make me a violin?" "Oh," he said, "I can't do that, I can't make a violin." So anyway, a couple days after, a couple nights after, he was singing again an' I asked him again, make me a violin. So in them times, people used to wear a pocket knife, eh, a pocket knife in the pocket eh? And we had a some kindlin' some boards, little boards in the wood box, eh? So he got a piece of board and . . . shape that almost like a guitar. Now me, you think I wasn't glad? Now he was makin' me a violin? Holy Moses! [laughter]. Well he shaped it you know, not like a violin, but about like a guitar. (Q-tape 8)

He got the thread to use for strings from his mother. Emile focuses on the domestic details of this scene in most tellings of this story.

So all right, now he [his father] said, "Go ask your mother for some thread." So I goes, and it seems like I sees her yet. She was mixin',

mixin' bread eh? And I said, "Mom, could I get your reel of thread, coarse thread?" "My god," she said, "I can't," she said, "I got only a small little bit left," she said, "on the reel." And she said, "I got to darn clothes," eh? Put patches on the clothes, eh? See? (Q-tape 8)

The thread was dear, "eight cents a roll" (Thomas 1983, 142), but his mother reluctantly surrendered some.

So, my gosh. So I never said too much, cause then I got right down-hearted like, you know, almost ready to cry. "Oh," she said, "OK then take it, but. . . . Tell daddy to look out," she said (laugh). So I goes, I said, "Mommy says for you to look out and not to waste the thread." "All right." So he took his pocket knife and he made some gaps, you know, and then put the thread in it, for to hold it, eh? Well he used to sound it. He [played] a little bit and he, foom, foom, foom, you know eh? [laughter]. A tight piece of line. So anyway, he got a bow, a little bow, with three or four strands, strands of thread on it. And then he looked in the wood box and he found a spruce, a little spruce with gum on it. So he rubbed that. And me, le, my little heart was pump-ing [laugh], God knows, about ninety I suppose [laugh], so glad for my violin. And that's when I started. Now, puttin' my fingers on that and with the bow and I used to sing [sings] a rhyme, I didn't know no jigs or anything like that [sings]. Foolishness eh? Foolishness. And look eh, I used to break a string and decide to get some more thread. Ah, ah, ah. But I could get something like now, like nylon twine, eh. Oh that'd be good, would stand a long time. Well, but I was practicing there all the time. My fingers was goin'. (Q-tape 8)

For two years Emile performed enthusiastically on his toy violin. "I couldn't play no reel or nothing but I was practicing all the time. Practic-ing the feet and singing" (Thomas 1983, 144). Watching Emile imitate his "playing" on the toy violin, it is clear that he was learning fundamentals of performance practice, musical style, and playing technique. He tapped his feet in rhythm, held the instrument, and moved the bow in the appropriate manner. He was internalizing the traditional idea and image of fiddling, if not yet the digital skills required to produce a melody, in a way reminis-cent of the early stages of the Suzuki training method. The advanced motor skills required for actual musical production, however, were not long in coming.

In the next portion of this story, which is occasionally told without the "piece of board" prelude, Emile acquires a real violin.

When I got the violin, [I was] twelve years old. My uncle, he said, . . . "Look, if Emile have a violin, eh, you know, . . . he'd play it" [laugh]. You think I never heard that, me? I run right quick to him. I say, "What you say? You gonna make me a violin?" "Anhh . . . yes, maybe when I gets a chance, I'll make you a violin. I'm gonna try." So anyway, he got old pieces of violin, but all stuck, you know, from an old feller, eh? And he never had no top, but he made a top with juniper. . . . But it took him a long time. Oh gee, it was all the summer, eh? Every time I used to see him I used to ask him, "You got my violin done yet?" And sometimes he get mad eh? "You breaks my backside," he says, "you [laugh] with your violin." So anyways, he made it, cat gut, cat gut string and bow. He had a horse that made a bow, a horse's tail, eh? And he brought it, and he could play a small little bit. (Q-tape 8)

Emile gives some indication of his uncle's limited skill in a humorous imitation of his playing.

So anyway, Jean Pierre, that was my uncle, that's him learned me how to play the violin. . . . So he use to play the violin when he was about three parts drunk. . . . He used to love this one, he used to sing it and then he'd play it on the violin. [Sings] "I'm free and easy, and janging along." He used to swing around [swings arms around]. [Sings] I'm like a blackbird on silver wings. Oooo, he'd go like that. So, he use to play that on the violin. He used to put the leg over the other like that [crosses legs, continuing to play tune badly, while swinging legs, crossing and recrossing them and clicking his toes together]. Brrrr. (Videotape)

His uncle teased him about living up to his family's musical heritage (Thomas 1983, 145) and showed him his first tunes.

So he showed me. . . . So, well in about ten minutes I could play it. Now, I said, "Now learn me a reel" [laughter]. So he learned me Devil Among the Tailors [sings tune]. One finger at a time, eh? So there, I got it, now my son [slap]. I usen't to eat [from playing so much]. . . . Well from that day, twelve years old [pause], I'm playin'. (Q-tape 8)

On another occasion Emile described in more detail what was apparently his only lesson.

Well okay, now I said, "Can you learn me one?" I'm going to play the one he learned me now, the first one. And I believes it's an Irish, Irish

Emile imitates his uncle Jean playing the fiddle.

tune. He could play a small bit, you know [plays slowly]. But now I plays it like that [plays at normal tempo]. Different now, see. But this is the way I start, he showed me [plays slowly again]. So I took the violin and I plays it. La. Now I said, "Show me the other turn" [plays second strain slowly]. So I plays it. La, I knows it. Start now playing it same like that, bow go back and forth like that. Now I played that about an hour I suppose. Now says, "Do you know any, step dance, something like, reels?" "Yes," he says, "I knows this one." Used to call it Devil Among the Tailors, eh? [plays a rudimentary version of "Devil Among the Tailors"]. . . . So he pass it to me and I played it. So, and I start. Oh I was all the week at it. I couldn't eat, had no appetite. I was right in the, heart and soul in that. And I start from that. Kept on going, kept on going, kept on going. (M-tape 81-502/C5319)

The intensity of his initial learning period is a theme he frequently sounds in this story.

That was in August when I seen him [his uncle] coming down the seashore with that [the violin] under his arm, not packed or nothing, but I could see, you know, I was expecting it any time. First thing he comes to the house and "here," he says, and he gives me. He made like this [indicates his violin]. It was pretty well made. He had strings on, cat-gut strings, eh. So all right. But when I passed the bow on and I tried to play the reel, I couldn't. I was all puzzled. Seemed like 'twas a dream. So he could play a little bit, so I said, "Could you start me one?" So that's the one now I played a little while ago. That's the one he start. . . . He couldn't play very well, you know. So, I knowed it. My poor father used to sing that, you know, so I knowed the jig. So I said, "play it again." So he played it again. "Now," I said after three or four times, "pass it along." And by the jeez, here I start . . . I was just as good as him then. And from that my son, I opened fire. I wouldn't eat or anything. Just maybe a piece of bread like that, and then a mouthful and put down the bread again, and across that stick again and give it to him, ya. How many times the old man, "Go on out and stay out," he said. We had a two storey house, you know. People used to come in, going to have a chat, you know, or something like that. "Go on," [very loud] he said, "go on, get upstairs, go on with that. You breaks my ears. Go on." So I used to go upstairs, and then the two feet, and I used to hit my feet [demonstrates foot tapping]. The loft used to crack, b'y. So I kept going, I kept going, I kept going. (M-MS 72-10/pp. 4–5)

I attempted on numerous occasions to find out how he proceeded to learn after this beginning but was consistently frustrated. According to Emile, he was self-taught. Apparently he had a store of music in his mind to begin working with, possibly from his father's singing and his uncle's meager repertoire. Although it is entirely possible that he never had even informal lessons, he must have had models to imitate and sources for expanding his repertoire during the next stage of the learning process, as he indicates at the end of one telling: "I keep it goin', keep it goin', keep it goin'. Until I was around fifteen years old. Then I start movin' around. An' I start hearing some air an' this an' that, you know" (M-tape 84-562/C7275).

Although no doubt exaggerated for humorous effect, Emile's characterization of this learning process does indicate that his uncle was far from an accomplished player and certainly not a teacher on whom Emile could model his own playing. From his relatives, then, Emile seems to have acquired an exposure to fiddle music, a sense of it as part of his family heritage, encouragement, and some initial help in acquiring an instrument.

As a novice fiddler, Emile first played for his family: "Oh well, [played for] my mother's father, and my brothers and sisters, sometimes young people. . . . When I got around fourteen we used to make a party at home. So I used to play . . . for square dances" (Q-tape 8). Within this family audience Emile's father played the mentor's role.

> So I kept goin' on, about a couple of months I was gettin' dere, my son. My father used to watch me, you know?
> Tod Saunders: Is that right?
> Tell me . . . how to hold the bow.
> TS: Your father knew a bit about it?
> Oh yes, but he couldn't play himself. But he used to tell me where to put the bow. (M-MS 86-143/pp. 157–58)

It seems there were no other fiddlers or musicians among this relatively private, familial group from whom he might learn. Later, as Emile began to "play out" in other houses and community events he began to expand his repertoire and skills.

> Oh no, I never heard nobody there when I played, clear of Uncle John. It's only when I started movin' out, you know. Oui? I was sixteen years old when I start travelin' eh? Oh then I met some old fellers, fiddlers eh? Oui? . . . They was funny fiddlers, funny eh? Yeah. Oh I'm able to play like them. So I used to play some of their old [tunes].

The first one I heard . . . an old feller was playin' . . . old Tim Goudet, le Goudet. I used to play that. That was his, at that time, that was his favorite, eh? So, that's the way it went. And I'm still goin' and I like it. (Q-tape 8)

Emile's narrative response to the question, "How did you start to play?" usually ends at this point. He had discovered his talent, gotten a violin, received his initial instruction, begun to play for his family, and was thus launched into the public sphere. The next event he notes is his first appearance at a public event, a wedding. Although the age he recalls may be variously thirteen, sixteen, or seventeen, clearly this represented the next step in his development as a performer: "Walter Young was his name. . . . He got married and that's the first wedding I played to. First I played outside the home. I played home, lots of times see . . . but [not] out. Thirteen years old, when I played for his wedding. Yeah" (M-tape 81-502/C5311).

At the same time he became established as an active performer at the informal parties held every weekend.

So, I kept goin', and kept goin' and ah—age of sixteen, I went out, I used to play for everybody down home, eh? 'Cause . . . on weekend we had parties you know. . . . Kitchen parties, eh? . . . When I started fishin' an' workin', but on weekends, now, I used to go and play . . . I got married and I kept on playin'. Yep. And after that, well, I started, they started to pay me you know, I used to go to [Campbell's] Creek, Boswarlis, Stephenville, and Cape St. Georges. They used to pay me a dollar a night. . . . When I was a young feller. Well, I was married, 25, 24 [years old]. . . . For 4 or 5 hours work you know. (M-MS 86-143/ pp. 158–64)

His achievement of full-fledged performer status was marked by the acquisition of a new violin.

Tod Saunders: But where did you get your first violin? Were you still using the one your Uncle John made for you?

Ah, well yes, oh yes. When I got that one, I was seventeen years old [shows violin]. . . . Yeah I paid 35 dollars for it. . . . It took me a year to pay for it. My father used to carry the mail, he used to get, ah, twenty dollars a month. . . . So, every three months he used to get a check— 60 dollars. So he gave me so much to pay for the violin. . . . I got her around here. . . . [From] an old, an old Scotsman, eh. (M-MS 86-143/ p. 159)

At the same time he was busily playing at house parties Emile was acquiring status as a performer for more formal events.

> I used to go up to Lourdes. . . . I was playin' for the Church. Build a church. Oh they used to go the hall, so I played. The more I used to go, the more I used to practice. . . . And after that, well, they went to get me. "Who's playin' tonight?" Well, somebody else with the cordine [accordion] or something like that. . . . Well, now when I go, they get Emile, they had lots of fun. (M-MS 86-143/p. 161)

Emile eventually became the most sought-after fiddler for the biggest social events in the region such as garden parties sponsored as fund-raising events by local parishes. The garden party was the pinnacle of public performance venues in the local context, and he frequently mentioned it as evidence of his stature as a musician in earlier years along with a list of communities throughout the Port-au-Port region at which he performed.

Further details of the stage that preceded achievement of this stature, however, are scanty. As Emile described his activities, he was "on the go" every weekend, closely observing other musicians, though none stood out as a mentor. More important to the development of his skill than such a model was his commitment to constant practice by performing at every opportunity. Emile shed some additional light on the end of the formative stage in his development as a musician in one early recorded conversation.

> Now them times there was no radio or nothing, no violin player around . . . you know. And when the radios started to come around and [we] started listening to Fitzgerald and all them fellers, you know, them old Scotch there, well then I was a married man. I had a family in charge, and I didn't feel like turning around now and turn my music now, change my music. I didn't have that in my mind no more. So what I learned then, well, I never improved. Because I never went, you know, and took the trouble and practised. That's the way the world goes, I suppose. (M-MS 72-10/pp. 5–6)

In other words, Emile's musical identity was firmly established within, and thus shaped by, the framework of the local tradition as it existed before the arrival of influences carried by various media.

Some impressions of the musical influences to which Emile was exposed can be gleaned from this oral evidence and corroborated by other sources. The radio stations to which Emile refers would have included those broadcasting from Sydney, Nova Scotia. These stations often featured fiddlers from that region, whose music contains a strong Scottish component.[10] Emile recalls learning a few pieces, also Scottish, from recordings played on his neighbor's gramophone. He first heard a gramophone before he was married, at about age "nineteen or twenty, something like that" (Q-tape 47). This would have been about 1932.

> Well now . . . old Lecour had got one. . . . He got one used to go with a crank eh? And there was a big funnel on it, eh? So that's where I learned them jigs. I learned Lord Macdonald's Reel and Cap le Fait ["Caber Feidh"]. Oh yes all them jigs . . . from the records, yeah. I used to go there sometime, especially on weekend, you know Saturday and Sunday afternoon, so we used to play that. But now every record you had to change the needle eh? . . . They was expensive too, eh? Expensive at that time. Yeah. But now you couldn't, he couldn't play too often. Had to spare the needle, eh? They play it twice, or they play a record, you know two side, and then next record, you could play it but would spoil the record. (Q-tape 46)

Emile could not recall who the fiddlers on these recordings were, but he identified them as "Scotch." Although Emile learned some items from recordings, they clearly played a minor role in shaping his style and repertoire. Radio came later, and Emile recalls becoming the first "in the cove" to get a radio in his mid-thirties (ca. 1945–51) (Q-tape 47). He recalls listening to stations from Charlottetown, Prince Edward Island, French-language programs from Quebec, and even Wheeling, West Virginia's station, WWVA. Traditional fiddling, especially that of Cape Breton, was frequently played on Maritime stations, as was the country music of the time. Emile enjoyed the country songs and learned from them "not too much, but a little bit . . . I was more after, for the jigs and all that now. . . . Oh yes. Yeah. I used to, I learned a good many on the radio, Bastringue ["La Bastringue"] and all that" (Q-tape 46).

Naturally the French-language programs had great appeal, and Emile recalled a comedy program that employed humorous characterizations similar to those he often used.

> We used to get a fella they call Seraphim, mean fella. Seraphim we used to call him in French. Used to come from Montreal. Oh I wouldn't miss that for nothing. Used to come on four o'clock in the evening. If I wasn't fishing, if I was home around, I leave my work and I had to come listen to the story. Yeah. His wife's name was Donelda

[makes noise], used to sound right rough, eh? [imitates voice again]. Hah, yeah. (Q-tape 46)

Media have continued to influence the local tradition. Joachim, for example, played a fiddle tune for me which he had learned from the John Allan Cameron television program from Nova Scotia. Emile adapted bits from several television commercials and programs into his act.

Although Emile was exposed to varied musical stimuli, his basic competency, achieved through learning the dance repertoire, and his primary role as a dance fiddler directed his musical development into the relatively narrow channel of traditional fiddling. The same pattern is suggested by the repertoire of other musicians of his generation. Willie Cornect from the community of Mainland, for example, played a variety of nineteenth- and early twentieth-century popular songs on the mandolin. He acquired the instrument and most of his repertoire while sailing to and from Barbados in his youth. He played for house parties, and his family was known for being musical, but he was never a dance musician and performed little of the dance music repertoire (Q-tape 1).

Emile's role as a composer developed as an extension of his activities as a performer. As he explains it, at first composing new tunes was a response to his own need for novelty and served as another means of pleasing his audience.[11]

> So I used to play for dances an' all that. We had no radio, no television, or nothing like that. So, I used to get tired. You gets tired [of] the same thing all the time, eh? You'll find, *fatiguer,* the same song. Same reel or same air. You gets tired. You want to hear something new. So I start makin' up things, eh, air, changing air, and all that. So [the dancers say], "Chee, where you heard that?" (M-tape 84-562/C7275)

Emile consciously worked to improve his composing over the years, as he stated in this answer to my queries:

> First thing you hears a new one, oh, well then! . . . Now, the other people goes, "Gee that goes good." Well from that, well you plays that for a while, then gets tired of it. Then try something again. That's the way it goes, oui? Yes, but after a while, you does that for years and years, eh? Well, you're getting pretty smart at it, oui? The same like go to school, oui? Getting your grade twelve. Same thing. (Q-tape 8)

It was not just Emile who apparently tired of the same old tunes. His audience seems to have appreciated hearing something new as well, an appreciation that was clearly important to him and enabled him to use composition as an additional device to entertain and interact with the audience.

> Another time I composed . . . [a piece], "Farewell" it's called. . . . I played it to a party and jeepers, fancy, everybody liked it, you know, eh? And Joe Farewell, him, he got on the floor and he danced, well it's just as well to say all night. We start seven o'clock, we finish two o'clock in the morning. For every dance on the floor, and that's all I played, that's all I played all night, "Farewell." Yeah.
>
> People didn't get tired of it?
>
> No. And after that . . . I went out with a horse and a couple of my family come with me too, and when we came home [it] was right calm, eh. And the moon shining so bright. Oh, beautiful. I used to hear people, eh? [sings melody of "Farewell Reel"]. Now, [it] was the tune called Farewell, eh? [whistles tune]. They know that because I played it all night [laughter]. So after that when they goes to the times, they go on "Give us Farewell." Well that's the way it works see, eh? (Q-tape 8)

Composing as an independent activity thus apparently evolved out of performing. Emile's initial pleasure in innovation was socially reinforced, and he began to exploit this talent. He discovered that such innovation was an effective performance device that served to heighten his status, and he began to cultivate composition as an independent skill.

Within Emile's formative milieu, recognition is given primarily to performers. The composers of traditional tunes are not known, nor are titles often used. Rather, tunes are identified with those who play them within a musical community. As I played some recordings I had made for a local enthusiast of traditional music, for example, he quickly identified the pieces not by title but according to the musician who frequently used them to "warm up" (Q-tapes 2, 3, 15 and field notes 1984). Even authors of tunes known to be of local composition may not be so acknowledged. Rather, these compositions are identified more as the proprietary tunes of their performer/composers. Most players have a few items they claim as of their own making, which are played primarily, if not only, by that performer.[12]

Emile's activity as a performer and the development of his identity as a composer gained added impetus by the arrival of collectors, fiddlers, and enthusiasts from outside his immediate locale, carried by the waves of a worldwide folk music revival, folklore scholarship, a Newfoundland cultural renaissance, national interest in francophone communities, and government "multicultural" policies. Emile recalled his first contact with these various movements and trends through participation in a musical event that was part of the 1966 "Come Home Year" celebrated in Newfoundland. John Widdowson visited him as a fieldworker in 1964 and heard him shouting, "bring back the old times!" at a dance in Lourdes (M-tape 64-15/C115–117 and personal communication). Gerald Thomas cites a 1973 fiddle contest in Stephenville in which he placed second as having brought him to the attention of folk festival promoters when its participants were subsequently brought to St. John's (1983, 145). Emile played again in St. John's the following year, in Ottawa in 1975, at the prestigious Mariposa Festival in 1976, and at a festival in Massachusetts in 1977. Once launched, his new career as a folk festival performer quickly developed, helped by appearances in various media. During 1978 he was a guest, along with fellow Newfoundland fiddler Rufus Guinchard, on the nationally televised CBC program *Ninety Minutes Live* hosted by Peter Gzowski, where he "took right over as he usually does." Shortly thereafter he appeared on the local Newfoundland television program the *Root Seller* ("Profile" 1978, 7). The release of his first record album in 1979 was also crucial in giving him wider notice (Benoit 1979).

Subsequently Emile became so busy as a performer that a listing of only a few engagements serves to chronicle his rising prominence. He continued to receive media exposure, appearing on such radio programs as Neil Murray's *Jigg's Dinner* on OZ-FM, which featured Newfoundland performers and traditional music (Thomas 1979, 6), and the "nostalgic" CBC radio program *The Newfie Bullett* (Narvaez 1986, 71–72). During 1981 he appeared with Kelly Russell, Rufus Guinchard, and me on a series of four programs of traditional Newfoundland fiddle music aired on the CBC radio *Saturday Special* (*Evening Telegram* January 23, 1981). Gerald Thomas helped to produce a film portrait made by Memorial University's Educational Television Centre, in both English and French versions (*Emile Benoit, Fiddler,* 1980, and *Ça Vient du Tchoeur,* 1980), as well as a ninety-minute narration of one of his wonder tales, the *Black Mountain* (Benoit 1985). Several Quebec television programs also featured his performances, and he appeared briefly in a National Film Board production that portrayed folk artists from across Canada.

During the same period Emile's festival appearances increased and expanded to reach new audiences. After his appearance on Peter Gzowski's television program he was invited and went to perform in British Columbia, his first major journey by jet, which inspired his composition of the "Flying Reel." During 1980 he was a starring performer with the Acadian musical show *Pistroli en Atlantique,* which toured Atlantic Canada (*L'Evangeline* October 14, 1980).

That summer I facilitated his performance at a week-long folk music and dance "camp" sponsored by the Country Dance and Song Society held near Plymouth, Massachusetts. During 1981 he was invited to perform at a conference in British Columbia whose organizers had heard of him through his media appearances. Two French performers who participated in an international festival held in Newfoundland to celebrate the four-hundredth anniversary of its discovery were impressed by Emile and brought him to their festival in Nantes in July 1987 (*Ouest France* July 1987; *Presse-Ocean* July 3, 1987). Emile's inclusion as a performer at the Sound Symposium (Monahan 1983, 11; 1986, 12), a biennial festival of "new music" held in St. John's, reflects the growing recognition of him as a musician.

Emile continued to perform until shortly before his death on September 1, 1992, at age seventy-nine. Just as I left Newfoundland and completed this study, for example, the *Toronto Globe and Mail* covered his appearance at the Harbour Front, York Quay Centre, Shipdeck Stage along with the Newfoundland band Figgy Duff in a feature article (*Globe and Mail* July 17, 1987, Entertainment section). Subsequently Emile was awarded an honorary doctorate by Memorial University of Newfoundland. Working with the band Figgy Duff during his last years he traveled widely and recorded a final album with them.

Comparison of Emile's musical life with that of many other prominent traditional musicians of his generation indicates that his experience was not unusual. His musical knowledge and skills were acquired in a fairly typical manner. A guiding aesthetic and system of meanings acquired during his earliest years were set within the social world he knew as a child and young man. The articulatory skills he needed to actualize the identity of fiddler were developed as an adolescent. The unique realization of these dynamics which make up Emile's fiddling competence served as his primary expressive identity throughout his adult life. His stature as a musician was maintained until changes in patterns of entertainment and especially dancing caused a decline in the kind of events at which he had been most prominent. He continued to perform in the contexts that persisted, however, and to pursue other opportunities that arose. During the latter 1960s and early 1970s he encountered the growing cultural revival occurring in Newfoundland and the worldwide interest in folk-cultural expressions suitable for staged presentation. His willingness to participate in any and all such events, his skills as an entertainer and musician, and his success at adapting to new settings catapulted him to prominence. The values inherent in this new milieu reinforced certain of his own attitudes toward performing and composing, facilitating a further flowering of his musical creativity.[13]

∾ The Research Relationship

At the heart of this study is a student-teacher relationship that grew into one of mutual exploration as Emile responded to my questions about his creative process. It is a record of my encounter with a talented individual, strong personality, and the music through which he expressed himself. Because of his prominence as a performer, his hospitality, and his willingness to be interviewed, Emile was recorded by many people in a wide variety of circumstances, and much of this material has been deposited in the Memorial University of Newfoundland Folklore and Language Archive.[14] I have also paid close attention to evaluations, whether encountered, implied, or elicited, of his behavior by these interviewers, his friends, neighbors, and members of his various audiences. Not surprisingly, he is viewed somewhat differently by his fellow francophones from the Port-au-Port, his other interviewers, and his audiences in St. John's or further afield. All these reactions, as well as Emile's commentary on himself and his reception, have helped to provide a more complete picture of the man and his music. Nevertheless, this study remains essentially the product of my encounter with Emile, as subject, teacher, and friend.

I have adopted a chronological approach for this presentation, dwelling on important steps in the development of my relationship with Emile, illustrating its nature at the time, and reflecting on the factors that contributed to its character. Not only did Emile show me many faces over the years I knew him, but my responses to him, as well, were varied and changed over time. My understanding of his personality grew both as I saw him react in a variety of social situations and as I matured. My appreciation of his musicianship developed as I saw him perform in different settings and play with other musicians.

Emile's willingness to reflect on his music making with me grew as my perseverance demonstrated commitment and my skills developed. I can recall his wife, Rita's, humorous recollections of my efforts to play Emile's tunes when I first visited them. During my last visit, his son Mike expressed admiration for how well I had learned his father's tunes, and Emile took pride in having taught me. The level of our discussions deepened considerably as I questioned him about details of various compositions and his compositional methods. Once Emile understood my interest in composing, he became willing to expose himself by playing unfinished pieces for me, in effect trying to create as I listened. In the latter stages of this project he often volunteered thoughts and observations related to the issues I was investigating without prompting. Having found his own rationale for our work together, he became much more of a self-reflective co-worker than a subject for study. He explained his understanding of this study as follows:

> It's an experiment, eh? You know, [I] suppose you could say, that's the way he [i.e., Emile as my subject] makes up my reels and all that, eh? Give an idea to somebody else how to do it, eh?
> Yeah, exactly right.
> Sure, sure. It's like I say, if you got to depend, [if] you do like somebody else, eh, it's not the same [as doing it yourself], eh? You do what you got to do in your mind, your intention, well it's gonna be different. It could be some of them could come with the prettiest thing that ever was put out in the world, eh? If they does it on their own, what they got there. If they try to develop it, eh?
> Yeah, work on it.
> Yes, yes, yes that'll come after a while. That'll be important, eh, to the world, eh? (Q-tape 46)

Although the development of our research relationship could be subsumed under the simple rubric of increasing rapport, closer examination yields insights useful in the analysis of Emile's musicianship. Presentation of our story effectively introduces this man and my interest in him.

Before I arrived in Newfoundland in the fall of 1977, I was involved in the revival of traditional music and dance. I learned to play the five-string banjo, had begun to play the fiddle, and was teaching contra and square dancing several times a week in the New York City area. I was a "folkie." Although I was inspired and nurtured by this social scene, I had also encountered more strictly traditional musicians and dance events, both at festivals and "in the field" and I looked to these as models to be emulated. In search of what I then believed to be a somehow more genuine, unsullied, and lesser-known tradition, I went to Newfoundland, where I felt there would be an unstudied dance tradition, traditional music and song in abundance, a burgeoning local revival, and an institution within which to work. I wanted very much to encounter traditions firsthand and thus to come closer to what I perceived as the inspiration for the revival movement; my purpose was also to deepen my understanding of the elusive quality that seemed to distinguish "traditional music."

When I first met Emile in 1978, he was well-known throughout the province as a traditional fiddler and storyteller. He had appeared at folk festivals in St. John's and elsewhere, been interviewed on national television, and recorded an album of his own compositions. He was a striking individual whose weatherbeaten face testified to the hard life of which he often spoke. His performances were imbued with abundant energy and communicated a great intensity of feeling and commitment. He often introduced his compositions with extended narratives recounting the circumstances under which they were composed, circumstances that often evoked gales of laughter but occasionally somber reflection from his audience. These and other stories were brought to life by his talent for humorous characterization. Emile's availability and my interests and background led to our meeting, and we began to associate with each other quite naturally. He was outgoing, talkative, and pleased to share his music with an enthusiastic student. Though his style of performance attracted me, I was most impressed by the large number of his own compositions. Here, I felt, was a musician who had learned to play in an almost archetypal traditional environment and had internalized the spirit and logic of this music to such an extent that he was utterly fluent within the idiom. Fiddle music seemed to gush spontaneously from some wellspring within him, made convincing by its authoritative style. I had never encountered such a prolific composer of fiddle music before and felt, along with most of the other revival musicians in St. John's, that Emile was a very special musician from whom to learn something of the essence of traditional music. I began to avail myself of every opportunity to play with him, recording his music and learning his tunes. Later, as a student of ethnomusicology at UCLA, I concluded that an extended study and analysis of Emile's compositions and creative processes would provide valuable insights into the nature of traditional music.

I continued to seek Emile out whenever he came to town, establishing a friendly acquaintance with him. Our meetings were usually in the context of his performances at local clubs (bars). I was one of several aspiring musicians from St. John's who attended these performances, usually playing a few tunes toward the end of the evening. At the St. John's Folk Festival in the summer of 1979, however, we spent more time together, and in response to his suggestion that with a little more time he could easily teach me to play in his style, I expressed an interest in visiting him at his home in Black Duck Brook. He reiterated the invitation, and I took him up on it, although I believe he was surprised when I turned up several weeks later.

Still a relative newcomer to the province, I took advantage of the academic break over the summer of 1979 to visit various parts of the island while trying to locate an area for possible field research. I spent a few days camping at parks on the west coast before finding the courage to go to Emile's as I planned. I arrived somewhat anxious about my reception because I was unannounced save for our informal conversation in St. John's. I found that Emile was at work in the fields but his wife, Rita, whom I did not know, greeted me. True to his word, however, Emile made me more than welcome, and I stayed on for fifteen days.

The ethic of hospitality that seemed to govern Emile's openness to visitors was expressed in one of his stories. As Emile recounted it to me, a neighbor had told a fellow worker at the lumber camps that he could always count on a welcome at his home. When the man arrived unexpectedly, however, he was away and his wife did not have enough food prepared. The visitor demanded that she light up the stove and make him something to eat, insisting rather roughly when she objected that she didn't know anything about him. When the man of the house returned, he took the visitor's side, scolding his wife for not treating him better—a friend should feel free to treat his house as his own. I found the story a bit disturbing because it seemed painfully hard on the wife, but Emile insisted that such behavior as this man's was reasonable for someone who had been offered hospitality and that he had been right to abuse the wife. I hoped there was no direct parallel to my situation.

Despite an uneasy beginning, I seemed to have made a positive impression. As Rita later recalled that visit, I worked hard bringing in the hay and helping Emile put new siding on his house but didn't play nearly as much music as others who had come on similar missions to learn music from him. She thus viewed me as an aspiring fiddler and an apprentice to Emile, a category already established by other visitors to their home, and appreciated my efforts to lend a hand where needed. Other visiting musicians had apparently limited themselves to a more musical exchange.

For me this first taste of fieldwork was an intense and unfamiliar experience. My interests were more diverse than simply playing music, and I made an effort to involve myself in Emile's activities, both in exchange for his hospitality and to discover more about the local culture. With Emile's cooperation I was able to record continuously while we played our fiddles, and I informally interviewed him (M-tapes 81-502/C5309–C5318). Using these tapes, which were made with extensive field notes at that time, I have been able to reconstruct much of that crucial first visit.

Emile played many tunes for me, a few of which I learned in the traditional manner, by following his example. I found it much easier to learn the melodies of the tunes we played than to imitate his bowing. As Emile expressed it, I had good "fingers," that is, I could play the left hand, but I couldn't seem to "catch that friggin' bow." We worked for many hours on just a few tunes. The method seemed to work because he soon began to praise my efforts.

⮑ Life Stories

While we worked together, Emile told me about his life. I recorded several narratives concerning his development as a musician and introductory stories to some compositions that were already familiar to me from his performances in St. John's. To illustrate the tenor of our talks, I will relate some of what he told me. I asked extensive questions about his experiences as a musician in various settings, but I will address this material later as part of a discussion of Emile's musical life. Here I shall consider what I was learning of Emile as a person through the life-story narratives he related. As the visit went on, our conversations became more personal. Emile "performed" many of his life stories during my visit for his audience of one, using them to share his experience, state his beliefs, and exemplify his values, as well as to present me with a positive image of himself. They will serve us in the same ways, as well as to provide material for discussion of his personality (Titon, 1980).

Several interrelated themes dominated his conversation, prominent among them the hard times he had endured. "My son, I had a hard life story. If were to tell everything. My poor boy, it's a wonder that I'm alive. It's only the courage and the will (to keep going). Only for that, I'd be dead for long ago. Fought my [way] through boy, in a hard, hard way. Although there's people in the world got worse that I got." He made this point by contrasting his youth with life today, a common theme in his narratives.

Yes my good boy. Oh we got a good life now, good God almighty, the life of Riley [laughter]. But the young ones complain. I wouldn't complain, not after what I passed through. To see now, how easy it is. Now, it's not only you can eat, I'm able to eat too. . . . I seen going to bed like that, nine o'clock, ten o'clock, hungry, "Mommy can you uh, get a piece of bread?" Ask my mommy for a piece of bread. And she get a piece of bread put butter onto it. We had a cow you know, homemade butter on it. One slice that's all, like to get two but got to save some for tomorrow. (M-tape 81-502/C5311)

These and other such statements emphasized Emile's ability to survive hardship. Having the courage to keep going is a valued character trait he repeatedly stressed. In the following story of his birth, these themes are represented in a humorous way. It is a narrative he often used to introduce himself to new audiences in public performances at the time.

In them times it was hard time. Hard to live. Yeah, there was nothing, just to grow, it was hard to make vegetables grow, hard to make hay grow and hard to keep cattle and you couldn't get enough food for them. It was hard on everything, every way you get up was hard. And went on, so here I come in the world. Now, you might think it's a lie, but it's a true story. The doctor, they had a doctor but you had to go across the bay, [it] was twelve miles to go across with a motor boat. But, I was born in March [and] they went across, hard winters [then], and they went across with a horse. And they got a doctor. So good enough. Doctor came out, his name was Doctor MacDonald, he was called, and [they] come home, so he born me. Now he said, I was a pound and seven ounces. Now that's hard to believe, to see the size that I am now [laughter] hard to believe. And he said like that, "For to save that child now, you have to get some raw wool and wrap him in and keep him under the stove and keep fire and you got to keep him in there for eighteen days." So, that's what they done. Now there was no nurse bottle or nothing like that. And my mother couldn't nurse me because she was weak, a weak woman and all. She was very weak. The food wasn't very good and then . . . she had no substance in her at all. But you take a piece of bread, little piece of bread and put little brown sugar, little brown sugar in and they had a rag they put that in, they tie it on and then they put that in my mouth and I suck on that. . . . But I almost choke [laugh]. Once I almost choke, so they find the little rag, the little, what do they call it, the little nipple, tie it on the leg of the stove. So I wanted to live you know [laughter]. I wanted to live. So, it [the string] used to go so far, but it wouldn't go in my throat, and then it keep me going like that.

Audience member: They had it tied on the leg of the stove?

Oh yes, yes. I said that's where I started to get the sound of the violin [laughter]. So anyway, went on. So, at eighteen days they took me out of that and kept me warm and kept feeding me and then I got all right. Got strong but I was still like that. I just cut myself a little bit . . . [and] I would faint. And if I be an hour too long before eating I'd faint. Faint, faint, faint, all the time, faint. Now listen, it's a funny story but it's a true story. It's true. So it went on like that until I was seventeen years old. When I cut myself or hurt myself, I faint, pass away. But seventeen, let go. [You] believe that story, that's finished. That story's finished. (M-tape 81-502/C5319)

During my first visit I was much impressed by Emile's tales of surviving serious injury, and I requested that he retell these in a later performance, hoping to share my perception of Emile with the audience. I found him somewhat reluctant to do so, although he did oblige me with a brief story (M-tape 81-502/C5321). Apparently these were not part of the performance repertoire he felt appropriate for presentation on stage but had emerged from our more personal relationship in the context of my visit to his home. In a later conversation between the two of us he retold these stories to emphasize his commitment to fiddling and the strength of his will to "keep going" no matter what happened.

Now that's what is hard, what I used to find hard, when I used to fish eh? I used to fish, my hand there now all, you know, full of blister and oh, you know, cracked, you know, with salt water and the hand line and the hooks and all that, you know. Ahhrrr, sore yeah, sore. The rest full of, water boils they calls it, you know, oui? And play, play the same. I go, oh about half drunk, you know, on home brew [laughter]. And I cut my two fingers here eh? [holds up first two fingers of left hand]. And I used to play. Cut them off, right off, in the jointer, because I had a workshop eh? Jointer, yeah? And I was putting in a sleigh runner, eh? . . . You think that my hand never slipped off, well my son, my fingers went right in, and whacko! You could see it. Look. Cut the bone and all. . . . So anyway, then I goes to the house and I got a pan of cold water, not me, but they give me a pan of cold water and I put my hand in it. And I put down my head right to the floor, sitting on a chair but my head right down. and by and by the light came in. Yeah if I hadn't'a done that I would have passed out. But I didn't. Almost went, almost. But I didn't. So all right, so I took some rag and I got some gum, you know, balsam they call it, and put it on, and then I packed it. So that happened on Monday. Saturday I had to go and play. That's true as God in heaven. Saturday I got to go play. So all right, I got some band-aid. Now you know well, there was crust on it, you know eh? I took a band-aid and I put it over the finger, the end of the finger eh? . . . Went up and honest to good heavens, look, well I was about half shot I guess. My clothes was full of blood, oui? The fiddle, full of blood. And I played, I didn't mind that, I played all night. Oui? I never stopped playing. Next Saturday, gone again. And I worked, worked [in] my workshop like that. I cut the two fingers right off, was took here [shows first joint] flicko, flicko. Only the bone, the end of the bone there, but half drunk, leave her go. They's dead after. Not at first but after, you know, three or four minutes, oh yeah, yeah. (Q-tape 8)

On another occasion he broke his little finger badly.

I broke this finger here. [It] comes across, right across my hand [shows]. Well I took it, I took it, there was three bones coming up, I took it and I put it back in place and press the bones together. I went to the house. I almost passed out too. But I band it and I took the two fingers together and I stayed like that for eighteen days, eighteen days and I never stopped working. . . . This one there used to hold the little one eh? [shows how the fingers were bound together]. Cause they were tied together, the little one couldn't move. Eighteen days, la. But if I hadn't done that, I had six miles to go to a doctor, so when I got there, when I would have got there he would have said, go to the hospital now, get that finger cut off. See? He said, would have been dead eh? But at the time I broke it, I just pressed it back together. It was alive, when it was alive. So I saved my finger.

Another one here [a finger], I got hooked in the bandsaw. . . . Tore it all right out, all the skin come there. And I kept working. Band it and ahnn. I went in the lumber woods and I, I put two thousand feet of pine through the mill. I got it sawed and then I hauled it home. I had a two-ton truck. I made two trips. I got my pine home and I started working. So. That's the reason I'm tough today, oui? Tough. 'Cause I was born with that, you know, I, I, I was trained, trained the hard way. My brothers, they couldn't stand the half I can stand and they're younger than me. (Q-tape 8)

Toughness in the face of hardship, especially physical pain and injury, is one of the character traits Emile wishes to present in these stories, along with the resourcefulness to cope with such situations. These recollections, though not part of his public performance repertoire, are clearly well-defined narratives which he used in more personal situations to exemplify these traits. These values are not unique to Emile but seem to be shared by the men of his community, as I have heard similar stories from others, some even more horrific, especially from his younger brother Joachim. John Scott has noted the importance of being able to "take it" in his study of Newfoundland sealers. He explains the importance of this character trait: "In a society which offers livelihood only through physical labour . . . the emphasis of the group will naturally be on physical development. . . . In the labour created society, hardiness becomes the basic requirement in one's being able to provide a living for himself. . . . The characteristic of hardiness manifests itself in the ideal of having a good reputation as a worker—a fellow who could 'take it'—and this is equally true for all the traditional occupations in Newfoundland" (1975, 141–42). In the context of sealing, the "willingness to take risks and to take them to the brink of disaster" is viewed as the epitome of such toughness. In Emile's community it would seem to be the strength and will to "keep going" no matter what.

The climax of these conversations was an evening during which Emile told me about various supernatural experiences he had had. I did not record them at the time, but during my fieldwork in 1986, while visiting with a third party in a situation similar to mine years before, Emile spontaneously told some of them again.

I seen the chalice in the sky. Seventy men seen it with me, because I told them come see. And they look at it and they ask me what it was. Well I said, I ask them what it was. They said it's a chalice. They ask, they said, "what is that? Is that the last of the world?" That's what they said, "Is that the last of the world?" Well, I said, "The last of the world," I said. I said, "That's the lord," I said. "That's the chalice." I said. And, "Look. You see the sacrament in the white?" It was about that size, I suppose, *right* white. . . .

In the sky?

In the sky, yeah.

This was in the woods, was it? In Stephenville?

It was I suppose in March in 1932. In the woods yeah, the lumber woods. . . . Yeah, there was seventy men there they all come to see. Some used to ask me, "What is that? What you seen? A caribou? A moose? What you see?" All kind of stuff like that. I said, "Come see what you see. Come see what I sees." So like that. Well, [if] I would've tell them after, [they'd have] said your eyes done that. Well my eyes done that? Well it must be their eyes done that too, then. Is that right? Sure. They all seen it. And they all forget about it.

Didn't bother about it.

No. All, all forgot about it. It's only me kept it in mind. I didn't forget. 'Cause I s'pose I seen it first eh? Another time I was here [in the kitchen] sitting down six o'clock in the morning. Now me I'm eating my breakfast. And I had a rosary up there on the wall. You see the nail there yet, le. . . . So I had the rosary [there] and I look [and I] seen something [indicates that the rosary was swinging]. Like that. Going swingin' like a clock. Going like that, going like that.

Going back and forth like a pendulum.

Yeah, yeah. And I was lookin', lookin', lookin', it was like this. I look around see if there was any birds or something. No birds. [It was going] like that, click, click, click.

Isn't that strange.

Oh I'm sure it was [a] minute. By and by it stops. That's funny. So I goes, me, and I takes it and I swings it. . . . Well, it stop.

[Didn't swing] very long. . . . You got any idea what it was?

No. No I have no idea. I told that to somebody, I said well I s'pose somebody wants a prayer or something. I says prayers for the soul all the time. All souls. . . . I pray for the soul. You pray for the dead, the body, any kind of graveyard I pass, well, I always make my sign of the cross and pray for them, you know. It's not outlawed, it's not [against] the law. Nobody can punish me for doing that. I mightn't help them but it's not hurting. I'm not harming them. Oui? So, why not? I'm not harming anybody. Ask God to forgive them for all what they done. All that. So all right [pause]. Well that's the way. (Q-tape 9)

A deeply religious faith is exemplified by these and other such tales, as is a strong sense of the mysterious. The story I found most powerful of the entire visit combined the themes of courage, religion, and marital fidelity. Emile recalled how his first wife sometimes made extreme demands on him and disapproved of his fiddling. When he returned from a long, hard day in the woods she insisted that he move a large number of heavy flour sacks in their storeroom. Emile obliged, lifting them for many hours with his back bent over. When he finished, he found he was unable to straighten up. For more than a year Emile was essentially crippled, but he continued to work despite his terribly awkward position and the pain it entailed. A doctor told him there was little hope that the condition would improve. In a desperate frame of mind Emile went to bathe in a nearby stream at dawn on Easter morning, breaking the ice to do so, because he had heard tales of the curative power of the stream on that holy day. After that he quickly recovered through the power of God.

Other tales bear witness to the efficacy of faith. Emile spoke, for example, of crossing the bay as a boy in a small boat with his father. Surrounded by huge waves, they feared for their lives, but his father stood in the bow and made the sign of the cross as each wave came toward them, and the waves subsided. Emile never forgot the lesson of this experience. When we later left to drive across the island in my car, Emile licked his finger and made a small sign of the cross on the windshield to protect us. The spiritual world and its power, these examples make clear, was very real for Emile, and his faith informed his life.

During this visit Emile told me stories that encapsulated his beliefs, values, life experience, and self-image, affirming those aspects of himself which he felt both were and would be highly valued. In particular, he emphasized his religious faith, commitment to the marriage institution, toughness, resourcefulness, and status, thus impressing me that he was a simple but capable man of high moral principle.

Gerald Thomas has commented that Emile projects a constant stream of comments in his narratives which represent "social and moral values that few people might care to question in public. Indeed, he manages to project through his tales and anecdotes a philosophy which is shared by most of his peers: it stresses the virtues of honesty, love of family, religion, friendliness, respect for one's neighbour, and the need to make full use of one's talents" (1985, 296).

Thomas, who, as I have, maintained a research association with Emile for an extended period, has also attempted, in a study of storytelling in French Newfoundland, to characterize Emile's personality in general terms. He finds humor and spirituality to be essential traits that shaped Emile's behavior (1983, 146–47, 151). My own experience reinforces Thomas's assessment, although with slightly different emphases. Certainly a strong religious faith is one of the values by which Emile guided his actions, in his family life, in his work life, and, not least, in his performances. This faith may in some way underlie the traits of strength, toughness, perseverance, and courage which he presented to me. *Courage* is in fact one of the words used admiringly to describe Emile's behavior by others from his community in a variety of situations, including his music making. Emile's courage, supported by his faith, often carried him through difficulties encountered in unfamiliar performance settings. He seemed to draw the strength expressed in his drive to "keep going" from these values.

Another, less serious side to Emile, however, was more readily apparent. For, despite the importance of these values to him and the strength he drew from them, Emile's public image was primarily that of the "clown" and many, if not most, people would describe him more as a comedian than a musician. Thomas attributes this to Emile's expressed desire to "make fun." In an echo of the fishing story recounted earlier, Emile says, "Ouais, ouais, ouais, je—me garâcherais à la mer si j'pouvais vous faire rire (1983, 146). [I would do anything to get a laugh.] And, indeed, in my experience he would stop at nothing to get a laugh.

"Playing the fool" was as much an element of Emile's performances as was making music. This in fact was one of the traits that attracted me from the first. I found it a refreshing change from the relatively self-conscious and serious presentation of traditional music I was accustomed to in the revival context.

The freedom of his approach, however, was one that revivalists often find disturbing. At a concert performance he gave in just such a setting, for example, I heard some negative comments to the effect that people wished he would play more music. His manner of presentation did not fit the models to which this audience was accustomed. Searching for an analogy, one friend identified Emile as "the Victor Borge of the fiddle." While providing a humorous characterization of Emile's performance style, this comment calls attention to tensions within some performance situations and Emile's strategies for dealing with them.

In retrospect, I realize that my first extended visit to his home was crucial, for though I came to formulate generalizations about Emile's personality and its expression in his music making long after our initial meetings, the themes of courage, faith, and humor clearly informed Emile's self-presentation during my initial visit to his home. Likewise, my role was established during this period, and a foundation of mutual respect based on shared experiences was laid for the future.

Toward the end of my stay in Black Duck Brook, for example, Emile was asked to play for a dance and concert in St. Fintan's, a community some distance away, off the peninsula on St. George's Bay. I drove him to this event and recorded the performance. On the way we picked up his eldest son, Gordon, who accompanied Emile on the guitar.[15] This concert was important in building our relationship because I met his son and shared the experience of a public performance near his home. At the dance Emile's reputation in the region was confirmed for me by an encounter with a man who recalled Emile from the days when both had worked in the woods. "Still keeping on the old way?" he asked Emile, who replied that he was. "It was a good way," and he didn't see any reason to change. The fellow said he remembered Emile from train rides when he would entertain the men as they rode along in much the same way as he was at St. Fintan's that night (field notes 1979).

The next concert to which we went was an even more important occasion because it was an unfamiliar situation for both of us. Emile had been asked to play for what was described to him as a festival in Grand Falls, a community in central Newfoundland, to which I had agreed to drive him. I was going home to St. John's, and Emile was traveling on from there to Toronto to perform during the following week. When we arrived in Grand Falls we discovered that the "festival" was in fact a gathering of motor-cycle clubs from throughout the Maritime provinces. They had arranged a motel room for our accommodation, but the audience and setting were unlike any festival he or I had ever seen. Nevertheless, Emile made the best of this unfamiliar environment. Unsure of how to entertain this audience, he opted for the clown role, mimicking the slow-dance style of couples at the bar we were in by taking a large dog in his arms onto the dance floor. The awkward situation throughout the entire weekend stimulated a lot of conversation between us as to his philosophy of performing: what different audiences expected, what Emile felt he was doing as a performer, and how best to achieve this (M-tapes 81-502/C5316–5318).

By the time we drove on to St. John's, Emile and I had established a strong relationship. I had been recording and practicing his music for almost three weeks, showing great interest in his life and opinions, and helping him in his work. As we prepared to separate, Emile explicitly acknowledged the relationship we had established, indicating that he had become used to having me around and was sorry we lived so far apart that meetings would be infrequent; otherwise, he said, I'd be able to catch on to his music very quickly.

Although often interrupted, our relationship continued in the same vein during the following years. I eventually did "catch on" to Emile's music. I am one of a number of people with whom Emile established a relationship based on his role as a folk performer. Gerald Thomas became Emile's "manager," helping him in financial negotiations with various employers, often steering those interested in traditional performers in Emile's direction, and providing a "home away from home" for Emile in St. John's. A few full-time "revival" musicians worked regularly with Emile, occasionally incorporating him into their performances or providing accompaniment for his playing. And I became a musical confidant with whom he shared his musical knowledge and experiments with new possibilities as well as serving as an assistant of sorts at various performances. Cast in the role of protégé, I attended almost all his concerts during 1985–86, helping Emile by being an active audience member with whom he could interact, by performing with him, and by giving him an occasional "spell."

Although we met frequently in St. John's during the year following my first visit to Black Duck Brook, our next extended contact was in August 1980, when I brought him to a week-long folk music and dance camp in Massachusetts known as Pinewoods. His role there was to teach fiddle, something he had often expressed a desire to do, to play for a French-Canadian dance class, and to tell stories. I accompanied him as a fellow performer, teacher, and general facilitator for his participation. This, once again, was an unfamiliar environment which Emile conquered in his usual style, by storm. I was able to record most of his official performances during this week as well as many informal sessions (M-tapes 81-502/C5319–C5326).

During the following year we continued to meet in St. John's, which he visited almost monthly. I often played with Emile, along with others, at his club engagements and occasionally put him up in my home. I left Newfoundland in September 1981, and our relationship lapsed until my return in 1984, although we did meet during my occasional visits. I had told Emile of my interest in working with him on this research project, a desire he encouraged, apparently pleased at the recognition it implied and happy to help me in my career. Thus I formally began this project in the summer of that year.

A new stage in our relationship began. During the course of my investigations, Emile's understanding of the kinds of information for which I was searching grew and he became more comfortable responding introspectively. He was performing monthly in St. John's, and I was able to interview him on each visit as well as record most of his performances. I also made several trips to Black Duck Brook. The St. John's interviews were in some ways more productive because he could focus his attention entirely on musical activity. At home in Black Duck Brook, just as on my first visit, there were many other demands on his time. My visits to Emile's home continued to be important, however, in maintaining our personal relationship and provided opportunities for me to interview other members of his family, as well as musicians and others from the Port-au-Port.

Emile emerges from the intersubjective framework of our relationship as a man who valued his independence and had the courage needed for self-reliance in the face of hardship, but who also played an integral role in the life of his community, who ascribed to its values, and who measured his success in its terms. This combination, reflecting a cognitive style unafraid to tackle novel problems, be they medical, mechanical, or musical, and hazard novel solutions, a value system that cherishes "independence of judgment" while accepting and responding to others' reactions, and a strong belief in the potential of one's own contribution incorporates some important "ingredients" identified as contributing to creative ability (Perkins 1981, 270–72). In later consideration of Emile's ideas about music and its place in his life I will explore further the basis for his demonstrated creative ability. The analysis that follows represents my effort to understand the music composition process "from within" and thus explore another's world of experience through its presentation in symbolic form.

2 ~ There's a Spirit in the Violin

A Musical Worldview

All musicians operate within a framework of ideas, some shared, some idiosyncratic, which direct the impulse to musical expression. This conceptual web spreads beyond the realm of sound normally considered in cognitive studies of music to connect music making with other dimensions of personality, life experience, and social identity (Koskoff 1982; Sloboda 1985). Musicians' musical worldview,[1] their idea of the musical universe and relation to it, is of fundamental importance in shaping compositional and performance processes and thus the observed "sound object." This is as true among "folk" musicians, who are often regarded as lacking developed and articulated aesthetics, theory, or philosophies of their music, as it is among "sophisticated," "formally trained" musicians (Marshall 1982).

Questions concerning informants' views of the nature and origins of music largely concentrated on the study of non-Western musics until recently. It apparently was assumed that Western folk musicians knew what was meant when speaking of music, and the issue never arose.[2] Western ethnomusicologists and folklorists, working in their own language among folk informants, have not often addressed these questions. They tend, rather, when concerned with informants' conceptualization, to focus on identification of native distinctions among kinds of music.[3] But even individuals from the same culture may vary greatly in their conceptualizations of music, which are extensively interwoven with ideas drawn from other realms of experience (Koskoff 1982, 367).[4] Investigation of informants' worldview and its actualization in performance is more common and has a long history in folklore studies.[5] Even among such studies of singers, however, the emphasis has been almost exclusively on song texts and repertoire, not musical features of performance.[6]

A problem in working among folk musicians is how to discover these ideas if they do not constitute a recognized realm of discourse. I have identified core concepts by searching for recurrent and related images and metaphors within many hours of recorded conversation, both formal and natural, made in a wide variety of contexts with Emile and others.[7] These concepts permeate a wide range of ideas about music, underlying imagery in which the nature of music, musicality, and the social roles of music are expressed, as well as evaluations of music and musical performances. I have chosen to focus on the identification of several important ideas around which concepts cluster, following Douglas Hofstadter's view of a core concept and what he playfully calls an "implicosphere" of related ideas (1985, 246–47). This view emphasizes the essential importance of the relationships of association and implication among concepts, rather than the distinctions among them, a perspective more often emphasized in semantic studies of musical cognition.

Despite its problems, analysis of language, or rather talk about music, continues to be the most common means through which researchers have tried to discover their informants' conceptualizations. Apart from performance and attentive listening, verbal language is, after all, our primary means of inquiry and written discourse our dominant mode of communication. Although inherently limited in its relevance to musical experience, as emphasized by Charles Seeger (1971, 1977, 16–30), it remains an inescapable medium, not only for ethnomusicological discourse but also for research, despite the acceptance of performance as a research methodology, first proposed by Mantle Hood (1960) as the concept of "bi-musicality" and subsequently integrated as a standard research practice into the discipline (Nketia 1986, 5–6). Though language has been criticized as a limited research tool and linguistics as a faulty model on which to base musical analysis (Feld 1974), talk about music has recently been rehabilitated as a valuable source specifically by Steven Feld (1984) and by implication in the many language-based studies of musical cognition.

Generic terminology offers one window onto Emile's inner musical landscape. The ways he categorizes music indicate the options of which he is aware and from which he chooses, or refuses to choose, when creating music of his own. In folklore studies different oral genres are each seen to have their "own rhetorical features, vocabulary, disposition toward reality, use of descriptive language, types of characters, and symbolic meanings—all of which mark it as a distinct form of discourse within oral tradition" (Ben-Amos 1976, xxx). The different genres of music recognized by Emile similarly exhibit characteristic musical features, particularly instrumentation, form, and rhythm, and constitute distinct "forms of discourse" with their own range of symbolic meanings invoked by Emile's choices among them.

A distinction between music and nonmusic is the most basic categorization to be made. Emile would seem to have a rather open view not generally associated with traditional or folk musicians. He stated on numerous occasions that "anything can be music," implying that almost all sounds have the potential to become music. Indeed, for Emile, music *is* the world of sound.

This view was most clearly demonstrated during his participation in the Sound Symposium, a "new music" festival held in St. John's during 1984. On this occasion he was asked to perform in a free-form group improvisation as part of an ensemble that included a wide variety of instruments.[8] Emile reported that he was happy to participate and understood the musical concept as follows:

> When I was down to the Sound of Music [that is, the Sound Symposium event], I went there for the Sound because I was a composer, I compose, eh? So they ask me there for the Sound, and so I used to make sound, you know? They used to make sound too, the rocks with a piano [a prepared piano piece] and all that, for to make sound, some different sound, eh? So I used to make different sound on my violin too, you know? Jeepers Christ I was at home. I got a letter, for to see if I'm goin' back there this year. . . .
>
> So how did you, what did you think of that? What did you think of that kind of sound?
>
> Well yes, I knows.
>
> Is that music?
>
> I knows about it, eh? Sure, yeah, they never knocked me out on it, because I knows about it. Oui? Because it's sound, eh? Anything at all, you can compose anything at all, by the sound of something, eh? Your note, eh? It's like a note, your sound is a note. Oui? Just [like] your talk eh? Your imagination is a sound eh? (Q-tape 46)

As Emile indicates here, he was uninhibited as a participant, although his contribution to the performance was somewhat limited by the range of techniques at his disposal—much of it "sounded like fiddle music," as some members of the audience commented to me.

During another conversation about the process of composing, Emile explained the musical potential of sounds: "The sound of anything, even the sound of a fly, huh, flying, eh? Sound, everything is a sound. . . . All kinds of sounds, all kinds of things, all kinds of imagination that comes in here [indicates head]" (Q-tape 20). Generally it would seem that Emile refers to these as possible sources of inspiration in the world of natural sound around him rather than as music per se. Such comments do, however, indicate Emile's experimental approach and open mind toward musical possibilities.

Although the broad category of music is open-ended, Emile nevertheless recognized major musical genres that reflect the types of music to which he had been exposed within his traditional milieu and, to varying degrees, through the media and in his travels. The further away these musical idioms are from his immediate experience the less clearly defined these categories become and the less important in terms of their associated meanings. Those musical genres with which he grew up had the strongest identity and carried the greatest semantic weight, while those that appear occasionally on the television and radio were relegated to a largely undifferentiated realm of "other stuff" such as "country" and "rock and roll."

The most significant distinction among musical genres is perhaps that between singing and instrumental music. I have often heard the term *music* used to refer to musical instruments themselves, implying that singing represents a significantly different category of activity, reflecting the traditional practice of unaccompanied singing in the region.[9] This has of course changed with the influence of country music models disseminated largely through the media and more recently those of rock and roll, both of which are now widely imitated by younger musicians. Older distinctions survive, however, in such questions as "Did you bring your music?" directed to guitar-playing singers and referring to their instruments.

Although he sang on occasion and performed as a singer in local concerts, Emile considered himself a fiddler. Within the musical realm of "fiddling," the musical genre most important to him, Emile distinguished Irish, Scotch, Canadian, American, French, and Newfoundland styles and tunes. These stylistic distinctions are not purely musical, and classification depends primarily on extramusical information about the performer or melody. The musical component of this judgment is not rigorously described or applied. Such judgments, when they are made, are based on a combination of knowledge about the performer, the repertoire, and particular diagnostic traits. Irish players, such as myself for example, tend to employ many melodic ornaments, an aspect of technique which Emile referred to as "fingers" and a relatively smooth bowing technique, with many slurs. The Scotch use unison notes played with the fourth finger, bowed ornaments, and fewer slurs. They often play medleys of tunes with changing rhythm. The Scotch repertoire is well-known, coming from Cape Breton through various media. Canadian players are basically those who sound like Don Messer, the popular radio and television performer. He played with fewer ornaments and a rich, almost violinistic tone. His repertoire is likewise well-known. American fiddling is like that heard in bluegrass and country music on the radio and records. It is marked by frequent use of double stops and the "shuffle" rhythm. Emile used the French category in two ways, either to identify the better-known French-Canadian players such as Jean Carrignan or, and more usually, to refer to the music of the older generation of French speakers on the Port-au-Port. Technique has little to do with this classification. The Newfoundland category, as well, is not based on musical characteristics but on the pedigree of the fiddler or the tune.

The most important musical category of all for Emile was "my music," as opposed to the music of others. Emile used the term "my music" primarily to refer to his own compositions, but it may extend to traditional pieces, which might also be identified with one of the style groupings listed above that Emile incorporated into his active performing repertoire. The frequently used phrase "one of mine," however, refers only to his own compositions.

In addition to terminology, my analysis of musical worldview includes larger units of linguistic meaning such as metaphors, proverbial phrases, and narratives.[10] I have employed several techniques to gather together significant statements for analysis which Emile and other musicians from his community made in the course of general conversation as well as during directed interviews. Proverbial expressions and traditional narratives have been considered to express ideas held generally within the community. Frequently repeated comments made by informants during our conversations about music making, including literal statements as well as metaphoric images, are seen to express their consciously articulated ideas. Emile's concepts in particular have been further delineated in terminology he developed in response to my repeated questioning. The essential inter-subjectivity of this "emerging special language" requires reference to the musical events by which it was evoked to understand its meaning (Fabian 1975, 194). I have explained this newly coined idiosyncratic language by referring to the musical demonstrations that often accompanied its use, for when our mutual exploration of musical concepts through linguistic means reached the limits of verbal articulation Emile often expressed his ideas through music.

Within the recorded conversations that I examined are many general statements of belief, as well as proverbial expressions used in connection with performance and several traditional narratives that convey my informants' ideas about the general nature of music. One of the most strikingly recurrent themes I found is the comparison of fiddling to speech. When people wish to express appreciation of a good performance, for example, they often say that the player can "really make it talk," and to encourage a player to greater heights of expression one calls out, "make it talk!" Both of these are common proverbial usages and reflect shared community attitudes.[11] This speech analogy is similarly employed in negative evaluative statements, though not proverbially as far as I have found. Emile, for example, often described poor fiddling in general as unclear and imitated it by mumbling. Good fiddling he likened to grammatically correct speech, that is, the listener can understand what the musician is "trying to say."

Bowing, which Emile considered to be the essential characteristic of his playing style, he said, "is like your tongue . . . and it has to come down hard on the beat. When you bring the bow down like I do, it draws music right from the heart. . . . Fingers make the people happy, but that bow's got to work" (Wegenast 1979), a statement that links two crucial ideas about the nature of music with his conceptualization of technique.

Emile's conception of music as talk is revealed as well in his identification of a specific bowing technique that serves as a marker of heightened involvement and expressiveness, what J. H. Kwabena Nketia refers to as an intensity factor in performance (1981, 28). Emile called this technique the "talking bow," a term of his own devising. It was a distinguishing feature of his energetic performance style, which he described as particularly appropriate for use in his own compositions, indicating its importance to him, even though he occasionally employed it as well when playing traditional tunes.

The talking bow is a feature of his playing style that Emile tried to impart to his students. When I heard Kelly Russell, a younger fiddler from St. John's, inspired by the revival, who learned many tunes from Emile, play for the first time after a long absence, for example, I was struck by his use of this bowing effect and commented on it to him. Kelly replied that Emile had been "after him" for becoming "lazy" in his bowing. This phrasing of the critique reflects the high value placed on rhythmic accent because of the role of fiddling as dance accompaniment. Not only is fiddling referred to, described, and realized in these ways as talk, providing the basis to infer that it is also so conceived; fiddling can also serve as a musical metaphor for talk. In Emile's performances, for example, I found that fiddling might be used to imitate conversation or even as a "conversational" medium itself.

Musical conversation is given traditional formulation in several widely distributed fiddle tunes played by Emile, which are known by some variation of the title "Old Man and Woman." Samuel Bayard gives several examples of tunes that are arranged to suggest "either an old man and his young wife, or a quarrel between an old man and wife" by playing the first part slowly and subsequent ones more quickly (1982, 200). His example from Northeast tradition is clearly cognate with Emile's old "Old Man and Woman," a tune commonly called the "Growling Old Man and Cackling Old Woman." As in the performance of a similar tune Bayard cites from a Don Messer collection as "French" (1982; 79, 576), Emile did not employ changing tempo to personify the speakers, but rather pitch, augmented by gestural characterization and verbal commentary. Although reference to the argument analogy is traditional practice, Emile's rendition is perhaps the most "conversational" I have ever heard. The following transcription, from an interview made in 1972, illustrates Emile's dramatic presentation of this piece. Asked to play the "Old Man and Woman," Emile proceeds to compare the different pieces he knows by this name.

> The old way's the best way too, 'cause it sound like the old woman, the old man. . . . Now that's the old man [plays low strain (A) of the "(Growling) Old Man and Woman"]. Now you know darn well he's so good, so kind. But, by-n-by comes the woman. Geeeee [laughter]. She's got a few drinks in her or something [plays a fragment of the high strain (B)]. [Emile imitates voices arguing and then continues to play the "(Growling) Old Man and Woman" repeating strains, AABBA and ending with a fragment of A]. . . .
>
> Audience member: Try the new way.
>
> Yeah the new way now [plays the "Old Man and Woman"]. Yeah, that's not so good, now. Seems like the two of them getting ready to go to a club or something like that. Now, it's not the same jig. It's called the "Old Man and Old Woman," but [it's not the same]. The

other way see, the old man and the old woman. . . . Like married life [imitation of bickering conversation]. (M-tape 73-45/C1426)

A student collector described a similar performance of these two pieces which included "a high pitched imitation of an old woman screaming at her husband [you leave me] 'all alone all the time,' [but] the old man, well, you know, couldn't help it," also noting Emile's comment that the old way "sounded like the old man and woman, too, eh? That's the real 'Old Man and Woman'" (M-MS 72-10/p. 9).

Emile clearly prefers the "older" tune because of its verisimilitude to the sound of the argument and the implied characterizations, which he finds amusing. The conversational, "talking" quality of the music is again an aspect of positive valuation. Emile often included similar humorous characterizations of arguments between married couples in renditions of traditional narratives, as, for example, in his telling of *The Black Mountain* [AT 313, The Girl as Helper in the Hero's Flight] (Benoit 1985; Thomas 1983, 335–56, esp. 350–52) and frequently discussed with me the difficulties of married life in his own experience and the values on which a successful marriage should be based. These related themes were of great personal importance to Emile, and they infused his performance of the "Old Man and Woman" and help account for his fondness for these tunes.

A more idiosyncratic realization of musical conversation occurred during one party at which Emile and an accordion player, Art Stoyles, became involved in a competition of sorts. The two were not accustomed to playing together nor familiar with the same repertoire of melodies, for Art particularly liked tunes from several European traditions learned from foreign sailors in the international seaport of St. John's. In this situation each tried to follow the other as he played a piece. Cooperation soon became competition as the unstated musical conversation developed into a sort of duel: "Can you do this?" "Oh yeah? What about this?" Each musician played a short burst of notes that became progressively less and less "musical," further from the norms of their respective playing. At first each played fragments of his most unusual repertoire items, but soon they were almost simply making noises on their instruments, Art hitting the keys seemingly at random and Emile running his fingers up and down the fingerboard producing no discernible melody. Although not a typical musical practice, the ease with which both fell into this mode of performance, if one may call it that, indicates that the conversational concept was extended thus in this particular situation.

A natural concomitant of the conception of music as talk is the identification of music as the personal voice of the individuals who perform it. This conceptualization permeates Emile's analysis of fiddling styles. Asked, for example, to explain the difference between his music and that of other fiddlers, or between Scots, Irish, and French fiddling in general, he often compared music to differences in language, saying that "I talk my way, you talk yours." "Same like me and you talking, eh. My sound is not the same as yours, like your sound. Like Gerald there [referring to Gerald Thomas's different accent]. It's all different sound" (Q-tape 30).

If each fiddler's style of playing reflects his or her particular voice, the music is a personal statement. Each musician, Emile believes, can and should search to find and develop an individual style, as distinctive as the sound of his own voice. This view is fundamental to his understanding of composition. His compositions are closely bound up with experiences he wishes to memorialize. Their titles and the associated narratives he usually performed along with them infuse his compositions with the beliefs and values according to which he lived and by which he wanted to be known and remembered. Emile's music, as he repeatedly said, "comes from the heart," and he believed his compositions were a legacy to leave behind after his death.

The concept of music as individual voice and expression may also be applied to groups. Thus regional styles may be identified more by the national origins of players than the presence of purely musical markers. Requests for "French" tunes, for example, are likely to elicit pieces learned from French-Canadian performers regardless of their playing style. Much of the opportunity for performance and composition which Emile had during the last twenty years was a result of the public policy of multiculturalism in Canada and a revitalization of Newfoundland cultural identity (Thomas 1985). Seeing himself in this context as a representative of French Newfoundland culture, Emile viewed his music as an expression of that identity.

It should now be clear that a generally held view of music as "talk" underlies how Emile conceived of music and music making, both in performing and composing, how he understood the significance of these activities, how he went about realizing his communicative intentions in performance, and how he evaluated the performances produced. Clustered together with this core idea are such related formulations as "music making as conversation," "music as personal voice," "music as ethnolinguistic voice," "music as personal expression," and "music as ethnic expression." There is strong evidence that these concepts of music and music making are widely shared within his musical community and that in conjunction with his life experience and personality they assumed particular importance for Emile.

A second core concept in Emile's musical worldview, which has a shared cultural basis but has been even more elaborated in Emile's personal context than that of music as talk, is the association of fiddle music and the supernatural. This is a common theme among Celtic legends, which often link the fairies and related beings with music, and it is found throughout Newfoundland.

The conception of music as supernatural appears most often in relation to the nature and source of its power. In one legend that is well-known in Black Duck Brook, for example, the Devil appears as a fiddler. As Emile tells the story, people at the party are compelled to dance by the Devil's supernatural music, which is played in an unusual tuning for Emile, the scordatura a e′ a′ e″ tuning. In a characteristically humorous twist, Emile describes how the dancers' feet and legs were slowly worn away as they danced on and on. Emile begins by setting the supposedly true events in Barbados, a distant locale, nevertheless known to Newfoundlanders through the rum trade:

> They told me now, the fella told me the story, that [it] happened in Barbados, wherever it's to. I don't know, I wasn't there. In the old times I suppose, in the sixteenth century, whatever. And he used to make sprees in home. You know, every Saturday they gather in the place and then make a home spree, eh? Get a cordeen [accordion] player or a violin player and then dance. So that evening, that Saturday, there's a bunch came there, that neighbor's house, and they say, "What about a spree tonight? Eh? That'd be all right boy, gee." Never had a spree there before, you know, that was the first time. They'd had it everywhere else. "What about here tonight? Be all right." "Yes, boy," calls out, boss of the house says, "Yes, it'd be all right." Quite a change you see, for a time, be all right. "As long as you can get a fiddler?" "Yes," he said.

> The host is sent out to find a fiddler, but none will come.

> He had to go about a mile I suppose where the fiddler, cordeen player was there. There was two fiddlers and two cordeen players. "Sure, he'll be able to get one." So all right, go on, all right. The boss of the house is gone. Went there the first one he asked to come he says, "Can

you come and play for our spree tonight?" "No," he said, "I'm engaged somewhere else. I got to go somewhere else." To that place over there, wherever it was to. Ah well, fine, say, "I'm gonna get the other one."

This scene is repeated as each of the musicians refuses to play.

Ah well, fine, say, "I'm gonna get the other one." So he went to the other fiddler. Well the other fiddler was in bed. Was sick. Ah, "Can't go. Sick." "Aah, after a couple drinks of home brew you." "Nah, don't talk to me about that." Say, "I don't want to hear it. Nah, don't feel good. No I'm not gonna play for nobody tonight. No spree tonight. Nah." So all right, he had to let him go, he couldn't get no sense out of him. So he gone to the other cordeen player. When he got there that feller he was, he was sick too. . . . So he goes to the other violin player and the same thing too. Nah, couldn't come, they couldn't come. Nobody. There was one and had to go play, the other three they was sick and they didn't want to go. So he went back and he told them about it. "Go on back again." "Nah." One guy said, "You sees me." Well he goes to that fat fellow over there, named by the name, and, "Tell him it's me wants him. He's my good buddy, he gonna come." All right, he's gone. Believed them. "Nah, buddy or not, I'm not goin'," he said. So he come back. Jeepers cripes they jumped on him [shouts], "You never tried hard enough. You got to try harder." "But you, I know, aahh." But then they start, "Go on, go back." "No," he said, "I'm not goin' no more." "Go on, go on. We wants a spree tonight. We want a spree." Well he says, "I got, I'm goin', but remember, if I don't come with a fiddler this time, I'm not comin' back. I don't care if it's, suppose the Devil, if I don't come with a fiddler I'm not comin' back. So I'll be clear of you then."

Having broken the traditional interdiction against calling aloud upon the Devil, the beleaguered host sets out.

So all right he's gone. He never walked too far [gets up and walks] cripes here's a fellow with a violin case comes, a black hat, black suit, white shirt, black necktie, a pretty man, wow [laughter]. So he got, he saw him he said, "Hello gentleman," he said, that young man, you know, is taken his time. "Not much," he said, "It don't look you're too much in a hurry." "No," he said, "I'm in no hurry." By gol' then he tell him the story. He had went for some fiddlers, cordeen players but he couldn't get none. He said what he had said now, "I'm going to find one suppose it's the Devil I'm gonna find one." Ah, the Devil laughed, "I'm not the Devil," he said. So all right. Said, "Will you play for our time?" "Sure, sure." So all right, gone.

When the host returns with his newfound fiddler the party begins.

And when they seen him comin', oh they all, everybody got in place for the dance. There was eight couple. They never wait until Devil sat down for to start playin'. They're on the floor all [stamps] goin', my God, "Come on, come on," you know, right wild [laugh]. So all right, fiddler took the violin out of the case and he sat down and he start, and he put his violin like that [tunes violin a e′ a′ e′′]. That's the way he had his violin tuned. Now he started [plays double stop] and when he done that, holy blue, their hair stuck on their head like that, whoosh [plays "Devil's Reel"]. "Yeee hoo, yee hoo, yee hoo." Goin' right to it.

One of those watching soon notices something odd about the fiddler's feet.

There's one of them sittin', they were all sittin' around you know, waitin' for their chance and their feet goin' [stamps] you know, for [them] to be finished, [so] they'd get on the floor. And one of them seen, he look at his feet. [Whispers] "Horse hoof, he had on his feet. Horse hoof." And then they start, [whispers] "Horse hoof." "Horse hoof." And then the first thing they, every, all around the house noticed. And they took off through the windows, the doors. They all left the eight couples there on the floor, goin' right to it.

Fright may have chased them away, but concern for the dancers left behind brings them back to discover what has happened.

And then they all went home and they start talkin' about it, they never went to bed that night that's all they were talkin' about, bunches of them, "Did you see?" "The Devil." "Yes." "The Devil." "Seen," you know, seen his feet, horse hoof. So all right. Next day, they said, "What happened?" Now the people never come back. They were still dancin'. And then they was uneasy. Everybody was talkin', talkin'. So the afternoon, there was one guy that, well a couple guys they went and they looked to the window and here they was already, their half leg that was wored out and they was goin' [stamps] and goin' the same speed all the time, same speed all the time. But the Devil was gone. There was no Devil, but the music was there. The man was gone but the sound of the music was there [sings tune and stamps]. That was the Devil. Well. Gone home, talk again. "Yes they're wore as far as here [points to shin] already. Bien, bien, bien, what's goin'." Couple of days after they comes back, look here, they was to their knees. And it kept goin' like that. After three or four days, week and a month after they went back, it was only the hair on the floor [sings tune] [laughter]. Long while after they went back, you hear the reel but there was no more hair left. It's a true story [laughter, applause]. (M-tape 81-502/ C5319)

Nine other examples of this legend have been recorded in Black Duck Brook by Gary Butler, demonstrating its traditional currency (1985, 1011–1108). He considers it a "didactic legend" focusing on a prohibition against casual invocation of the Devil by name. It does not, I think, convey a sanction against dancing itself, as might be inferred. In fact, when asked directly whether this story implied that dance music was somehow evil or "of the Devil," Emile emphatically denied this association, in keeping with his generally positive conception of the social role of music. The legend does, however, suggest a supernatural source for the compelling nature of dance music.

Dance accompaniment is one of the primary social roles of music, and the image of music to which one "can't sit still" is high praise indeed. Emile ascribed this compelling power to his grandfather's near legendary playing: "He could make you cry, he could play and make you cry, and then he'd turn it the other side, you had to go. Sick or not you had to go. It'd go right through you" (M-tape 81-502/C5311).

As well as the power to compel people to dance, Emile refers here to another aspect of musical expression, the power to make one cry. But because Emile's performing persona was largely shaped within the high-status role of public dance musician, a preeminent position among the musicians within his musical community (Ashton 1981), which he held from young manhood until these dance occasions declined in importance in the early 1960s, he valued dance fiddling most highly, as he indicates in the following comments:

Now you take Harry Harview, he was good violin player, but, when play for [a dance], they wouldn't, they wouldn't get outta their seat.

But he could, a nice violin player, nice to listen. . . . They wouldn't
dance. They would listen to him all right. Soon [as] I take it, holy gee,
everybody on the floor [stamps].

Couldn't sit down.

Yeah, you see? Eh? That bow. Dart. You there, gotta go, you see. . . .
See, fun eh? You want fun. You hear those, nice fiddlers, but they
don't give me, not too many gonna give me courage to go dance eh?
But there's some now, they gonna play, holy gee, you gotta get up, you
gotta get up. You got that bow, that machine, that dart there. (M-tape,
81-502/C5311)

The "dart" that drives the dancers is the strong rhythmic articulation valued
by Emile that makes for fiddling one can "understand" and is exaggerated
into the intensity marker of the talking bow.

Human musicians depend on technique to actualize music's expressive
power in performance, but the nature of music's power to move people to
tears or compel them to dance is personified and conceived as supernatural.
The traditional melody called "Les Marionnettes," for example, also links
supernatural legend and music. This tune was sung or played to bring down
the northern lights (aurora borealis) and, once again, compel the lights,
that is the marionnettes, to dance.

I heard that when I was a young feller but, all gone, never heard nobody singin' it for a long long time. . . . And we used to sing that,
that's the one that could make them dance eh?

Did you sing it or play it?

Oh we sing it or play it, anything at all. Oftentimes sing it and the
same thing as music. [When they sang it] them sheets [of light] be
goin' flashin' and . . . they disappear, and first thing, whoosh they're
down here again, whoosh they goes up again. And when you sing they
comes. Oh yes. (Q-tape 51)

Emile considers the marionettes to be the souls of unbaptized children,
who wear long blue robes cinched at the waist. They live in the North,
thought to be the location of hell.

"Les Marionnettes" has been cataloged as a children's rhyme (Laforte
1976, 89), but it is known on the Port-au-Port primarily as the "Gigue des
Marionnettes," a tune, reminiscent of "Yankee Doodle," that can compel
them to dance when sung or played. Butler quotes many similar statements
of belief, several of which identify the marionettes as souls compelled to

dance by the Devil, demonstrating an association between this belief and the Devil as fiddler legend based, I surmise, on the notion of supernaturally compelling music.

Emile also knew and performed with its traditional tune the legend of the "Hangman's Reel," in which miraculous fiddle music saves a condemned man from hanging (Wilgus 1965, 1980). This story is also reported from several other informants, primarily musicians, by Butler (1985, 113–14). In this legend the music is portrayed as supernatural in origin.

Emile related several of his own compositions to supernatural experiences. The "Skeleton Reel," one of his most often performed pieces, commemorates and is usually accompanied by a lengthy narrative account of his encounter with a spirit (Thomas 1983, 148–50, 368–70). The elements of the story are quite consistent from one telling to another (M-MS 80-406). Emile identifies his age as about seventeen and explains that he was walking home at night from a visit to his girlfriend. He mentions that both he and his parents were quite religious, in particular that he always makes the sign of the cross when passing a graveyard for the sake of those buried there, a practice I observed as well in our travels together. While passing the graveyard on this occasion he noticed a skeleton beside him. Unafraid, he asks what he can do for the spirit.

> I look on my right side here's a skeleton standin' by my right side, so I turns around and I looks at him like that. And I wasn't frightened, not a bit in the world, and I says, "What you wants?" And he didn' answer. So I said, "If you're under the protection of God," I said, "tell me what you wants," I said, "and I'll do it for you." So he don't answer. So I said if you're under protection of the Devil I said, "Go on, in the name of God." So he disappeared. He's gone.

Subsequent encounters are similar, but the skeleton becomes more intimidating.

> So it went on like that, for to make the story shorter, I had to go over a mile, about a mile an' a quarter or something, maybe not that, I don't know, anyhow it's a long ways, and he done that all the way. I used to walk about twenty-five or thirty yards and here he was, so I talk to him the same things I said, until I got down the shore here, right here in this, this is the place where I'm talkin' now. So when I got down below to the shore there, mister man, I looked like that on the side and here he was about twenty-five feet high I figure, or could be

thirty, I don't know but I figure about twenty-five in the air and he was about fifteen feet wide and the arms on that and the bone I could see the bones, eh. Oh my good heavens. I fell down back first and I found a piece of wood a big piece of wood on the bank you know. So I fell on that and I lost conscious, lost my senses.

When he recovers some time later he is shaken but struggles home.

So all right by and by I don't know how long I was there, ten minutes, fifteen minutes, twenty minutes, I don't know but I come to, an when I come to, the water was pourin' off of me, pourin' off, same like I took a bucket of water and threw it on me, I was soakin', soakin', soakin' wet. So I looked around, nothing to see, nothing, nothing in the world. Nothing. Gone disappeared, I couldn't talk to him that time, that's all, he frightened me, that's all. So okay. So I try to get up, fall down. I used to get up, fall down the legs, couldn't get no use of my legs you know, they were gone, see, couldn'. Well after a while, well I got to. I got up on my legs but I was goin' same like I was drunk eh, goin' this way an' that way, zigzaggin'.

A final encounter occurs just as he arrives home.

So I managed to come up to this house, I, and to climb up that hill up there, an' when I put my foot on the platform, for to open the door I looks in the corner here he was there again. Like I seen him before, you know, standin', standin' there lookin' at me right at the corner the platform. So I went in. So when I got inside the door, my father jumped up and mom, mom cryin' "Petit a faire." Oh they say what's wrong, what's wrong, what's wrong. Only I didn't want to say nothing because the old man didn't want to believe in ghosts, he didn' believe in that, him. No. If I would have tell him, no get mad see. So I didn't want to say nothing so, I went to bed. But I never slept that night.

The experience was so traumatic that its effects lasted for quite some time.

Hah, and I was two years after that I couldn't go out in the night, that I had to get my brothers or I had to come down before day, before dark, I couldn' gain the night. I couldn't go outdoors, or I have to have somebody with me, my sister or my brothers. But, the way it went, two years, two years and a half before I was, I got bold again. So that passes.

The experience was so powerful, so "true," that he felt the need to memorialize it through music.

> But now I compose a reel, an' I said, for to remember my, my fright, I'm gonna call it the Skeleton Reel and that's the way it goes. (M-tape 78-239/C3581; Thomas 1983, 368–69)

In other tellings he concluded as follows:

> Je l'ai baptise Le Reel de le Squelette. Comme ça, mon histoire vivrait toujours. Et c'est, c'est la varité. . . . Ca c'est la varité. [I baptized it the Skeleton Reel. So my story would live forever. And that's the truth.]
> I had that in my mind all the time, all the time, all the time. So I composed a reel. And . . . I said I'm gonna call that the Skeleton Reel, because, I said . . . that reel . . . would be so true . . . that I said that, that the story will go go on forever. . . . So, and it goes like this. (M-MS 80-406/p. 24)

Although the tune was composed and named long after the original event, it served later, as Emile said, to recall the experience, "to remember my fright," and to provide an opportunity to pass the memory of this experience on to others. By associating the narrative with a fiddle composition, Emile took a step toward "traditionalizing" this personal experience narrative so that the story would "go on forever."

A more recent composition, "Brother's Farewell," which commemorates the death of Emile's brother, serves as an omen of his passing in the story of its composition. Emile's brother, a fiddler himself, had been in the hospital for some time with cancer but had never mentioned the fiddle during Emile's numerous and regular visits. After he returned home on the day of their last visit, however, Emile received a surprising phone call.

> So, that day, the last day that we went to see him, he never spoke of the violin either and we stayed there 'till six o'clock. So anyway six o'clock we went back home. He had his sense and everything. Good. And around ten o'clock I had a phone call from our first cousin, she was just from the hospital and she said that he wants for you to go in and play his farewell. Now gee that, I found that funny, but I said "I'm just from the hospital." Well anyway, that's what she told me. That was the truth. I thought 'twas a lie, but it was the truth.

That night Emile composed a new tune, "Brother's Farewell," and went to play it for him the next day.

So ok. So . . . I took the violin and it wasn't long before I had one composed for his farewell. So finest kind. Next morning I went, got there it was ten o'clock. When we got there he said, how is me, he said. I said, "Brother how are you this morning?" "Not bad," he said, "not bad." I said, "Is that true you want for me to come to play your farewell?" He said, "Yes it's true." I said, "Well I composed one," I said, "for you, last night. I'm gonna play it for you." So, he said, "Very good," he said. And he was looking at me and listening and he was smilin', and with his two hands like this [as in prayer]. You know, smilin' and lookin' at me. And soon as I was finished playin', he got in a coma and next morning he was dead. Now *that's funny*. That's a funny story, but it's a true story. (Q-tape 17 and videotape)

The tune is played slowly, with rhythmic freedom, but as in the characterization of his grandfather's playing, sadness and melancholy are not effects on which Emile wishes to linger.

So anyway, everybody want for me to play it after, I used to play it. And they used to find it all right and after a little while, they say it takes little over a week to forget about death, well anyway I forgot about it and I turned it the reel, in a, that piece is kind of a rock-and-roll or whatever it is. But I call it the "Caribou Skin Nailed Around the Circle" [referring to a *bodhran,* a traditional Irish drum]. "My Brother's Farewell," the "Caribou Skin Nailed Around the Circle" and then there's another one goes after, "Wayne and the Bear." That's another story too, that I composed too. (Q-tape 17)

As perhaps a further antidote to the serious tone of the first two pieces in this medley, "Wayne and the Bear" is a humorous scatological story of misadventures while hunting in the woods.

This story of the "Brother's Farewell" is one that Emile told frequently after the event. It clearly conveys the high level of emotion with which he invested his music and the importance of composing in his expressive repertoire. By reworking the melancholy "Brother's Farewell" into the "rock-and-roll" "Caribou Skin" he created a vehicle for conveying his attitudes toward death and how one should respond to it. The piece has been well received by concert audiences and in his home community as well. His brother Joachim, inspired by Emile's composition, created his own farewell, which Emile adopted and dubbed the "Brother's Answer."

Emile also frequently associated music with the world of dreams.

Music, it seems, is "like a dream" in that it comes from somewhere else and touches us with an experience beyond the quotidian. This association is given traditional sanction through the widespread titling pattern for tunes: "So-and-so's Dream."[12] Emile describes the composition of a melody while dreaming in the narrative introduction to his tune "Emile's Dream":

Well, three years ago, 1980 I s'pose, hey! Far as that goes. I went to bed that night, that's a special night now, it was in March, you know, cold weather and this and that. So 'round three o'clock in the morning, 'hweet! I wakes up with a *dream*. Mais, it was so beautiful in my brain, in my intention, I jumped right up, and I went and I hooked the violin, and I played it. I played it for *half* an hour. La! I had no tape-recorder at the time . . . I had a sister not too far from where I live, so I got on the phone an I start. Croo! A-croo! A-croo! A-croo! J'ai ring and ring. . . . By and by she got up. And she wasn't pleased! "My what in heck is wrong with ye?" Well anyway, well I said, "Maggie that's your brother Emile." Ah, I said I had it, euh, that important, "It's emergency." "Euh, what is wrong?" Well I said, "Look euh—I dream, I just dream about a eight"—a jig you calls it in . . . English— and euh, "I want for you to get that tape-recorder you got there and tape it, because I'm afraid to lose it, ferget it, or whatever." She said, "Yes, yes yes yes yes, yes, yes." Well okay, she got it. So I played it. La. Good enough. Not too long you know, just a couple of turns, couple of notes, whatever. Then I went back to bed. Next morning I got up seven o'clock . . . La. Got up, light the stove and I takes my violin. Then I'm searchin' for it. I'm lookin' for it. And I tries, non! Gone, gone, gone, gone! For one it's in my life that I had dream something I love so much and it's *gone*. La. So I gets on the phone. She wasn't out, to the phone again. "Hello what d'you want, what d'you?" "Oh yeah, yes, c'est encore, encore le meme, c'est le, that's Emile, your brother." Yeah, yeah, rer-rer! I said "I wants to get that, I lost it, I wants to get that tape-recorder out again, and play it for me." So she got tape-recorder. Just a couple of notes, okay. So I took the violin. I played it. And after that I *never* forgot it. And I'll never forget it and there's the way it goes heh! It's *Emile's Dream* I calls it. (Thomas 1982, 10; see also 1983, 370–71)

If the association of the Devil and fiddle music can be seen as a transformation of its connection with other supernatural figures such as the fairies (Halpert 1943, 42), perhaps Emile's ascription of music to the world of dreams is a more contemporary rationalization.[13]

Emile had a strong belief in the supernatural and placed great importance on spiritual faith in his life (Thomas 1983, 141–51). For him cultural attitudes associating music with the supernatural have been integrated with these beliefs and values, strengthening the importance of this conceptual cluster for his understanding of the origins of music and the source of its power to move us, as well as underlying his motivation to perform and compose. Belief in the supernatural character of music provided the linchpin in his conceptualization of his role as a composer and the composing process, as he virtually stated in a conversation we had during my first extended visit to his home. Although I sensed at the time that this was a serious conversation, its full significance did not become clear to me until this analysis was undertaken many years later and I could place it in the context of my greater knowledge of his biography, personality, and music.

After several days of playing and recording tunes during the summer of 1979, we sat together in his kitchen until late one night while Emile told me much of his life story. As we talked, he played a few more fiddle tunes and I asked him yet once again where a piece I did not know had "come from." He answered as follows (quotations that follow are from M-tape 81-502/C5315):

> Yes where that come from? I don't know myself. Oui? There's musician, you know, it's hard to, he can't, he don't know.
> Where they come from.
> It's like a dream. Where it all come from. Four strings, four fingers and sheew, eh? Play and play and play and play and all different kinds of notes in there eh? And when he look up, he don't know where it come from.

Emile's expressed attitude here is that the sources of music are mysterious and hidden even from the musicians themselves. This attitude informs Emile's musical worldview even though in later conversations I was able to coax him to reflect and report on his compositional processes in more detail. At the time of this original conversation, however, I tried to prompt further discussion of the subject by referring to Emile's frequent response to this question and description of his music as "coming from the heart." He proceeded to characterize music as somehow "in" the violin, waiting to be discovered.

It's from the heart yes, and what is the, what is that? What's in there [points to fiddle]?

What's in the fiddle?

Yes. There's something in that fiddle that we'll never know, eh? There's something sacred in that fiddle. We'll never know. We'll never know. We'll never learn it. Nobody in the world will learn it. It could take another thousand years, to learn what is in the bottom of that violin.

This statement reflects an attitude toward the fiddle itself as the source of music based on a tactile, concrete approach to music making. This way of thinking about music, together with the concept of its spiritual nature, which he reiterates, accounts for the difficulty I experienced in prompting Emile to abstract the process of composition from its physical realization.

Continuing to explore the implications of this idea, Emile ascribes these qualities to the violin in particular, his medium for musical expression:

My son I guarantee you. You can play all kinds of stuff on that, all kinds. There's nothing in the world you cannot play. Eh? If you know where to put your fingers. And you take any other kind of music [here he uses *music* in a concrete sense, meaning an instrument] you'll get fooled up on it, eh? You know, there's not enough notes there to catch everything there in place, in the right place. You take the violin it's all there. Even that guitar, eh? There's a lot of notes in it but still they can't catch it like they catch on that, oui?

The "notes" available to Emile on the violin were those familiar to him from traditional tunes he knew and earlier explorations of his own. In practice his compositional technique often involved searching among these possibilities for new combinations that met the criteria he described as balance and rhyme.

Emile explained to me how he composed a particular medley of tunes, the "Wedding Waltz," which incorporates and was based, he says, on the traditional tune "Irish Washerwoman":

I'm gonna play you one now that I compose, off of the Irish Wash-woman and the Rigydoo [the tune known widely by several names, including "Old Ragadoo," "Little Beggerman," and "Red Haired Boy"]. So I'm gonna play everything. So this is the way music is composed, off the notes from this here and there, and then change it in a different kind of direction and bring something, something new eh? So the Wedding Waltz, the one I'm going to play you there, so you gonna take notice it comes from the sound of something. (Videotape)

The way he looks off into space while discussing the experience of composition creates in the listener an impression of the music as "out there" somewhere to be found. He gestures, as well, above the fingerboard, indicating that it contains the notes among which he searches for the composition.

At the climax of this extended conversation about the nature of music, which I have been following and explicating, Emile paused and slowly spoke a few sentences, giving them added emphasis: "Yeah. Guarantee you, my son. The violin, just, there's a ghost, there's a spirit. Know where he comes from. Yeah. No wonder he's the master of the world. Violin is the master of the world" (M-tape 81-502/C5315).

This is a statement of musico-religious creed. The exact source of the vivifying spirit of the violin remains unclear, but Emile believes in it. Fiddle music comes from a spiritual realm. It draws its power from that source yet exerts its influence in a secular context, and it is a powerful influence, especially within Emile's subjective experience. For Emile the violin is indeed the master of the world. It is the means by which he exerts control over the domain of musical sound in composition and performance; through musical composition and performance he makes his voice heard, influencing those around him, and it is through its means that he has achieved the status and notoriety he desires and enjoys as a performer.

Emile then went on to substantiate his belief in the power of fiddle music with observations on the popularity of the fiddle and to elaborate on his concomitant love of its sound.

In three part of the world that's their love, that's their music, violin. Three part of the world that's livin'. There's only one, one quarter that loves some other kind of music. Wouldn't like, love the violin. But the other three part all loves it. That's the best that's goin'. Although they can't play it, but they like to hear it. Well me, I just hear somebody just pass the bow on the strings, just that, not playin' at all, just that, it affects me, yeah, it touches me.

Yeah. Just the sound.

So that's the reason I says anybody plays good for me. They all plays good for me. Yeah, because I love that violin so much when I hears the sound, no matter how he plays it, I loves it. Yup. I loves it. 'Cause I don't care who plays, suppose he don't play as good as me, or better, I don't care. But I likes to hear it, eh. What he can do, I like it. Oui? Because it's so special [pause]. That violin is so special in the world [pause]. There's no sweetheart nothing, can stand his ground like that. That baby can, eh. No sir.

Emile here ascribes a power to the violin in terms especially meaningful to him—the strength that must be evinced by a true "sweetheart."

I again tried to prompt further reflections, and Emile responded by referring to the musician's search for self-expression, linking this conceptual cluster to ideas associated with the concept of music as talk.

Just think of all the thousands of people, right. All doin' their best to play it, you know.

Yes, yes, yeah. They like so well to, to, to push it out the way that they got it in mind, the way that they believes in it, eh? Ah c'est, c'est, c'est wonderful. It's a mystery you see. It's hard to understand. Yeah. Me I plays too, a long time I'm playing but, still, when I plays, and I'm, you know, [when] I feels to play, because it's not all the time you feels to, you like to hear it but you don't like to play it yourself, but you're tired and you know you don't feel for it eh? But, when I feels for to play the violin. Well I know there's something there I can't get, but I like to get it. Huh. It's there. It's boiling in the head, but I can't get it. But I [would] like I could get there, eh? Same like it's far away and you can't get there. Same like you fall in a well now and you're trying to get up with no ladder. Yeah, I know so well there's something else at the bottom of that, I can't get. I can't get it. Holy gee. Get on your nerve you know eh?

Composition is a search to find something far away, an effort to climb unscalable heights or plumb depths, all at the same time. However one might interpret these images in psychological terms, it is clear that the creation of music had for Emile the character of a spiritual quest; a quest that he believed is shared by all musicians: "Yeah. There's something there I can't get and there's a lot of people, good fiddlers, and I hears them playing and I knows there's something over there they like to get and they can't get it eh? Oui." This quest is part of the essential nature of making music.

Another important type of imagery in the way Emile describes the "search" for music which is composing revolves around the emotional power of music. This is encapsulated in the phrase "it comes from the heart," which Emile often used to explain the source of his music. Indeed, Emile's emphasis of this phrase led me to use it in the title of this book.[14]

> My music is from the heart because I love the violin. . . . So that's the reason I said, the music or anything, it always affects your heart. Woman or anything, it all comes from the heart.
>
> Tod Saunders: So like, you falling in love with a woman is like falling in love with music?
>
> Sure. Why sure. Its not coming from the head. There's a pain there, pain in the heart, eh. (M-MS 86-143/p. 169 and accompanying tape)

The "pain" in one's heart to which he refers here is part of what motivates him to compose. It is the pain of loss, of transience. One of the losses he seems to feel is the passing of his traditional cultural milieu. This attitude is exemplified in the shouts of "Bring back the old times!" with which he punctuates a dance performance recorded in 1964 (M-tape 64-15/C115–17). At this time the local dances had declined, and this event represented the very first stirrings of the cultural revival to come. Recreating the pleasurable times of his youth, and with them his status as a public musician, was clearly one force motivating him to perform. This attitude is associated with a conservatism that views the society of his youth and its values as a better world, despite its hardships or perhaps because of them, which is evoked by his performances. Performing provided an opportunity for him to expound this philosophy and extol its virtues.

Another more intimate kind of imagery relates to the feelings associated with composing. During a visit I made to his home in March 1987, Emile described to me how the sound inside him, for which he searched when composing, was the sound heard at his mother's breast. We are each the product of our childhood home and what we have to offer, what we can bring into the world out of ourselves, he explained, is to be found there. He occasionally worked this idea into the birth story discussed before by explaining that as he suckled on the bit of milk-soaked bread hanging under the stove he had played with its string, making a sound that entered him at that time and for which he searched when composing.

> Elaine Pelley: And where do you think your musical inspiration came from? What do you think inspired you to play? . . . Can you tell me that little story again?
>
> Yeah, well when I was born I was a pound and seven ounces. . . .
> Now my mother, she was a sick mother, sick woman, an' she had no

milk, eh? No breast, no food. But now, they used to take a piece of bread with a bit of brown sugar and a piece of cotton and they used to put that in that and soak it in water, or cow's milk or something like that and tie it, then put it in your mouth. . . . And now they tie the piece of line on the end of the rag, to the leg of the stove.

EP: And you were under the stove, trying to keep yourself warm?

Yep. Now my joke, eh. So, I was a sucking on that I suppose. I used to hit on the string, you know, playing with the string [in a laughing tone], with the string eh. I used to make a sound. So, it went in my head, in my head. (M-MS 86-139/pp. 89–92 and accompanying tape)

Although he jokes about it here, the idea that the "sound" of his music came to him almost at birth and remains within to be rediscovered through compositions that can evoke the crucial experiences of his life is central to his motivation as a composer and performer.

As a final comment in many discussions of this nature, including the one from which I have quoted at length, Emile would often justify the value of music and composing in social terms. "There's no sin in that. That music is a wonderful thing to have in the world. Makes a lot of people happy. Makes a lot of people happy. Yeah" (M-tape 81-502/C5315).

Although making music had the character of an inward spiritual journey for him, it was also a means to evoke pleasure in others. This attitude toward the role of music, stemming from his role as a musician in the context of "house" parties and public "hall" dances (Quigley 1985, 57–100), is closely connected with his motivation as a performer (Thomas 1983, 146). As a result, creating and performing new compositions both satisfied his inner drives and generated external justification for its importance.

Despite his talent as a narrator and entertainer, widely recognized in his community, where he was known for his antic humor as much as his fiddling (Thomas 1983, 146), Emile identified himself first and foremost as a fiddler.[15] Close examination of his musical worldview allows us to understand this sentiment more fully.[16]

I have identified several significant conceptual poles around which Emile's performing and compositional activity centered. Music is thought of as talk, personal voice, and individual expression; it has strong emotional associations with the halcyon days of his youth; and because it is viewed as drawing power from a supernatural source, making music has the character of a spiritual quest. These conceptual clusters overlap around the experience of composing, providing support for this activity. The density of associations around the idea of composing reinforces its connection with many other aspects of Emile's personality and life experience to which I have alluded. This saturation of concepts produces a crystallization of great power in Emile's life, as his compositions become, for him, a spiritual voice of supernatural power in the secular world; composing them is experienced as the discovery of this voice in himself and the world around him. It is the combination of these attitudes, drawn from a common cultural store but reinforced in his personal context, that underlies Emile's great commitment to performing and prolific activity as a composer. It shapes the way he realizes these ambitions, as well as how he understands and explains their meaning and significance in his life.

One may agree with Charles Seeger (1977) on the essential distinction to be made between speech and music, while recognizing that how people talk about music, especially in "lexical and discourse metaphors" to use Feld's terminology (1984, 13–15), reveals much about how music is experienced. Both ideas about music and musical ideas, as John Blacking has distinguished these cognitive realms, would seem to be susceptible to this mode of analysis. Although he considers that musical ideas "are always nonverbal and more often performative then propositional," and ideas about music "are propositional and are generally expressed in words," verbal expressions can nevertheless provide guidance in the elucidation of both realms (1986, 9). Indeed, it is especially important to seek connections between them for they interpenetrate one another deeply and essentially. Not only do ideas about music provide the framework within which musical ideas are understood (the social and ideological ground from which they spring), as Blacking recognizes (1986, 9), musical ideas serve to actualize and realize people's ideas about music in sound. Subsequent chapters explore the structure of Emile's musical thinking directly, but his impulse to musical expression took form within the context of the musical worldview characterized here. How Emile thinks of and about music is crucial to what he does with it and how he does it.

3 ~ Catching Rhymes

Compositional Processes

A moment-by-moment account of composing is difficult to document, for it is a solitary pursuit. I have, however, caught glimpses of these private moments, sometimes while listening and recording unobtrusively, often in an adjacent room, as Emile composed, or as recorded on the tapes of compositional ideas he sometimes made as an *aide-mémoire* (Q-tapes 14 and 45). Emile was most likely to begin to play his most recent composition alone at home, most often early in the morning, taking pleasure in a new creation and fixing it in his mind. He played tunes and bits of tunes which he recalled from the past, allowing his fancy to lead him without concern for the quality of performance. His fingers roamed over the instrument almost at random, attentive to pleasing combinations. The formless, unpredictable, fragmentary melodic result is difficult to follow or transcribe, but such music making without the constraints imposed by performance practice is the crucial context for composition, one that could occur only when he was alone.

Emile's composing process may be envisioned as an intimate pairing of musical experimentation and evaluation. Ongoing modification and eventual selection were based on his aesthetic values. The components of the compositional process, illustrated in figure 1, might occur unconsciously or in full awareness. A tune could be created very quickly, these steps occurring almost simultaneously, or over several days or, through successive repetition, over longer periods. Whenever the act of creation can be

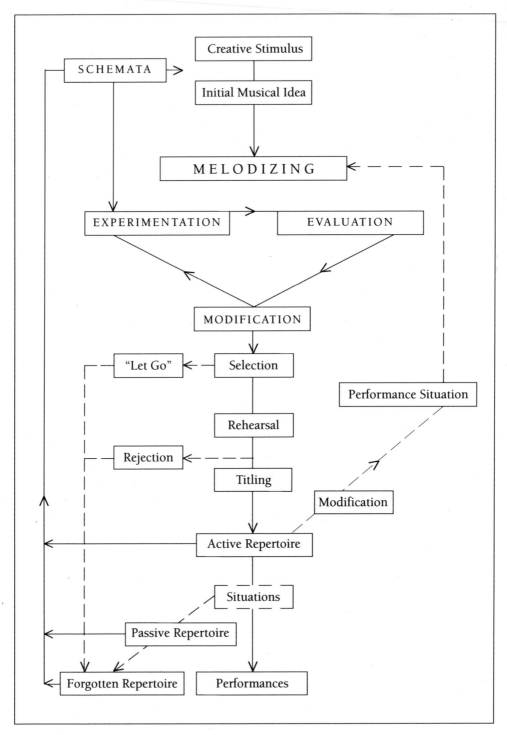

Figure 1. Components of the Compositional Process

clearly monitored, however, these components are present, and other cognitive research supports the conclusion that they occurred even when the product seemed to emerge fully formed.

Several methods of inquiry into the "central and fundamental" musical process of composition have been identified: examination of the history of a particular composition; examination of what composers say about composing; observation of composers working (Sloboda 1985, 102–3). Although these techniques were formulated with composers who create written scores primarily in mind, I have been able to adapt them to the study of an oral tradition: I recorded several tunes at various stages of their development; I interviewed musicians at length about the process of composing; I recorded the composition of tunes on request; and I was present for the spontaneous creation of several new pieces which I was able to record. I was also able to play back some of these performances and note Emile's commentary on them, as has been suggested might be done to study improvisation, because elicitation of a simultaneous account of the process would be difficult to obtain in this situation (Sloboda 1985, 149).

One problem with using composers' own accounts of their methods as source data is that they may tend to explain what they believe should have happened rather than what they actually did (Nisbet and Wilson 1977). Since the dynamics of this process are linked to what may or may not be easily recalled (Ericsson and Simon 1980), it would seem that the more remote the actual experience, the more likely the account is to be conditioned by expectations. These observations buttress the case for using "protocols," a subject's introspective comments recorded simultaneously with the process being examined, as data rather than recollections. From an ethnomusicological or folkloristic perspective, however, such information, strongly shaped by the informant's beliefs, can be crucial for the discovery of how composing is seen within the musical system itself.

Many, indeed most, previous discussions of generative musical processes focus on either improvisation or composition, concepts that are often seen as opposed to each other but neither of which seems completely apropos of the musical creativity evidenced by Emile.[1] Nettl argues that both are instances of the same musical creative process and that all performers "improvise" to some degree, in the sense that all musical performance combines to some degree both premeditated and on-the-spot decisions (Nettl 1974; see also G. Smith 1983, 32).[2] In this view, variation in performance becomes a form of improvisation (O'Súilleabháin 1987).

Scholars of folk and traditional music have generally been more concerned with processes of transmission and variation than with generation,[3] usually portraying traditional music as consisting of a received repertoire of melodies that are varied as they are transmitted through time and space (Bronson 1969, 144).[4] The concomitant focus on particular items and the ways they are realized by performers generally implies a "tune family" model of divergence leading to the development of new tunes, a model that has been progressively recognized as inadequate for this repertoire.[5]

Although the scholarly myth of "communal creation" and the devolutionary premise that change is primarily the result of error or forgetting have long been abandoned and the intentional and often innovative role of traditional performers is now generally acknowledged, the nature of the processes by which musicians manipulate their musical materials has remained largely a matter of speculation. Samuel Bayard writes that "many a player with expertise on his instrument and a headful of tunes and formulas could be capable of something more than merely varying melodies. It seems most likely, in fact, that a good player might at any time consciously try to produce a new melody. The character of the music itself suggests that he could go about it in several ways" (1982, 7). Nettl posits an "imaginary but perhaps realistically conceived folk composer" to illustrate a variety of ways in which a "group of similar tunes can come about" as well as to what extent the composer may innovate (1983, 112–13). Reflecting on the possibility of "collective musical creation," the Romanian scholar Constantin Brailoiu writes in a similar vein of the "primitive" creator, who, "truth to tell, nobody has managed to apprehend" ([1959] 1984, 106). James Cowdery argues that the study of "tune relationship" can be transformed into "metaphors for the study of folk composition." For, "ultimately, folk composition can seldom be studied directly" (1990, 93). My access to Emile's compositional practices thus represents a unique opportunity and a valuable laboratory in which to examine these issues empirically and in some detail.

Emile usually made very few on-the-spot decisions in performance, only a bit of ornamentation and slight variation. Composition is conceived as a process quite distinct from performance in this tradition. Emile's compositional intention is to produce a "tune" that can be recalled and performed with very little variation. This intent was a prime constraint shaping his creative process, for he must compose without the aid of musical notation to fix the products of his musical imagination for subsequent evaluation. Various possibilities must be held in the mind and played several times over for aural evaluation without losing the overall scheme. As he commented about the creation of a medley of tunes, "Picadilly Slant," "West Bay Center," and "Making the Curve to Black Duck Brook," while driving to his home: "But you know I'm gonna tell you the facts true, the way I compose it there. I had the notes here and there, you know. When I got home, well I took the violin, I practice it, but it wasn't the same thing, because you never do things twice the same. Because [even] when I compose something now and I put it on the tape recorder, gosh, it takes me an hour before I can get like that, right, you know? The rhyme. . . . Well c'est ça" (Q-tape 17).

Because Emile's creative intent was to produce fixed compositions yet his methods were conditioned by the ephemeral quality of his aural/mechanical medium, I would characterize his creative process as one of aural composition. Under favorable social and psychological circumstances, the act of composing was initiated by a creative stimulus that led to generation of an initial musical idea. Its purely musical aspects might arise spontaneously and be linked with some extramusical association after the fact to produce a titled tune or be intentionally generated in response to some particular extramusical stimulus. Emile then developed this musical idea through a combination of experimentation, evaluation, and modification in a cyclic process to produce a fixed melody. He then intensively rehearsed this melody to transfer it from short-term to long-term memory and firmly establish its extramusical associations. At this point he titled the newly completed fiddle tune and entered it into his repertoire. The new tune might then be modified intentionally or varied accidentally. It would be further evaluated in light of audience response and its appropriateness in particular situations. Emile might then further modify the tune, but more usually he either retained or abandoned it. Evaluation of tunes in use was a continuing process, and over time successful compositions might suffer from overuse and be dropped from his active repertoire, although possibly retained in his passive repertoire and available when needed (Goldstein 1971). If not called up from memory at least occasionally, however, tunes were eventually forgotten, their musical components decomposing to rejoin the fertile soil of musical possibilities from which new compositions might spring.

I have shown that Emile's motivation to musical creativity springs from his particular personality, values, and opportunities or lack thereof, which produced a predisposition toward this form of self-expression. Believing his music making to be a continuing inward search for his own "sound," Emile constantly explored musical possibilities. The transformation of the products of his musical experimentation into a part of his repertoire, however, occurred primarily within the social framework of music making. Emile's unsolicited accounts of tune creation, which usually serve as tune-title narratives, for example, generally emphasize the situation that triggered their composition or in which they were premiered and titled. Composing provided Emile with a means of capturing and preserving particular experiences in his life, their associated emotions, and especially the values and beliefs they exemplify. Particular compositions might result from important experiences such as his brother's death, his encounter with the skeleton, and his first flight on an aircraft.

In many instances, however, a new composition was created without such an overt external stimulus. Without an extramusical association, however, it was unlikely to enter or last long in his repertoire. Thus more mundane experiences were called into service. Older compositions chronicle everyday aspects of his life in Black Duck Brook; more contemporary tunes reflect his new experiences as a performer and were often named for people he met. Titling occurred in the final stages of composition, tying the new composition to an experience associated with its crystallization. The newly titled tune then became available for use in his repertoire, often carrying with it strong associative meanings derived from the context of its composition. Emile would seem to be intrinsically motivated to experiment with the musical materials at his disposal. This activity served his desire for self-expression in a lasting form, linking it to extramusical events. The connection ran both ways, however, so that external events or experiences he wished to perpetuate might provide the stimulus for a particular composition.

Although most of Emile's tune-title narratives do not refer to an initial musical idea and Emile did not recollect the starting point for most of his compositions, he did tell a few such stories that reflect his beliefs concerning the nature of music and musical creativity. My own observations of tune genesis provide more mundane examples of his generative heuristics.

Emile characterized all sounds as potentially musical, but especially sounds with a particular texture or tone quality that he could imitate with a high-pitched nasal whine of a pulsing rhythmic intensity. Such sounds in Emile's environment on several occasions triggered the creation of new tunes. The high strains of both the "Bandsaw Reel" and the "Flying Reel," for example, were so inspired.

> I got the sound of the wings, eh? I was in the hind seat, in behind the
> wing, eh? And listening to that [makes a high-pitched nasal hum],

you know, a sound [makes the sound again]. And I didn't sing it, but I had that [sound in mind], you know? So I took the violin and I played it. It was easy, easy to play and I play it right low. After a little while I got it and then I open up [laughter]. Jeez cripes, they started getting up. They started getting up from their seats. Oh there was about twenty-five or thirty all in line, to go to the washroom, they wanted to know what was going on [laughter]. So, the pilot, not the pilot but the waitress, he was a man.

The steward, yeah.

So . . . I went up, he put me on the telephone for fifteen minutes. Played. They all went, sat down in their seat [laughter]. So I played the Flying Reel, so I told them there that I just compose it. So anybody had a tape recorder, now, on there, I guess they picked it up. . . . Yeah, it was all right.

It struck me that both the plane, that wing sound, Flying Reel sound, and the bandsaw [sound], are both real sort of [makes whining sound]. Sort of high pitched.

That's right, yeah.

And I wonder whether, well, it just seems interesting. I mean does fiddle music always have that kind of penetrating sound?

Oh yes, when it happened . . . it was a shot of grease eh? [referring to the "Bandsaw Reel"] And it stuck eh? And it squealed [imitates noise]. Squealed eh? *Gee* [Emile's tone of voice emphasizes act of noticing this sound], that there, that'd make a nice, that'd make a nice jig, nice reel. So I went home and I, I never played all the reel, but just the start of it eh?

What was the start of it? Do you remember which part was the start of it?

Oh yes, yes, yes. Well the squeal is, this here is the squeal eh? [Plays high part of "Bridgett's Reel" by mistake]. Bien, bien, bien, bien. I'm sorry [plays high part of the "Bandsaw Reel"]. See? [plays trill between a″ and b″].

That bit there is the [sound of the saw]?

[Voices high-pitched whine to imitate sound of bandsaw]. . . . That note. So I keep on, and then. Well I never played the whole, the whole thing right at once. When I got it there, then I worked on it eh? [plays "Bandsaw Reel"]. (Q-tape 30)

It is clear, especially from the conclusion of this discussion, that the triggering sound has a direct correlative in the emphasis on the a″ note, reinforced in the case of the "Bandsaw" by the repeated upward movement to b''. This seems to be what distinguishes it from "Bridgett's Reel," which he begins to play by mistake, as he corrects himself by trying to stay up on the a'' longer than he does in "Bridgett's," an effect achieved by repeating the a''-b'' combination. The "Flying Reel" employs a similar melodic realization of the sound of the jet engine.

On another occasion the sounds of his truck while driving seem to have stimulated a musical response.

> I'm gonna tell you this story, a good enough story. I was coming from Stephenville, five or six years ago. And when I got to Picadilly I was alone. I start to think about you know, sounds . . . with the truck I suppose and the road and this and that and I got a sound [hums] or something. So I start [to] hum that at first. I didn't sing it but I had it in mind. I was practice, practicing in mind and after a while I got it, [a] good sound. And when I got in West Bay . . . another sound again, came. So, it was the same sound but a little different. And when I got Lourdes another sound again. So, Making the Curve for Black Duck Brook. And when I got home, we were three brothers, we play the violin the three of us. So I . . . played another one . . . I comp[ose], I calls it the Brothers Jig. . . . So ok, Picadilly Slant first and then I turns on West Bay Centre." (Q-tape 30)

This story describes the stimuli for a medley of tunes named after places along his route driving home. Usually he focused more on the place names than the way the initial idea was generated, but in this instance it was not so much an introduction to a performed tune as a response to my queries about how musical ideas occur to him. The sounds of Emile's truck seem to include both the sound quality of the tires' hum and its rhythmic character. "Making the Curve to Black Duck Brook," for example, he says was inspired by turning the truck around a sharp corner toward home from Lourdes, which made his tires squeal, especially in the fall of the year when the road was wet (*Emile Benoit, Fiddler* 1980).[6]

Environmental sounds occasionally stimulated a spontaneous musical response from Emile, and he translated this musical impulse into terms he knew and could manipulate. Thus a high-pitched squeal inspires melodic motifs centering on the a'' which move among the adjacent notes. These are variations of the note combinations with which he was already familiar and suggest possible routes to follow.

The seeds of a new composition are to be found among the melodic ideas with which he was familiar from the repertoire he already knew.[7] When the initial musical idea was not spontaneously evoked, Emile consciously searched through known tunes for fertile ideas, and he often explained the sources of his compositions in terms of the known tunes from which ("off of") he had "taken" the new "note." This is how he explained the genesis of the "Part Time Fisherman's Reel" in which the first phrase of the "Bandsaw" second strain is shifted down one string to provide the initial musical idea. "I composed the Part Time Fisherman's Reel. Part Time Fisherman, it's almost the same [as the "Bandsaw Reel" which he had just played]. I got the note off of that" (Q-tape 30). "Calamus [Candlemas] Day Set" is such composition consciously developed from an "old-time" set tune (Q-tapes 45 and 46).

Sometimes the relationship between tunes taken from one another, as here, is clear, but at other times what has become of the original "note" may be more obscure, as in the case of a medley of tunes he called the "Wedding Waltz" (see figure 2). "Now, you take this, the Irish Wash Woman, [and], how they calls that? The Rigadoo? Well anyway, they compose that on the Irish Washwoman. And, I compose a waltz, I calls it the Wedding Waltz, but I took a note off the Irish Washwoman and the Riggydoo" (his usual title for the tune and song known as the "Little Beggerman") (Q-tape 8).

Emile seems to have self-consciously created the "Wedding Waltz," itself based on the "Riggydoo," combined the two, and then incorporated further musical associations as they developed. His observation that "they compose" the "Riggydoo" "on" the "Irish Washwoman" is a conclusion based in retrospect on his own train of musical thought.

While this process of "taking off" a tune may be explicitly perceived and acknowledged in this manner as well as consciously employed, it is also implicit in the compositional practices I have documented even when unacknowledged (Q-tapes 14 and 45). Emile typically began relatively private playing sessions by rehearsing his most recent compositions and then departing from the known. He might try to reconstruct partially recollected tunes or explore the possibilities of musical motifs that occurred to him.

An initial musical idea may also be generated from a distinctive physical characteristic of its production. This seems to be the case for "Noel Dinn's" and "Madeleine's Glass of Lemon Pie," both of which employ a motif in which an a', played on the d' string with the fourth finger alternates with the d''. He seems to have become fascinated with this technique, unusual in his repertoire, and used it in these two tunes which were composed at much the same time. In another instance, Emile observed that repeated

Figure 2. Notation of the "Wedding Waltz" comparison

Wedding Waltz

Riggydoo (I)

Riggydoo (II)

Irish Washerwoman 1

Irish Washerwoman 2

playing of a high trill between a'' and b'' initiated his composition of "Delyth's Desire" (Q-tape 30).

In this same conversation he described the general process of beginning a composition:

> What's the first thing you think of when, how do you do it, if you know that you want to make one up?
>
> Yes, I [was] just doing like this [plays the trill from "Delyth's Desire"] on that. . . .
>
> The Delyth's Desire one.
>
> Yeah . . . I was fooling [plays up and down a scale with trills].
>
> Sort of like the Roaming Scott one.
>
> Yes, yes, you fools around and first thing, you finds it.
>
> . . . You find a little part that you like. (Q-tape 30)

Perhaps the fundamental cognitive act that provides an initial musical idea is what has been called "noticing" (Perkins 1981, 78–83). Emile might notice an ambient sound that evokes the tone quality or rhythm of fiddle music and translate it into a melodic idea. He might notice a particular melodic figure in a piece he already knew and use it as the starting place for composing a different melody. He might focus his attention on a particular physical aspect of sound production and work from this kernel. This act of noticing, which results in an initial musical idea, may be evoked spontaneously or Emile may set out intentionally to generate novel note combinations and physical sensations. But however these are generated, Emile must first find a melodic starting place when composing.

As composing became an important and distinct activity, Emile developed several heuristic devices consciously to generate such possibilities. As the preceding conversation suggests, allowing his fingers to wander through patterns he knew while exerting a minimum of evaluative constraints was the primary means by which Emile generated new possibilities. These wanderings take the form of rhythmically free melodic movement of traditional types, such as arpeggios, short scalar passages, and ascending or descending interlocking thirds, within particular fingering patterns. But as subsequent examples of Emile actually composing will show, such explorations are made within a flexible envelope bound by traditional phrase structure and thus do not extend indefinitely without form.

His use of this self-conscious generative heuristic technique contributed to the formal innovations in some of his compositions which begin with fixed free rhythmic melodies, externalizing a formerly internal and often unconscious process. If nothing struck his fancy enough to be noticed as a potential initial idea, Emile was likely to try moving in unexpected melodic directions, altering some pitches and changing tonality. This practice seems to be reflected in the shifts between major and minor tonalities in a composition such as "Roaming Scott, Welcome to Holiday Inn." But this response verges on the developmental phase of the compositional sequence, reminding us that the stages I have distinguished are primarily analytic concepts. In practice much may happen so quickly as to seem simultaneous and unconscious.

Once Emile noticed an initial musical idea, he began a process of nearly simultaneous experimentation, aural monitoring, evaluation, and modification through which he developed the idea into a *tune*. This process is suggested by Emile in the following comments:

> Do you think, the idea for a new piece, do you get it in your fingers or in your head first?
> In the fingers first. Yeah, you get the sound, and then it goes to your head, eh. Well to your ears, eh, and then it goes in the head, the cells in the head, yeah. Move them fingers and you get all the sound. Now,

with that, you hears it, eh? Whether it's right or not, or wrong, you know, you hears it, oui, in your head. Well you're trying there, you're thinking and thinking and thinking to see if you can match something that'd suit the sound in your, right, in your head. So by'n'by you got it. (Q-tape 8)

On one occasion that can serve as an example of his typical procedure, Emile willingly complied with a request to compose something while recording (Q-tape 49). He began by playing a short scalar passage from d' to g' sound a typical intervallic opening for tunes in D major. As he progressed, this melodic unit was quickly stabilized and repeated, at first too many times in an experimental fashion, to create a phrase. A leap up to the d'' and scalar descent provides a link for a slightly varied repetition of the first melodic unit a step higher, a jump back to d'', and descent to the tonic d' to fill an entire strain. (See figure 3.)

If not especially memorable, its units being so predictable, this demonstration is effective melodically. Challenged to create something quickly and under scrutiny, Emile seems to have relaxed his selective criteria, accepting a mediocre solution rather than continuing to experiment with more possibilities as he did in the creation of more genuine compositions.

The second strain of this demonstration composition was more difficult for Emile to "catch," as he might say. In its rendering he seems to intend that it move up to the octave tonic, through a standard arpeggio. He tried several patterns reiterating the c♯'' and descending to the a' or e' and made tentative moves toward extending the melody in the later passes through the strain. After a few minutes and four passes through the entire tune form, for example, twice for each strain, Emile stopped, the second strain still unfinished.

I then prompted him to set this new "composition" to a dance rhythm. He immediately began at a dance tempo in $\frac{2}{2}$ meter which he maintained throughout. Both strains underwent variation though the high strain, more so in the subsequent performance. The tune seems to have an "extra" cadential phrase, a relic of melodic units generated in the previous compositional phase but not fully integrated because this demonstration was not completed. (See figure 4.)

Emile's demonstration of composing, though revealing, is somewhat distorted by the nature of its performance. Emile felt constrained to produce something on demand and quickly. As a result, he did not seem to

Figure 3. Notation of Emile's composing at my request

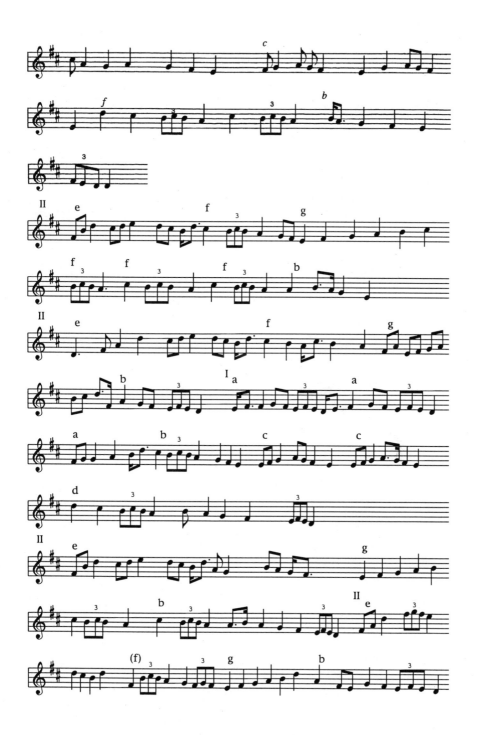

Figure 4. Notation of Emile's demonstration tune

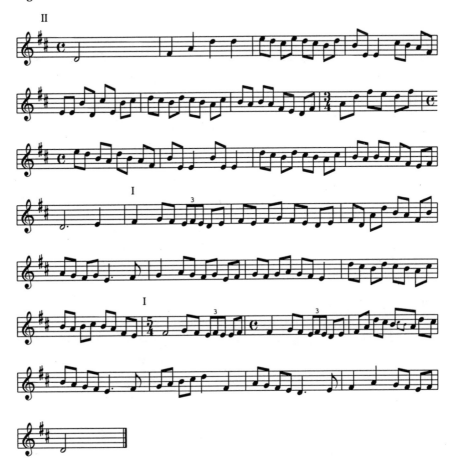

notice any striking characteristics in the initial musical ideas. Rather, the first patterns that came to mind and fingers were employed without much evaluation and simply extended to complete the strains.

During the Christmas season of 1983, Emile responded to my questions about his compositional methods by offering to play a piece he was currently working on: "Now I got one here that I'm starting," playing ascending runs. Although he felt uncomfortable, feeling that "you gets fooled up . . . [when] somebody's there listening" (Q-tape 30), I encouraged him to ignore me and he proceeded to play the unfinished composition destined to become "Madeleine's Glass of Lemon Pie," which I have dubbed "Proto-Lemon Pie." One can find in this example bits of the tune he had played just previously, echoes of other similar tunes, repetitions of particular melodic ideas, and melodic experiments that had not yet been stabilized. (See figure 5.)

Emile began by playing an ascending arpeggio from a, labeled (a) in the transcription, that establishes a D major tonality. Several repetitions of the idea in quick succession led him all the way up to a''. He continued with an echo of the tune played previously, "Delyth's Desire," (b). He followed, a motif marked (c) in the transcription, with a distinctive repeated interval using the fingered a', which he identified as a crucial musical idea that would be retained no matter how else he modified the tune. An ascending scale led to a repetition of the idea. The following phrase experimented at descending back to the tonic d'. Emile then returned to the initial phrase but continued into a new experiment, leaping between notes of the G, D, and A chords. He then descended again to the tonic.

The major ideas essayed, Emile then experimented by changing the order of phrases. He started over again, altering phrases somewhat as he went. A new idea was tested at the point marked (f), which extended the melody down to the g string. After another pass, he returned to try this idea again, generating a new phrase, labelled (g), employing an ascending G triad.

I have grouped multiple variants of the similar musical ideas together in figure 6 to illustrate their progressive development. Emile varies their rhythm and length, struggling, it seems, to compress his ideas into the one or two measures allotted them within the finished form.

It would seem from this example that Emile held several melodic ideas in mind while crafting them to fit one another. The overall two-strain form, one high, one low, and each ending on the tonic, provides a flexible envelope within which he may experiment but to the boundaries of which he must always return. That is, he will experiment with a melodic idea, allowing it to stretch beyond the length appropriate to a fiddle tune but must try to bring it to closure on the tonic. The closing phrase thus becomes an important anchor to his flights of fancy. The opening phrase would also seem likely to serve this purpose. Both, of course, are subject to revision as the distinctive melodic figure is developed. The challenge is to compress musical ideas into a form of limited length rather than expanding them. Emile concluded this illustration of the composing process with the following comments:

Now something like that. Now, I'm going to get that, you know, after a while I'll get it.

Figure 5. Notation of "Proto-Lemon Pie"

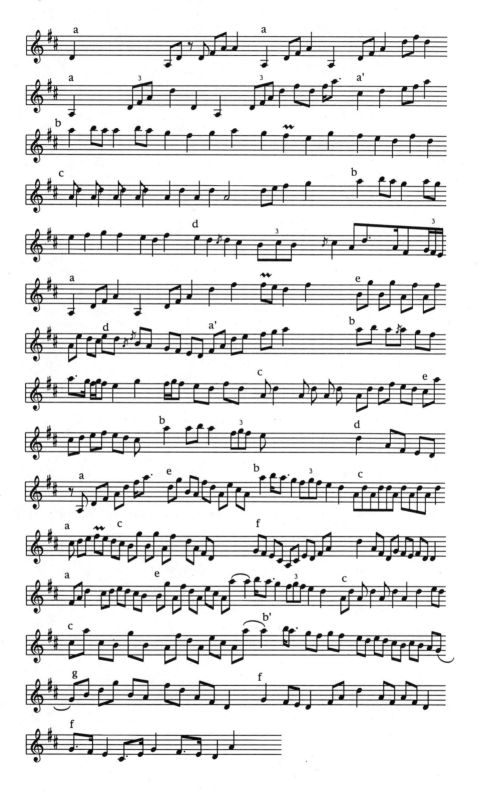

Figure 6. Notation of experimental melodic units from "Proto-Lemon Pie"

a

b

d

Figure 6.

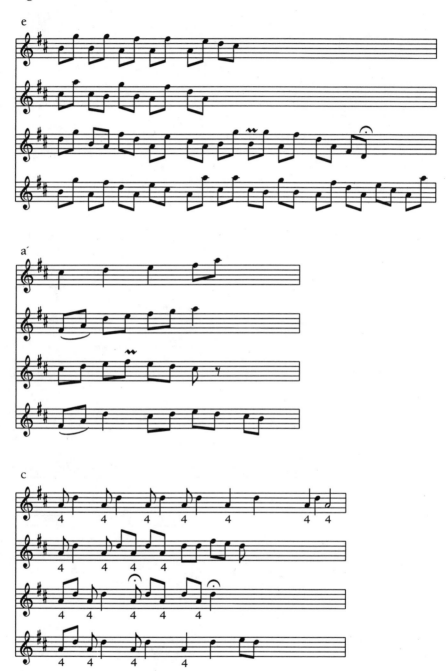

f

Next time I see you.

But I can't go play that tonight, I can't, I just you know, I got to work that by myself . . . I got to be quiet, you know, myself, and then it's, relax there, the music, the sound there. (Q-tape 30)

He needed solitude to relax the severe constraints of performance, quiet for the concentration necessary to listen, evaluate, recall, and modify his experiments. Some months later he recorded the finished product along with his other recent compositions, providing an excellent opportunity to study the process of development.

Examination of the finished tune reveals that Emile retained a relatively free-rhythm introduction that sounds much like this compositional improvisation although its melody had been firmly fixed. It combines the motifs marked (c), (f), and an amalgam of [a] and [a']. The second strain of the introduction is played closer to the meter. After repetition of these strains the tune switches to dance rhythm using some of the same units but adding a new descending phrase of descending interlocking thirds, quite common in his repertoire, together with a scalar descent. Although there is no doubt that this is the tune on which he was still working when I recorded him during Christmas of 1983, it was much refined by the time he began performing it.

These examples reveal at the core of Emile's compositional technique a process of melodizing which I characterize as cyclic. It is initiated by a musical idea that is realized as a melodic motif played as an experiment. This is aurally monitored, evaluated, and subsequently modified accordingly. The eventual output is a fixed melodic unit. In practice, however, additional cycles are begun immediately following the initial experiment so that experimentation is always within the structural parameters of the fiddle tune form. This form requires several motifs in sequence which must "suit" one another, requiring that they be evaluated together and adjusted to one another. Thus from the very start Emile is shaping a whole tune, and evaluation is happening at several levels. The new motif is evaluated itself but also in relation to the initial motif, which is retroactively evaluated together with the new experiment.

This sequential experimentation may continue but is limited by the formal constraint requiring repetition. This bounding within a recursive framework distinguishes melodizing from improvisation per se. Having learned what he knew of musical possibilities by playing a traditional repertoire, Emile appeared to play naturally in the customary repetitive form composed of several related motifs even when melodizing with generative intent, not in an endless stream of concatenated motifs. In practice, then, the melodizing process might be best envisioned as a spiral through time, the modification cycle for each motif overlapping throughout, continuing until evaluative standards are satisfied, modification ceases, and exact repetition is achieved. It seems that Emile melodized within a flexible overall framework provided by the fiddle tune form, which effectively limits the number of motifs generated in sequence and to some extent directs the form of his experimentation.

Crucial to this model of the compositional spiral is the genesis of melodic units usable in the fiddle tune form. These units were created from musical materials and along patterns with which Emile was familiar. It is this aspect of the aural compositional process which seems most formulaic. The clearest example of a "formulaic" approach is found in what Emile calls "rhyming" or playing "rammages." This is how he identifies his former practice of creating new tunes, often while playing for dances, and "letting them go."

> Oh well I'm going to tell you, that's a long time that I'm composing. On the first I didn't put no name on.
>
> How come?
>
> Well now I was tired of it, tired playing that one. You know, fed up. Like you say, everybody gets tired of the same thing all the time. So, and then being in a party or something, a time [festive gathering], I play something else eh? A rhyme eh?
>
> What do you mean, a rhyme?
>
> You know, rhyme [sings "mouth music"]. As long as it suit.
>
> So you wouldn't have composed it beforehand.

No, no.

Just like making it up on the spot.

Yes but it's gone, it's gone. Well I might play it maybe for a half an hour or something like that, but it's gone, it's gone. So next time I goes back again I might play it again, you know. I gets tired of that. Another one again. I compose some rhyme again, everybody going full swing. Oh, you know, new eh? You know, sound funny, you know. Good and eh, different. So people [get] up [to dance], eh? (Q-tape 30)

These comments suggest that Emile did on occasion create "rhymes" while performing, continued to play them for a while, sometimes remembering them for another occasion, and then forgot them when their novelty had worn off, a process that certainly sounds improvisational. Emile's use of the term *rhyme* to describe these musical products, however, is revealing: *rhyme* refers primarily to a structural principle of tunes while rhymes are not necessarily or usually complete pieces in themselves. Emile explains that a tune must rhyme, but by this he generally means that the notes of a melody must "sound together" in consonance. The concept of a rhyme thus refers to a melodic phrase constructed from one chordal fingering pattern. His performance of rhymes does not necessarily cohere into a fully elaborated tune.

That Emile's improvisational "rhyming" produced the substance of fiddle tunes without their form is supported by a 1964 recording of his performance at a local dance (M-tape 64-15/C115). On this tape were several pieces I did not recognize. When I played this tape back for Emile to record his comments, he identified an especially odd-sounding one of these in a deprecating manner as "rammages," a local word meaning "bits and pieces" (Gerald Thomas personal communication). Emile elaborated his commentary in English, describing the piece as "foolishness," "language you don't understand," "nonsense," and "like a hash" (a one-pot meal of many different foods). The piece consists of his playing short melodic segments maintaining the same meter but without ever shaping them into a repetitive form. These melodic motifs seem to be taken from other tunes in his repertoire.

Playing rammages is both formulaic and improvisatory, but it does not produce fiddle tunes. It is rather like externalizing one part of the compositional process, that is, a generative melodizing device, without bringing it to completion, by suspending all "formal" constraints and allowing the play of melodic ideas to flow freely. Because it occurs during dance accompaniment performance, however, the rhythm must be maintained. It is perhaps this aspect which is most reminiscent of improvisation, for there too the composer/performer must evaluate his product instantaneously even while shaping the next phrase. There is no time for reflection and correction of the choices he has made; he must go on. The result is a restriction of experimentation and a reliance on known, fixed melodic material drawn from other repertoire items, phrase units that are combined and not repeated enough to coalesce and be recognized as a "tune." The result in Emile's rammages is freer formal play, employing juxtaposition and combination of fixed melodic phrases drawn from other tunes, what Jeff Titon calls preforms,[8] that is, paradoxically less inventive, again in Titon's terms (1978, 96), because these preforms are not experimentally transformed as they are during Emile's melodizing in a conscious search for new note combinations.

Is this spontaneous composition which Emile reports, and I observed, as "rammages" improvisation? It would seem to be spontaneous composition in performance, as Nettl has characterized improvisation (1974), through variation using preforms, but occurring here in a tradition that hampers rather than facilitates the process. Invented on the spot from bits and pieces of other tunes without the opportunity to fit these musical units into one another, performances do not achieve a repeatable form and are "let go," like other improvisatory music which is notoriously difficult for performers to repeat once the moment has passed. The musical product is likely to seem fragmentary, both to Emile, who deprecated the recorded performance, and to knowledgeable listeners within this tradition, who try to perceive the "tune." Emile's occasional willingness to risk such performance in public is a mark of the courage that supported his compositional activity.

By transferring this improvisatory technique out of the performance milieu to a private situation, however, Emile was able to harness it for his compositional ends, disciplining his melodic inventiveness to polish his creations into more finished and memorable form. Because Emile was not performing while composing, he could reflect on each possible choice as he tried it. He must, however, retain his experiments aurally because he had no means to preserve them for later consideration. Moreover, Emile's only means to externalize musical choices for consideration was to play them. Thus a composing session might sound like improvisation, for he played continually throughout. This melodizing, however, was in the service of generating units that would fit together in the short repeatable melody of the fiddle tune form and was not a "finished" form in and of itself.

When given a portable cassette recorder by his children, Emile discovered its potential to change this limiting factor and began to record "works in progress" (Q-tapes 14 and 45). He did not actually work with the recorder on, however, preferring to wait until he had as close to a finished product as he could get in a particular sitting before recording. As a result, the tape recorder became more useful as a means to increase his compositional output by saving new tunes with much less effort than was needed to "fix" them in mind through repetition than as a true aid to the melodizing process.

Scholars have emphasized the range of variation among related melodies in fiddling tradition as a whole, yet for Emile and other performers of his musical community a fiddle tune exists as a whole repeatable in its performance with a limited degree of specific variations. Different musicians might acknowledge having different versions of the same tune and, indeed, a single musician might know more than one such version, but these would be considered distinct entities. There is no provision for the gradual unfolding of melodic ideas in performance through variation, which is of limited extent and is static rather than progressive in character. The characteristics of this tradition, which are described as dense and narrow by Nettl (1982, 11–12), channeled Emile's desire to create new musical statements into composition through melodizing, rather than the more improvisatory rhyming in performances that produce rammages.

When Emile did create in public performance, he went through a disturbing period while the "tune" took shape. The audience would perceive that he did not seem to know what he was doing because of the unacceptable degree of variation from strict repetition. Emile's courage, however, often carried him through such uncertainty to a melodic line he could repeat and that would serve. Fellow fiddlers commented in these terms on Emile's first-time performance of an unfamiliar request at a small gathering following a festival performance in Stephenville (field notes 1984). Taking a slightly known melody and transforming it into a fiddle tune is the most common form of composition in performance I have observed. While he was performing at a bar one night, for example, a patron asked him to play "Danny Boy." Not too sure of the melody, Emile gave it a try but quickly transmuted it into a fiddle tune rhythm and format. This process is much the same as that described as "taking a note off" another tune. In this case, however, the whole melody is so used rather than just a small portion of it.

Learning a new tune may engender a similar transformation. On one occasion I played a piece on the accordion and he joined with me to learn it. Once again the tune was soon changed and a new piece, dubbed "Colin's Missing Note," created. After some experimentation it was transposed a fifth higher by shifting the fingering over one string and conforming it to standard patterns of core fingering.

This is an example of the "wholesale remaking" of melodies by traditional performers hypothesized by Ann and Norm Cohen as the traditionalizing process by which popular tunes have been given an oral-traditional character (1973). It places the locus of this process firmly within the musical cognition of the individual musician rather than a community responsible for "re-creation."

All these examples indicate that the result of Emile's constant disassembling of his repertoire for reuse and reshaping is a tightly interwoven web of compositions with countless interconnections at all constituent levels. While Emile clearly drew on melodic ideas familiar from his repertoire of traditional tunes and previous compositions, he also tried to develop novel tunes by "changing the notes," as he would say, that is, by transforming them. Typical transformations include rearranging the notes of a triadic motif (one may compare, for example, "Kibitzer's" and "Ron Hynes'"), or he might change the sequence of step motion in a melodic phrase constructed within the same tetrachordal "finger area" (as is the case with portions of the "Bandsaw," "Skeleton," and "Skipper's" reels). Changing rhythms is another way to create one tune from another (as "Brian Tobin's" has been from "Martin White's").

To summarize components of the compositional sequence considered thus far, the core process of development from an initial musical idea is one of continuous experimentation, evaluation, and modification. It may operate on initial melodic units ranging from entire tunes and strains, through phrases, to short melodic fragments. Whatever the size of the unit with which he begins, Emile proceeds to experiment by playing within a loose fiddle tune template delimited by its formal constraints. The number of potential musical units with which he can experiment at one time is limited by the need for repetition, which requires that they be held in short-term memory as they are modified in light of their evaluation. Individual phrase units are evaluated for their qualities of balance and rhyme. The two strains must contain contrasting but complementary phrases at different pitch levels and generally finish with identical units. This process may take from a few minutes to a couple of days. It may seem to occur spontaneously, and its processes appear unconscious, or it may be consciously directed.

This process of melodizing is facilitated and directed by relatively flexible schemata. These operate at all constituent levels, providing the standard length and shape of entire tunes and strains as well as possible melodic material. Fingering patterns play an especially important role in guiding choices at the smaller phrase levels. The first strains of "Kibitzer's Reel" and "Ron Hynes'," for example, clearly contain units constructed within the same fingering patterns. The most common of these would be appropriate within only a few tonalities, thus further limiting choices easily "at hand," to borrow David Sudnow's terminology (1978). This multilevel use of schemata constrained Emile's choices within each tonality, producing a repertoire with a high level of similarity and consistency among and between its different items.

Such dependence on schemata for guiding creative thinking is generally associated with models of improvisation in music and folklore.[9] Schemata that are able both to provide "ready-made" units and to serve as plans for exploratory thinking, however, have been identified as an important component of creative work in general (Perkins 1981). Their use need not imply that the thinker is any less inventive or interested in producing and perfecting useful, that is, "creative" innovations within any given realm of operation. Indeed, their use seems to accompany the work of especially prolific producers, whose "fluency" of production depends in part on their having a large repertoire of unconscious units and patterns on which to draw. These schemata provide mental structures that "allow a person to perceive or act effectively by anticipating the organization of what the person apprehends or does, so that the person need not function as much from scratch" (Perkins 1981, 161–74). Emile's compositional practice is clearly directed toward innovative goals while strongly reliant on schemata. From the creator's viewpoint, schemata are less constraints on his imagination than they are its facilitators, providing possibilities for exploration by "preselecting," in Emile's case for certain melodic "sounds" known to be fruitful.

∼ *"Comme ça, mon histoire vivrait toujours": Tune Titling and the Dynamics of Repertoire*

Once he had noticed and selected an initial melodic motif, Emile employed a repertoire of compositional principles in the process of generating additional units to fill out the fiddle tune form. Simple repetition is one solution, as in the "Breakwater Boys' Breakdown." Repetition with slight variation is common, often achieved through inversion of a portion of the melodic phrase. Repetition with slight variation also operates to generate eight-bar phrases composed of two four-bar segments differing only in the final resolution, as in "Reel de la Pistroli." Repetition at a neighboring pitch level in sequential manner is also frequent, as with one-measure units in the first strain of "Arriving to St. John's" or two-measure segments in "Bridgett's Reel."

So closely tied to the process of experimentation through which Emile developed his initial musical ideas as to be virtually simultaneous is their evaluation and modification according to criteria applied at several different levels. Each melodic experiment is evaluated as a potential phrase of a finished tune. Subsequent phrases are evaluated as potential components of a strain. The whole is measured against the model of fiddle tune form within which experimentation has proceeded throughout the composing process. The evaluative principles in terms of which melodic experiments are measured are expressed by Emile as the need to find notes that "suit," "balance," and "rhyme."

Notes that suit are limited to certain scales as realized within the basic fingering patterns "on" relatively few tonic notes. Emile employed those tonics most commonly found in local tradition. Melodies are built around triad fingering patterns of arpeggios and scalar passages within this gambit and that of the tetrachord available within first position on each string. Emile searched within the soundscapes defined by these parameters as he developed a new composition.[10]

When composing in the instances considered above, for example, Emile never moved outside the tonality defined by his initial choice of tonic and the associated fingering positions. Alternation between f♯'' and f'' natural, as in "Roaming Scott, Welcome to Holiday Inn," is a possibility he discovered for changing the "sound" of a tune without affecting its fingering, thus making it easy to implement. Modulation to different tonics and their associated fingering patterns does not occur within single compositions, although it is found in medleys of tunes that would have been created as distinct entities and might have led from one to another, as did the components of the "Wedding Waltz" medley.

When explaining that the notes of a tune must "rhyme," Emile often referred to harmonic relationships with which he was familiar. Asked directly "what it means when one [piece] rhymes with another piece," Emile responded with comments such as "there's two sounds, but they still meets together, eh. They sounds together" (Q-tape 20). Consonant intervals that he employed include unisons and octaves sounded with the open fiddle strings, fifths, to which the open strings are tuned, fourths as sounded by the first and second fingers on adjacent strings, and major thirds as sounded by the first and third fingers on adjacent strings. While searching for possibilities within the musical soundscape of a particular tonality, Emile was looking for notes and patterns that rhyme, that is, notes he knew would "sound together."

Exploring this topic on one occasion, Emile suggested we play "Colin's Missing Note" together, one on the G, the other on the D. Emile's expectation that our playing of a tune in parallel fifths, essentially one string "apart," would naturally "rhyme" indicates that his understanding of harmony was based on practical experience of playing a solo violin, in which such parallel notes are consonant. His harmonic concepts were not much elaborated through ensemble playing. He showed a relative lack of concern about the chords played by accompanists, for example. Most guitar players in his home community are familiar with only the basic I, IV, and V major chords in D, G, A, C, perhaps some seventh fingerings and the a and e minor, but probably not b or f♯ minor. Emile preferred such guitar accompaniment as his son Gordon provided, which often does not closely follow the potential chord changes implied in his melodies that young urban guitar players, more broadly influenced, tend to employ. What seemed to matter most to Emile in accompaniment was rhythm, not harmonic complexity.

Rhyming also refers to consonance in sequence, probably based on his experience of using triad-based fingering patterns. Thus the notes of a melody must suit by rhyming, particularly the melodic closure of a phrase, which must rhyme by returning to the tonic. During one interview Emile suggested I compose something myself in the manner we had been discussing. I complied and we used my efforts as a point for further discussion. Asked what considerations should guide the continuation of my initial phrase, he replied:

> You change it for to suit the sound, you come down now and suit the sound you got up there. Well the same like a person acting, he goes and he goes right, in place, and back again, eh? In music it's the same thing, eh, got to balance, eh? Got to balance. It's an answer, yes.
>
> So like question and answer? Down here for one part, right? Would you then do, the next part you go higher up?
>
> You got to suit, you got to make it suit, yeah. (Q-tape 20)

Where the melody "got to go," as Emile points out, is back to its beginning. The concluding phrase must rhyme with the initial phrase by "bringing the note" back to the tonic. Possibilities for extension of the initial musical idea into higher ranges and back down is largely determined by the tonality established in the initial unit for "it got to suit what you got up there." No matter where it goes, the melody must return to its initial phrase for it "got to balance" by providing an "answer" to the initial "question." The final phrase of a strain in particular must rhyme by providing a melodic cadence. Although so-called circular tunes are known in the tradition, Emile preferred a clear resolution to the tonic, as suggested by his efforts to rework one of his brother Joachim's compositions in the "Brother's Answer." Joachim's melody, composed as a response to Emile's "Brother's Farewell," never resolves to the tonic g'. Emile found this unsatisfactory and spent quite a while playing the piece over and over trying to find an interesting way to conclude on this note.

Despite the constraints imposed by his understanding of which notes will suit one another, however, Emile observed in conclusion, "But you [can] change it [the notes] in any kind of way, long as they suit," perhaps responding to my seeming desire for guidance and rules of composition to follow. For Emile, composing in this manner is not like following a set of guidelines that are guaranteed to generate acceptable tunes. Rather, he was searching for something new, trying to innovate within the parameters of acceptable musical organization by using the musical means at his disposal.

Melodic ideas that balance are likewise those which suit and answer one another to provide a sense of completed form. Rhythm is also important to this sense of completeness. In the same discussion Emile explained:

> Well balance, sure. If you, you does this, you plays it say [like this, plays "Colin's Missing Note," changing tempos at each phrase]. See you lose your balance there. If you jumps on that note you goes fast or you goes slow. If you don't keep time, well you lose the balance, you're just no good. Your reel's no good.
>
> So it's got to be even.
>
> Yes, yes, it's got to be there. Yes, yes, yes. Sure if you plays the violin you got to keep time. You got to try to have it even. Or else you gonna go halfways then turn, speed faster. Speed faster if you want, but keep faster. Keep the same distance again. Right? Don't go faster, jump slow again, something like that, if the reel or the jig or the waltz don't suit. It gotta suit. It gotta balance. It gotta go, you know?

Indeed, a good tune not only "gotta go," "It gotta fly, like a bird. It gotta fly, nice. Yeah" (Q-tape 20).

Not surprisingly for a musician whose musical forms serve primarily as dance accompaniment, rhythm emerges from Emile's comments as the paramount musical value. His brief comments on the quality of different tunes most frequently make reference to the "going good," "having a good beat," so that "it balance good" (Q-tape 8).

As he explores different combinations of notes Emile listens for possible melodic units that balance well. In his use of the tape recorder as a composing aid this process is externalized. He explains in the following conversation that after recording "all kind of foolishness," that is, unformed musical ideas,

> I listens to it and if I picks any sense in it, so, I do something with it. And if there's no sense in it, well if there's no sense in it for me, there's no sense in it [laugh]. . . . It's the balance, you see? Anything at all, down there [referring to the lower range of notes on the G string, where I have been attempting to compose something in his manner]. Balance is the thing. It's got to have the right, beat to it. Yes. Any kind of air, that's how you got to work it. (Q-tape 49)

In other words, melodic phrases must be clearly defined within the meter. This usually means a closed melodic phrase of two two-beat $\frac{2}{2}$ or $\frac{6}{8}$ meter measures. Coincidence of melodic markers of closure with the metrical frame is typical, but occasional discrepancies are found, most commonly involving added or dropped beats that do not disturb the basic pulse. "Hélène's Reel" and "Jim Hodder's," for example, contain such phrases. Some tunes seem to have extra phrases, producing longer strains than usual. This would seem to result from genesis during the melodizing process of more material than needed for standard form, as in the case of the composition created on demand which I discussed above. Sometimes variation from formal norms seems intentionally employed to add interest to the melody. "Ryan's Fancy Arriving," for example, is based on the traditional "Woodchopper's Reel," but its distinctive first strain phrase is lengthened through repetition, creating a somewhat humorous effect in performance. The "Flying Reel" repeats its first strain an unusual three times, perhaps compensating for its reliance on a single musical phrase. The "suites" he composed most recently are the most extreme example of departure from formal norms of tradition.

Once Emile generated an entire tune through this process of aural composition by selecting melodic units that met his criteria of evaluation, he was confronted with the challenge of preserving the product of his aural imagination. He accomplished this through immediate and constant repetition. As he says, his favorite tune is always his most recent. After all the trouble it takes to compose a new tune, it is surprisingly easy to forget. "Colin's Missing Note," for example, was so named because as soon as we had finished making it and playing it for about ten minutes (Q-tape 12), neither Emile nor I could remember the particular melodic turn that had most struck his fancy.

The tape recorder is a new aid to this stage of composition, as well as that of "searching," to which Emile was introduced by his children and researchers but which he began to use himself. "Emile's Dream" is one composition that owes its recollection to the tape recorder, although this was highly unusual at the time. After about 1984 Emile more systematically recorded many of his compositions, perhaps motivated by his increasing level of activity as a composer (Q-tape 49). It seems that he could generate many more tunes than he could hold in his repertoire, as demonstrated by the appearance on tapes of many "compositions" that were never actively performed. Some new tunes such as the "Basketball Quadrille," for example, do not seem to outlast the immediate context of compositions, while others appear to have been relatively short-lived, only appearing on recordings for the duration of a particular visit or performance "gig." Without the tape recorder it is likely that these would have been "let go," as he recalls were most of the compositions of his youth.

Titling is a crucial step in fixing new compositions in memory. At that point a piece entered his active performance repertoire and acquired a distinct significance, was given a performance role, and became a meaningful statement. The new tune was repeatedly rehearsed and consciously associated with its title until the two "sounds" were inextricably associated in his mind. Significantly, while earlier stages of the composition process were carried out by the musician in solitude, in response to internal, personal drives, naming almost always occurred through social interaction. Titling marked the point at which the new composition was offered to his audiences, and he often did so by asking someone to "baptize" the new creation. Moreover, tune titles that achieved common currency were those confirmed in use by the community of listeners and other performers. By titling his compositions in this public manner Emile indicated once again that he meant to give his tunes to "tradition" so that, as he said of the "Skeleton Reel," his experience might never be forgotten.

The titles of Emile's compositions may be conveniently classified according to their sources—places, people, and events—although in some cases these overlap. These are, in general, the most common types of tune titles throughout related traditions. Although their assignment to tunes may appear arbitrary and capricious, as it has to many regional collectors when viewed from a large-scale perspective, tune titles are seen, when an appropriate scale reflecting the operative musical community is adopted, to be meaningfully tied to the environment, experience, and worldview of musicians and audience. Emile's tune titles include the places, communities, roads, and natural landmarks that framed his life; the people he wished to entertain are memorialized in the titles of the tunes they enjoyed; and crucial experiences that exemplify his values and beliefs are recalled by tunes named for them.

The most common sources for tune titles are the names of close relatives and friends, people for whom he played his music, public figures whom he respected. Numerous examples of this practice could be cited. "Joe Smallwood's" was one of the first of his tunes to be so named. Smallwood was the Liberal party premier of Newfoundland for many years and the man who brought it into confederation with Canada. Emile celebrated his allegiance to the Liberal party and his interest in politics in several other tunes: "Brian Tobin's" for the Liberal member of Parliament from Port-au-Port; "Steve Neary's" for a prominent Liberal party politician in the province; and "Jim Hodder's" for the Liberal Member, House of Assembly, from western Newfoundland. Emile was politically active, attending party conventions as a delegate, often performing and sometimes composing tunes for these events. When Hodder switched party allegiance to the Progressive Conservatives by "crossing the floor," for example, Emile began calling this piece "Jim Hodder Crossing the Floor."

As his output of compositions increased in response to demand from a wider audience, Emile continued to name tunes for people, most often those with whom he worked. There are tunes for Noel Dinn, Pamela Morgan, Kelly Russell, and even for me, all musicians from St. John's with whom he frequently played. Gerald Thomas was a significant source of tune titles in the later period, often requesting tunes for various members of his family. Thomas is notable in this regard because he was often the first audience for a new piece. I also saw situations in which Emile played a new piece and requested suggestions for a title.

There are also tunes named for John Houston, the assistant director of the Disney film in which he appeared, and the artist who painted the portrait that appears on the LP album *Ça Vient du Tchoeur/It Comes from the Heart,* Gerry Squires. He did not know either of these people well or interact often with them; not surprisingly, their tunes never really entered his repertoire but were dropped as soon as the situation that spawned them ended. Such melodies might reappear to be retitled later, however, somewhat modified by the aural compositional process. A tune Emile identified as "Gerry Squires'," for example, appears on a recording made many years before they met (M-tape 64-15/C116).

Titles based on place names often commemorate the locations associated with their composition. The bars in which he performed in St. John's are so memorialized as is the recording studio, Clode Sound, used for his first LP (Benoit 1979). This tune likewise seems to be a convenient retitling of an older piece, called "Up in the Clouds" on another occasion, to satisfy a particular need (field notes 1987). Places around his home also often served as titles. This is one of the few medleys he commonly played before this recording. Thus it was not the musical concept of a medley that inspired him to group these tunes, though their reported genesis would imply some musical relationship, but rather the thematic relationship of the tune titles to his environment. In performance the titles of these pieces would create an immediate and shared image in the minds of anyone from the peninsula, an image that would clearly place Emile in the physical and social fabric of this region. More than once as we drove along this stretch of road, Emile recalled these tunes and related this story. In performance in St. John's and elsewhere it served as a kind of musical address or identification of his home turf.

The most idiosyncratic of Emile's tune titles are those that relate to memorable experiences and are often linked with more extended narratives. Some of these incidents are the basis for humorous anecdotes such as "Gerald Thomas' Burnt Potato Reel," or "Wayne and the Bear." Others are more serious such as "Brother's Farewell" or the "Skeleton Reel." Some of these titles have an active quality, for example, "Arriving to St. John's," different from those named after people or places. In either case the title is the name of a story as well as a tune and echoes the crucial details of the narrative to which it refers. One needs to know the story to understand the title, which may achieve a humorous effect through its very obscurity, as in the case of "Madeleine's Glass of Lemon Pie" or through odd juxtapositions as in the "Roaming Scott, Welcome to Holiday Inn."

Tune titling, then, was Emile's crucial means for giving his compositions meaning through extramusical associations. Once he had created a composition, he usually played the new piece in informal performance and if it was well received, gave it a name, most often suggested by his immediate environment or some recent memorable experience. The new tune was repeatedly rehearsed and consciously associated with its title until the two "sounds" were inextricably associated in his mind.

The title forms a link between tune and tale. Although Emile was familiar with at least some traditional titles for traditional tunes he played, he rarely used them in performance. His own compositions, which formed the bulk of presented material in almost every contemporary performance, however, were almost always announced as such and titled. At a minimum he would shout out a title such as, "Now 'Tootsie Wootsie'!"

The titles of his compositions in many cases encapsulated the associated anecdote he would narrate. These might be brief and simply evoke a particular experience, as in the case "Arriving to St. John's," or quite lengthy.

Most discussions, and there are not many, of tune titles note how widely the titles for particular tunes may vary and, vice versa, how many diverse tunes may be referred to by a single title. Many traditional tune titles have been called floaters. In Irish tradition, for example, there are any number of tunes called "Pigeon on the Gate." The reverse situation, many titles and one tune, has been noted by revival players who joke about the tune known in Scotland as "My Love Is but a Lassie Yet," in England as "Too Young to Marry," in Appalachia as "Sweet Sixteen," and supposedly, in some places they still call it "Statutory Rape." Vance Randolph has noted the frequency of both situations in his collection of tune titles from the Ozarks (1954).

This confusion led Samuel Bayard to describe the "tune-naming situation" as "chaotic."[11] No one has addressed the function and significance of tune titling or examined their use in performance contexts within a musical community at any length. This is unfortunate because I have found that the process of naming a tune can be an important meaning-giving act through which the musician and the audience connect the musical experience of the fiddle tune with their other individual and shared worlds of experience.

Tune titles were a crucial means for giving Emile's compositions extramusical associations. Once so "baptized," compositions served to carry the meaning of their associated tune title narratives. Emile's choice of tune in performance, for example, was significantly affected by his ability to use it in this manner. He played tunes named for people present, such as "Gerald

Thomas' Burnt Potato," whenever possible; he played tunes the audience requested by name; and he played tunes that incorporated narratives he wished to relate.

Some modification of the tune might occur at this stage in the compositional sequence but did not usually. On one occasion, for instance, shortly after composing "Pamela Morgan's Desire," he solicited my opinion concerning two alternative renditions of its lower strain, which differed only in the use of several triplets. The difference was so slight as to constitute an acceptable level of essentially ornamental variation in subsequent performances.

New compositions might be rejected at this stage as well. By continually asking for recent compositions I happened to record several that never reappeared after their initial performances. The "Basketball Quadrille" is one such (Q-tape 67). It contains fewer musical ideas than most compositions, only one for each strain, and simply may not have been interesting enough to impress itself on Emile's mind. His tentative experimentation with alternation between f''♯ and f'' natural in this piece struck me at the time as an effort to generate a more distinctive "sound."

The "Nagra Jig," which also never reappeared, however, is no less interesting than many other tunes in his active repertoire. It may be significant that both titles were rather strained efforts, made at my suggestion during the interview and not linked to any especially memorable event. In this they seem similar to the humorous titles that are entirely of the moment. Those tunes likewise lapsed from Emile's conscious awareness. The failure to connect a tune with a memorable extramusical association contributed to its demise because the choice of tunes in performance was made as much for their extramusical associations as their musical character.

A tune without a title was not yet incorporated into Emile's active repertoire or really "finished." Untitled compositions seem to be more tentatively "fixed" musically. The composition that was eventually dubbed "Fight for Your Rights," for example, appears on several earlier tapes with greater than usual variation. This example indicates that it is possible for a new composition to linger in this nearly finished state for some time, until it can be "anchored" to some experiential association. More commonly, untitled compositions were forgotten.

The evaluation of even finished and titled pieces was a continuing process that could lead to subsequent modification. This might be slight, as in the addition of a few more rhythmic accents to the dance-rhythm section of

"Madeleine's Glass of Lemon Pie," which occurred well after it had become a standard performance piece.

"Jim Hodder's" was modified in response to a particularly successful interaction with an audience. As Gerald Thomas recounts the events, he attempted to stir up some audience reaction at a bar performance by clapping along with its second strain. Emile began conducting him with his bow, thus creating a pause in the tune which was filled by clapping. The audience responded enthusiastically, and Emile began to incorporate the technique into subsequent performances, instructing people to follow Gerald's lead (Q-tape 58).

More substantial modification subsequent to the initial melodizing process might initiate a new round of aural composition employing the tune in question or some aspect of it as a new idea. The result is a long-term composition in which novel elements progressively accumulate, as in the case of "Roaming Scott, Welcome to Holiday Inn."

The preceding analysis would seem to account for both the traditionality and originality of Emile's compositions. He also produced a more radical change in form by progressively accumulating novel elements. In the later years the most distinctive pieces in his repertoire were short "suites" that begin in a relatively free-rhythmic format, which sounds rather formless to a traditional ear, before being given a dance pulse and rhythm. The first of these was the "Roaming Scott," composed in 1977 or 1978 and recorded on *Emile's Dream* in 1979. Cast in $\frac{2}{2}$ meter, it was played more slowly than dance tempo, and its two strains were of nonstandard length. He explained its genesis as "something that I composed" and "was a long time playing it by myself and I was kind of shy to play it in public." Indeed, "even I wouldn't play it to my family." When requested, however, he did play it for a visitor from St. John's, typical of the urban revival musicians who were taking an interest in his music at this time. "By gosh," he said, "that's good. That sounds good. Play it again!" So I played it again. "Well," he said, "that's beautiful! Gee I love that." So, good enough. I played it. So, I kept on then and I wasn't shy no more (adapted from Thomas 1982, 11–12).[12]

The tune, a product of "wandering" within a tonality, caught Emile's fancy but was not immediately cast into dance rhythm. He expected that this form would not be well received by his listeners and so kept it largely to himself. The visiting "Scott" who changed his mind was Scott Swinden, a geologist from St. John's working on the west coast. An accomplished bluegrass and old-time musician on the guitar and mandolin, he often sought out traditional musicians with whom to socialize while "in the field." He enjoyed this tune and encouraged Emile to perform it (field notes 1982). Emile quickly discovered that it was well received by audiences in the concert situations in which he increasingly began to find himself.

During this period and the years immediately following, Emile's compositional activity increased, and the associated process of free-rhythmic "searching" became more self-conscious. At the same time he was exposed to arrangements of fiddle tunes and songs in complex medleys by contemporary folk ensembles such as Figgy Duff (1980; 1983), with whom he worked and shared many stages. These factors apparently combined to produce conditions favorable to experiments such as the "Roaming Scott." At first, however, he remained unsure of their value, perhaps not having internalized the new aesthetics underlying this form, which were tailored more to the concert stage than the dance hall or "kitchen racket." Indeed, I have noted negative responses from some in his local milieu, who considered the nondance rhythm sections to be musically nonsensical. The value of the new form was confirmed by positive audience response to the "Roaming Scott," significantly brought from outside the traditional milieu. Encouraged, Emile began to explore further the possibilities of this new musical form, and the "Roaming Scott" provided a convenient starting place. Continued experimentation produced the altered and extended "Welcome to Holiday Inn" by 1981, which he recorded on *Ça Vient du Tchoeur/It Comes from the Heart* (Benoit 1982).

In "Welcome to Holiday Inn" the original "Roaming Scott" tune appears as the first "piece," as Emile describes it, of the new composition, but it has been slowed and incorporates new trills and slurs. The second "piece" is further slowed and played more freely. It employs musical material from the first strain, taking one-bar units and altering them somewhat, changing the melodic contour. Its second strain likewise follows its predecessor but compresses it by not repeating units from the first strain. This section also experiments with more alternation between f''♯ and f'' natural intonations and a stronger use of C natural than in the first section. The third piece shifts into dance tempo and uses C natural throughout, employing units from the first strain of the second piece and altering those of its second strain further in this process. The entire composition has the character of a musical train of thought, recording the process of Emile's exploration of possible ways to change the "notes" and "sound" of his original "Roaming Scott."

The new composition, a medley of changing tempos and shifting tonality unlike anything Emile had composed previously, was titled when Emile again encountered Scott at the Holiday Inn in Corner Brook, where he played it for him. Its success inaugurated a new genre of tunes in this form, including "Madeleine's Glass of Lemon Pie" and medleys such as the "Wedding Waltz."

Audience reaction was always important to Emile's evaluation of tunes at the stage of incorporation into his repertoire as evidenced by his emphasis on this in many tune-titling narratives. The "Lovers' Reel," for example, is named for the response of an audience of friends and neighbors on the occasion of its premiere. When Emile asked if they liked it, they responded, "No, we don't like it. We loves it!" And so Emile called it the "Lovers' Reel" (Russell 1979). In the traditional musical milieu, this attitude would have helped to keep his compositions within traditional norms; in a changed setting it fostered innovation.

Understandably, Emile seldom mentioned negative responses to his compositions. Those in this new form are an exception, however. He perceived his original "Roaming Scott" as "foolishness" because of its nondance rhythm, anticipating the response he expected from his audience although he found it appealing enough to continue playing, mostly for his private enjoyment. During a visit in March 1987 I observed the point of view reflected in this judgment (Q-tape 54). While we were playing together in an informal house party situation, Emile began to play some of these pieces and I joined with him. His son Mike, who had been playing accordion, was quick in voicing his opinion that anyone who played something like that, referring to the "Brother's Farewell," had to be "out of their mind." It seemed as though such tunes were barely even music as far as he was concerned.

The local aesthetic, formed in dance and house party milieus, clearly did not include music of this freer-form character, although fiddling of this expressive character is acknowledged in the traditional framework, as Emile's comments about fiddlers who "could make you cry" indicate. But such fiddling seems not to have been much practiced, and I never heard its like from other musicians in the area. Indeed, Emile's own firm grounding in the aesthetics of dance music is revealed by his transformation of every slow tempo introduction into a brisk dance rhythm. His reaction to others' music, almost always that of enthusiastic whoops and hollers, reveals the same attitudes.[13]

Emile's development of this new form demonstrates the reliance on his own feelings and opinions that characterized his personality as well as his willingness to respond to his peers' opinions. Within the milieu of local values, which viewed instrumental music as dance accompaniment or as evocative of its energy, he generated new ideas but kept to himself those that would not be well received. When they were greeted by a positive response in a changed milieu, he quickly exploited the idea further.

Once a composition entered Emile's active repertoire, its use in performances was strongly influenced by extramusical associations. Some tunes, such as the "Skeleton Reel," were performed at nearly every opportunity. This tune and others, however, could suffer from overuse, and Emile sometimes demurred when asked to perform it, responding, "I'm after telling that a thousand times" (M-MS 86-143/p. 173). Other tunes are more ephemeral, losing interest quickly, perhaps because of their musical character or possibly their association with a title and story that would seldom be called for at performance occasions. Such tunes were gradually forgotten, although they might linger in his passive repertoire for years.

His repertoire was subject to constant turnover. Components of both current compositions and nearly forgotten tunes provided material for generating new compositions. One result of this recycling process is the impression that the same tunes kept reappearing. This is because he constantly reused musical bits and pieces and shaped them along familiar lines, not that he transformed or recomposed whole tunes or used a small repertoire of "tune models."

The process of aural composition as exemplified by Emile is somewhat paradoxical in nature. Compositions were clearly generated from musical materials of a formulaic character at several constituent levels; these levels emerge from the disassembling of existing repertoire into musical components. This suggests that aural composition in this idiom is akin to formulaic models of improvisatory performance, but it is also self-consciously reflective and intentionally innovative in the manner of written composition.

The shaping of melodic units occurs within the framework of flexible schemata provided by the recursive fiddle tune form, which constrains the number and length of phrases, and a few tonalities and melodic figures found within familiar fingering patterns, which suggest melodic possibilities. The combination of these units into phrases and strains occurs within similar constraints and may be further channeled according to familiar patterns of harmonic progression.

Some underlying "deep structure" of tunes does not serve as a stage in the composing process, which operates, rather, through experimentation at the foreground level, facilitated by traditional schemata that operate on many musical components. Possibilities would present themselves to Emile's mind from his knowledge of traditional repertoire, and he evaluated them according to traditional norms. The musical formulas and model tunes with which he was familiar, however, served primarily as a starting place for imaginative transformation rather than as restrictive constraints. In fact, the constraints imposed by traditional aesthetic norms must be temporarily lifted to allow imaginative freedom for the generation of new compositions.

Emile appears to have acted relatively unselfconsciously, aiming primarily for melodic innovation within aesthetic norms closely tied to dancing, by composing in a formulaic manner approaching that of improvisation for many years. Further innovations occurred as the compositional process came under more conscious control when he began to take this activity more seriously in response to both external and internal stimuli. Constraints on form and tonality, consciously loosened to allow for melodic experimentation, became subject to alteration themselves. A new form consisting of medleys of related melodies in changing meters, tempos, and tonalities was developed which seems to preserve stages, previously less conscious, in the compositional process. Steps along the path of musical thought were externalized and preserved in the final composition. Although Emile apparently discovered the resulting form for himself, its flowering was facilitated by a shift in the values and performance settings of his musical milieu which encouraged its development.

Emile's musical communities thus played an active role in shaping his creative product, but not in the usual sense of "selecting" from among slight individual variations that which suits popular taste (Bronson 1969, 149, discussing Sharp [1907] 1965). The communal forces acting within the compositional process are more akin to the principle of "continuity" which exerts "flexible control" over variation resulting in "relative stability" postulated by Bertrand Bronson. "The variations of individual singers occur within the tradition, that is to say, in a habit of musical thought, the product of minds steeped in an idiomatic continuity. They are in no danger of radical departures from the traditional norm, because such alterations as occur to these minds are confined to the area of legitimate change" (Bronson 1969, 150).

But Bronson underestimates the creative element in traditional musical expression, distinguishing between "legitimate" and illegitimate" deviations, "not subtly but by a crude separation of arbitrary departures (willful substitutions, groping restorations, conscious creations) from such alternative or variant phrasings as are exemplified in successive renderings of a stanza or song by the same singer. The latter are 'legitimate,' and they move within, and activate, the genuinely positive and recreative part of tradition. They are, we may infer, the all-but unconscious expression of true musical instinct steeped in traditional habits of musical thought" (Bronson 1969, 146).

Here Bronson lapses into a stereotype of the unconscious folk performer. My analysis shows that it is just such intentional acts which he brands as illegitimate that characterize the creative process in Emile's "traditional habits of musical thought." Although Emile was an unusually prolific composer in his traditional community context, his compositional activity was not anomalous, as almost all local musicians claim to have made at least a few of their own tunes. It is because Emile was both so clearly steeped in the knowledge of his musical tradition and able to provide so many instances of composition at work that I have been able to examine the elusive generative processes of tradition in some detail. I expect that my conclusions will prove generally applicable to most traditional fiddling and perhaps apt for other such types of tradition as well.

This account of Emile's compositional process, along with other more recent tune studies (such as Goertzen 1983; Cowdery 1984), challenges the adequacy of the tune family concept, one of the few theories we have to explain the processes of tune genesis in the tradition represented by Emile's repertoire, fully to account for the contributions of creative musicians to their tradition. The musical elements of his compositions are so densely interconnected that its family trees would most probably emerge as an impossibly tangled growth. This may be because instrumentalists take a more consciously manipulative attitude toward musical materials than do singers, with whose repertoire the theory was elaborated (Goertzen 1983, 113). Cowdery has found similar complex interconnections within Irish-language singing tradition (1984). The more dynamic relational principles of melodic outlining, conjoining, and recombining which he proposes for the Irish tradition, based on examination of both vocal and instrumental repertoires, were developed to "show that Irish tunes are composed and developed in relation to other tunes in flexible ways, creating a changing repertory of tunes which all 'sound right'; [that] this changing repertory is certainly generative in itself . . . [and that] Irish traditional musicians operate in a world of melodic potential" (Cowdery 1990, 123).

These concepts and the weighted transcription model Cowdery employs to portray a tune group are also appropriate to describe many of the relationships within Emile's repertoire, however, cataloging all the routes of variation available to him, which might provide a map delineating strong and weak tune relationships, would likely be a never-ending task for in a sense, Emile seeks to discover and follow such routes himself. My examination of compositional practice shows Cowdery's concepts of tune relationships at work in the processes that produce them, but these processes also include intentionally innovative strategies not so well accounted for by Cowdery's analysis.

It is the transformational potential within the tradition that enables musicians like Emile to meet the challenges of change alluded to in my discussion of the innovations associated with the "Roaming Scott" (Hopkins 1976). This potential for transforming allows such a piece to be both traditional and innovative at the same time. Rather than the "alchemy of communal reinterpretation," as Larry McCullough has restated the conventional formulation of communal re-creation (Barry 1933), in reference to the compositions of Irish fiddler Ed Reavy, which "become traditional when . . . accepted by traditional players and subjected to the process of variation" (McCullough 1979, 10–11), the creative process of the individual composer emerges as the "primary alembic" of tradition (Ives 1979, 423).

4 ~ Fingers and Bow

Repertoire and Style

In this chapter I analyze the musical features of the tunes to which I refer throughout this study, based on an examination of Emile's conceptualization of them.[1] I explore his understanding of how musical sound is organized, especially its tonal and rhythmic principles, the structural elements of musical form ranging from the constituent elements of particular pieces to generic categories, and the technical knowledge he brings to the instrument.[2] In contrast to the ideas about music I examined in connection with my analysis of Emile's musical worldview, such more purely musical ideas as these have been surprisingly little investigated by ethnomusicologists using this approach, although several scholars, notably John Blacking (1981), have called for such studies. This lack is partly owing to the strong legacy of interest in cultural analyses in the field (Nketia 1981), as well as inherent problems in the discovery of such concepts. In most folk traditions, musical concepts are seldom articulated, making them difficult to isolate for analysis.[3] My transcriptions should be read with these musical concepts in mind.

Emile's playing techniques and musical concepts, both of traditional provenance and idiosyncratic, were acquired along with a traditional repertoire. The music to which he was exposed during his formative years established basic generic categories, concepts of musical form, tonal coherence, and rhythmic patterns. He developed his playing technique to accommodate these norms, and they are often embodied in his technique rather than as abstract concepts. His musical knowledge, comprising the cognitive resources on which he had to draw as a creator, is almost entirely derived from the traditional repertoire.

Ethnotheory is a term that refers to the world of musical ideas as reconstructed by the researcher, as distinct from the purely "native theory" of the informant. The term was derived from the anthropological school of ethnoscientific methodology, which was intended systematically to reveal informants' conceptual categories through semantic analysis. Application of the concept of ethnotheory to musical concepts has drawn researchers' attention to the variety of ways in which such ideas are represented (Feld 1981, 43–45).[4] A few of Emile's ideas, particularly those concerned with musical forms and genres, were explicitly verbalized. Some of these, however, Emile articulated only in response to my prompting, and he used relatively few idiosyncratic terms to convey a variety of meanings. The context in which this language is used and the musical examples to which it often referred require especially close attention to understand what Emile means to say. Some of the most basic of such concepts were never articulated verbally. These ideas might be expressed by musical demonstration or remain entirely unstated, revealed only by analysis of his practice.

During our conversations Emile identified several formal characteristics as important features of his fiddle tunes. He readily verbalized a two-part structure. Ideally, he felt, the first part should "lead" easily into the second and the latter, in turn, back to the opening. The entire piece ought to end on the tonic, and a "rhyme" was necessary for a satisfying finish.

Indeed, virtually all of Emile's tunes of the dance type have the two-strain structure that is common and widespread in the fiddling traditions of both North America and the British Isles. As is also typical, one strain is high, the other low in pitch. Although some regional traditions seem to favor one or the other order of these parts, both arrangements are found among Emile's tunes. Each strain is repeated in performance, although there are a few exceptions, often with slight variation in the closing phrase. The strains may be analyzed into two-bar phrases, of which there are rarely more than two in each, and these phrases are composed in turn of one-bar units, which may also repeat. These smaller subdivisions of the fiddle tunes were not often identified by Emile as such. The closing phrase of each strain is usually the same, serving to unify the whole by "rhyming."

Examination of Emile's compositions reveals the following common structures:

Some tunes, such as "Pamela Morgan's Desire," have only four-bar strains.

: A A′ :: B B′ :

: ab ac :: de dc′ :

Those tunes with eight-bar strains basically repeat the four-bar structure with slight variation producing a pattern of balanced phrase repetitions, as in "Reel de la Pistroli," for example.

: A B A B′:: C D C D′:

||: ab cd ab cd′:| |:ef gd ef gd′:| |

As in "Neil Murray's," for example, perfect balance is not necessary,
although a closing "rhyme" is almost always present.

: A B A B :: C D C D′ :

: ab cd ab cd :: ef gh ef gd′ :

Wider variation from the highly regularized norm is more common
in his recent compositions such as "Fight for Your Rights," with its four
interconnecting strains of different lengths.

: A A′ B B′ C C′ D D :

A A′ : aa′b a′′bb′ :

B B′ : cdb′ceb′′ cdb′ce :

C C′ D D : fghg f′ghg′ :: f′′ijk f′′ijk′ :

Although his standard performance format was to play single compositions, Emile sometimes performed medleys such as the series of tunes
"Picadilly Slant," "West Bay Center," and "Making the Curve to Black Duck
Brook," which would have provided variety and continuity within a lengthy
dance performance. As he continued to experiment in this extended format he explored the possibilities of progressing through related keys and
changing rhythms, as in the "Wedding Waltz" medley. Emile was influenced in developing pieces in this format by the practice of most revival
groups of young musicians with whom he came in contact and especially
Kelly Russell's arrangements of his compositions into medleys for his first
LP album (Benoit 1979).

Several of Emile's newer compositions departed far from the norms of
the dance tune repertoire. These open with a melody structured like the
dance tunes but played with greater rhythmic freedom and at a relatively
slow tempo. After several repetitions a dance meter and tempo is estab-

lished and the melody adapted to this framework. The "Roaming Scott, Welcome to Holiday Inn" is one of the more elaborate of the compositions in this form, opening with a metrical but non-dance-tempo two-strain melody, moving to a rhythmically freer section of changing tonality and unbalanced phrase lengths, before concluding with a dance meter section.

The bulk of Emile's compositions, however, are quite traditional in character, deriving from his acquired musical knowledge. This is one reason why they are so successful as "fiddle tunes," as virtually all his auditors agree. But because his particular musical worldview, which was not particularly idiosyncratic, combined with an open-ended concept of musical sound, a concomitant willingness to experiment, and a powerful commitment to self-expression through music, which *are* unusual. Emile continually explored his knowledge and skills for new potentialities. Although he was sensitive to his audiences' responses, which have varied, he was primarily attentive to his own creative agenda.

∾ Selected Compositions of Emile Benoit

The following collection of tunes includes primarily the compositions Emile actively played during the 1980s.[5] It is not a complete collection of Emile's repertoire or of all his compositions. Even such a corpus, were it possible to assemble, would not really capture the musical legacy I hope this study represents and helps to pass on. Emile's repertoire was in a constant state of flux and compositional turnover. He "let go" countless rhymes and compositions, and he continued actively composing and performing up until his death, well after the period of this study. The limited selection of tunes presented here has been chosen to represent the range within which Emile worked and to illustrate my analysis of compositional processes, the creative source that lies at the heart of his legacy.

I have arranged the following musical examples both thematically and in a rough chronology, using them much the way Emile might have, to tell a story. I begin with traditional tunes and compositions of an indeterminate older date which evoke his youthful experiences. The sequence of compositions then follows Emile's career as he leaves home, meets new people and plays with other musicians, traveling along with him through the stories he presented to audiences around the world.

The musical transcriptions, though based on specific performances, do not record all ornamentation or variations but rather provide a generalized representation of the tune. A more detailed analysis of performance practice in general follows. Pitch levels are as played, although Emile's tuning may sometimes have been slightly sharp or flat. Standard notational symbols have been employed together with a few special symbols drawn from common ethnomusicological practice.

Emile's First Tunes

We have already encountered Emile explaining how he started to fiddle. On several occasions he demonstrated those first tunes, which were taught to him by his Uncle Jean.

> I'm going to play the one he learned me now, the first one. And I believes it's an Irish tune. He could play a small bit, you know [plays slowly]. But now I plays it like that [plays at normal tempo]. Different now, see. But this is the way I start, he showed me [plays slowly again]. So I took the violin and I plays it. La. Now I said, "Show me the other turn" [plays second strain slowly]. So I plays it. La, I knows it. Start now playing it same like that, [my] bow [going] back and forth like that. Now I played that about an hour I suppose. Now [I] says, "Do you know any step dance . . . [any] reels?" "Yes," he says, "I knows this one." Used to call it Devil Among the Tailors, eh? [plays a rudimentary version of "Devil Among the Tailors"]. . . . So he pass it to me and I played it. So, and I start. Oh I was all the week at it. I couldn't eat, had no appetite. I was right in . . . heart and soul in that. And I start from that. Kept on going, kept on going, kept on going. (M-tape 81-502/C5319)

Emile's first tune, as played by Uncle Jean

Emile's first tune, as Emile has modified it

Devil Among the Tailors, as played by Uncle Jean

Calamus Day Set

The Calamus (Candlemas) Day festival in February was an occasion for dancing, and Emile took this somewhat unusual, perhaps only partially recalled, older tune, and reordered, added, and reiterated musical material to create a more standard form for the tune taken from it.

The old-time source

Emile's Calamus Day set

The Old Man and Woman Tunes

The first of these traditional tunes is commonly called the "(Growling) Old Man and Woman," and as explained in chapter 2, Emile performs it as an argument between an old married couple. The tune Emile called the "New Old Man and Woman" is likewise widespread.

(Growling) Old Man and Woman

(New) Old Man and Woman

Gravel Pond Reel

Emile's first LP recording, *Emile's Dream,* produced by Kelly Russell in 1979, included older compositions that had stood the test of time as well as more recent ones, with titles invoking his new experiences as a musician. Kelly was responsible for most of the pairings of tunes on this recording and the choice of singer-songwriter Ron Hynes to accompany Emile on guitar.

The "Gravel Pond Reel" is one of these older compositions, titled on the way to the dance, where it occasioned much enthusiasm.

Les Sabots

Gerald Thomas and Kenneth Goldstein visited Emile's home in July 1978 and recorded this then recent composition. It was paired with "Gravel Pond Reel" in the *Atlantic Fiddling* anthology recording (1980).

> Hien, a little while ago, and it was in April I think, my wife was wash-
> ing the dishes, and she had a pair of sabots on [wooden shoes]. And
> I could read [hear?], read [a] jig, you know, read something, [in]
> the way she used to walk, whether she was in a hurry. And she was
> going across the floor. So, I took the fiddle, I was sitting to the end of
> the table and I was watching her, you know. The . . . eyebrows were
> hauled down a little bit [chuckle]. No foolishness there, she means
> business. So, ok. So I start mumbling something, and the first thing
> here I gets a reel. So when I plays it, and I was watching her there,
> I was getting the swing of the feet you know. Well I said, "c'est ça."

When I played it, I got the name then. I said, "I'm gonna practice that
and I'm gonna call it the Sabots Reel." So, and this is the way it goes.
(M-tape 78-239/C3581)

West Bay Centre, Picadilly Slant, and
Making the Curve to Black Duck Brook

These three compositions recall places along the road Emile took to
travel home across the peninsula. Although he usually performed them in
a medley illustrating the story of their composition while he drove along
this route, as related in chapter 3, the tunes are among his extant older
compositions and may stand alone.

West Bay Centre

Piccadilly Slant

Making the Curve to Black Duck Brook

Brothers' Jig

Later appended to the preceding medley was the "Brothers' Jig," titled to commemorate Emile's playing of it for his two brothers. Emile incorporated this tune into the "Making the Curve to Black Duck Brook" narrative by explaining that he played this medley for his brothers upon arriving home and named the last piece for the three of them together. I believe that this is a later change, however, as Emile explained to me on another occasion that it came from an old song that "come into my mind" and was transformed into a jig, which he premiered for his two brothers and named to commemorate that event. Relatively simple to play, this tune was quite popular with the younger musicians in St. John's when I first arrived there in 1979.

Lightkeeper's Jig

This older composition was named for a lightkeeper who lived and worked "on the point."

Lover's Reel

This tune was named to characterize its first audience's enthusiastic response.

Happiness Reel

This is an older composition that Emile recorded with the "Lovers' Reel."

David's Reel

This older composition was played together with "Happiness Reel."

Arriving to St. John's

Once Emile was "discovered" by those involved in the Newfoundland cultural revival of the 1970s, he began to travel extensively to perform. Composed in 1976, this tune was titled to commemorate his return from the Mariposa Folk Festival in Toronto. He was playing it on the airplane when the captain said they would be landing shortly in St. John's.

Flying Reel

Inspired by the sound of jet engines, as recounted in chapter 3, this tune was composed during a cross-country flight in 1978.

Skeleton Reel

This reel was one of Emile's most played, and most requested, compositions when he first began to perform away from home. Its story memorialized a powerful experience of an encounter with the supernatural evoking the world of folk belief.

Michael T. Wall's Breakdown

The tune was named for a prominent performer of "Newfie" music in Toronto during the late 1970s. Emile explained how they met and the tune named:

> Well I had composed a reel . . . I never had put no name onto it. I never put no name on it, so I went like that, you know, and I used to play it and I used to love it and it was good. So when I got over there [to Toronto], I played it. I went ten days [to the Caravan Festival], I went thirty times on the stage. And I played it thirty times up there. So during that time I was playin' it Michael T. Wall, he's feller that come from Corner Brook, that's where he was born, but he's up in Ontario [now]. So that's where he met me and he liked the reel. So we start, you know, talkin' together and he said, "You got a name for that?" "No," I say, "I got no name. No." He said, "What about callin' it Michael T. Wall's Breakdown?" "Yes," I said, "that'll be all right." So then after that I used to call it, I used to tell the people, the audience, you know, that I was gonna play Michael T. Wall's Breakdown. (M-tape 78-239/C3581)

Emile's Dream

Often paired with "Arriving to St. John's," its story, recorded on *Ça Vient du Tcheour/It Comes from the Heart* (1982), has been recounted in chapter 3. This tune was paired with another early favorite of Emile's compositions and the title of his first album.

Diane's Happiness

Before Emile began traveling much to perform, renewed interest in folk music brought interested people to his home and made him new friends. Diane McIsaac, a public health nurse stationed in Port-au-Port, friend of the family, and frequent visitor along with others who appreciated his music in the 1970s, provided the title for this tune.

Bandsaw Reel

The story of this tune, mentioned in chapter 3, evokes both Emile's working life and his "ear" for music in the sounds of his environment.

> I had a workshop years back, when I was eighteen—now I'm thirty-seven, hah! So anyway, I was just working in my workshop, and first thing I went to start my motor, [because] I was making a boat, cutting timbers on the bandsaw. And first thing when . . . I hooked everything on. Nee-ee-ee-ee [nasal whine]. I give her too much grease. . . . But it was a funny sound, a nice sound. So I stopped the engine and I went back home, went to the house, took my violin and I made up a reel. And then I called it The Bandsaw Reel and this is the way it goes. (Thomas 1982, 15)

Part Time Fisherman's Reel

Emile took this tune "off" of the "note" of the "Bandsaw" sometime in 1983.

Ryan's Fancy Arriving

This tune commemorates a visit by the folk group Ryan's Fancy to film a segment for their CBC television program during 1978. The first strain is closely related to the traditional "Woodchopper's Reel."

Clode Sound Jig

It is not always easy to know when a piece was composed. Recorded on *Emile's Dream* (1979), this tune is described in the album notes as "a new one that came into my mind when I was at the studio [Clode Sound] to make this record." I noted the same tune played by Emile and his brother Joachim on March 12, 1987, but referred to as "Up in the Clouds." It may be that the "Clode Sound" title, which would not have been much called for in performance contexts, was dropped, or that the tune itself was older than its commercial recording and simply dubbed appropriately on that occasion.

Breakwater Boys Breakdown

The Breakwater Boys were another performing folk group active in the 1970s. While appearing with them in Lunenburg, Nova Scotia, Emile composed this piece recorded on his second album (1982), "An' I calls it, the Breakwater Boys Breakdown. An' this is the way it goes" (Thomas 1982, 15).

Neil Murray's Dinner Jig

Baptized at the Corner Brook festival in 1981, this tune commemorates Neil Murray, host of an influential traditional music program *Jigg's Dinner* on OZ FM radio for which Emile performed many times. Thomas reports that the word play with *Dinner* (after the radio program) in the title was his suggestion, adopted by Emile. On many occasions it is introduced merely as "Neil Murray's," as is the case with some other titles involving this kind of humor.

Motorcycle Club Rally Reel

My own visits were connected with two tunes in particular. Emile was in the process of composing this tune when we performed for a motorcycle rally in Grand Falls on our way back to St. John's from my first visit to his home in 1979. It was always rendered in both rhythms.

Colin's Missing Note

As mentioned in chapter 3, this tune resulted from the recreation of a piece I played on the accordion. Emile and I were never able to rediscover "the note" that so caught his fancy at the time.

Both of these tunes are relatively unremarkable, and neither became prominent in his repertoire; yet they would be played whenever we got together again after some time apart.

Colin's Missing Note

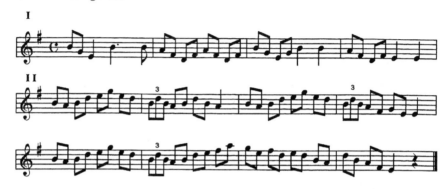

The "accordian double" source tune for *Colin's Missing Note*

Jim Hodder's

Emile identified himself as a Liberal and occasionally performed at party functions. "*Jim Hodder's*" was probably composed at the turn of the year 1979–80 while he was performing in St. John's. Emile explains, "Jim Hodder—a good guy, one of my best because he's a Liberal—I'm a Liberal an he is a Liberal heh! If he wasn't I suppose he was a good friend too but still not the same— . . . an so I composed for him too" (Thomas 1982, 16). Later, when Hodder, the Member, House of Assembly, for western Newfoundland, changed his party allegiance, Emile began introducing this tune as "Jim Hodder Crossing the Floor."

Brian Tobin's

Another political figure, the Liberal member of Parliament from Port-au-Port, was the inspiration for this title.

Martin White's

This tune results from a rhythmic transposition of the preceding, as discussed in chapter 3.

Bridgett's Reel

The name derives from Bridgett's club in St. John's in which Emile performed frequently, up to two weeks at a time, in 1981.

Kelly Russell's Reel

Recorded in 1982 on *Ça Vient du Tchoeur,* this tune was sometimes identified by Emile as the most difficult of his compositions to play, apparently an appropriate attribute for a composition named for record producer and fellow fiddler Kelly.

Kibitzer's Reel

Kibitzer's is a club where he frequently played in St. John's during 1985. It is described in chapter 5.

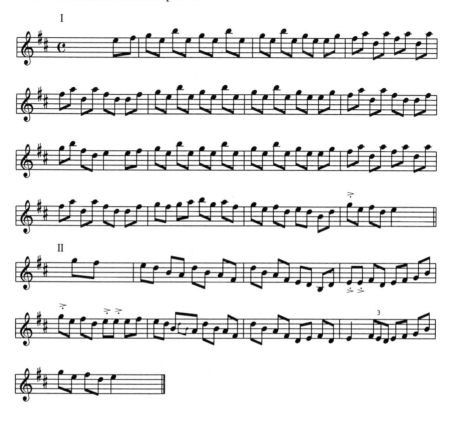

Le reel de la Pistroli

This tune title marked Emile's appearance on a television program of that name in Moncton, New Brunswick (letters refer to formal analysis earlier in this chapter).

Ron Hynes's Reel

Ron, a member of the new set of young musicians he met in St. John's, accompanied him on his first LP, *Emile's Dream*.

Noel's Din (Noel Dinn's)

The drummer and leader of Figgy Duff was entitled to a tune as well.

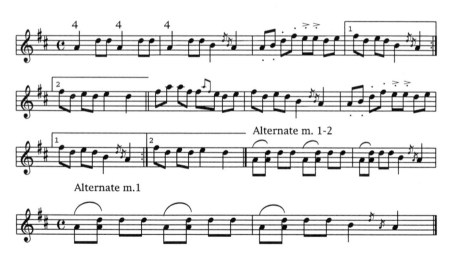

Alternate m. 1-2

Alternate m.1

Pamela Morgan's Desire

Composed in 1984 for the lead singer of the folk band Figgy Duff with whom Emile had begun to work, it is one of several titles in the "So and so's Desire" mold.

Roaming Scott

As recounted in chapter 3, the original "Roaming Scott" inaugurated an idiosyncratic compositional format employing relatively slow-tempo and freely played melodic introductions followed by dance rhythm transformations.

Original version

Roaming Scott, Welcome to Holiday Inn

The "Roaming Scott, Welcome to Holiday Inn" underwent a cumulative process of development resulting in the following elaborated form.

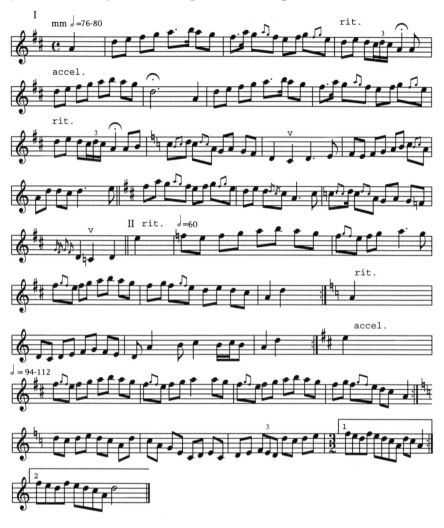

Hélène's Reel

Titled at Gerald's suggestion, this was composed in 1977 or 1978.

GT: Emile do you remember, do you remember a reel you composed, [you] didn't compose it in St. John's but you put the name to it
in St. John's, it was my sister's name?

Yeah, I do remember, yeah.

GT: Tell it in English.

Hien, I was to Gerald Thomas', and I had composed that reel. No,
to say the truth, I'm mistaken. Gerald Thomas was here [Black Duck
Brook]. So I had composed the reel. So he asked me . . . if I had a
name for it. I said, "No." Well he said, "This [is] my sister's birthday
today, you know." I said, "Yes?" "Yeah," he said. "She's thirty years
old." It's something like that, I believe it's thirty years old he said. So
I said, "Yes," I said, "What is her name?" He said, "Hélène." "Oh," well
I said, "what about I'll baptize that one Hélène's Reel, Hélène's Reel?"
"Well," he said, "that'd be nice." He said, "Whenever I writes to her or
I sees her or something I'll tell her about it." So this the way it goes.
(M-tape 78-239/C3581)

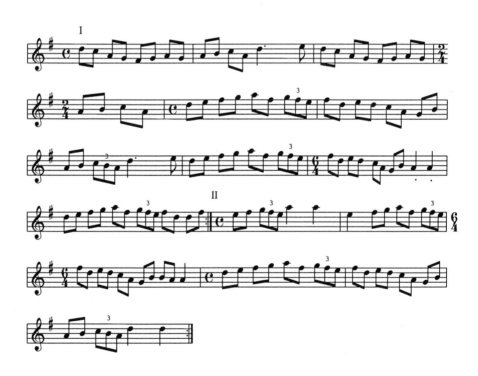

Delyth's Desire

Composed in 1983, this tune was named at Gerald's request for one of his daughters. The introduction was played very freely at first but became progressively standardized as Emile performed it with others, especially Pamela Morgan on the tin whistle.

Madeleine's Glass of Lemon Pie

Analyzed in detail in chapter 3, the story of the lemon pie made by Gerald Thomas's wife, Madeleine, captures a humorous moment at the dinner table of Emile's frequent hosts in St. John's.

Well anyway, this one here, I calls it Madeleine's Glass of Lemon Pie. The way I put the name on, she was making the lemon pie. And when the lemon pie was cook, she put [it] on the counter. She took the knife and put it under the piece and rose it up. . . . There was nothing on the knife! There was no lemon pie; all slipped off of it. So I seen that. So I was composing that piece. So I said, "Madeleine." She looked at me. She said, "What?" I said, "Pass me a glass of lemon pie please" [laughter]. You could put it in a glass but you couldn't put it on a knife [laughter]. So that's what I called it, Madeleine's Glass of Lemon Pie. (Videotape)

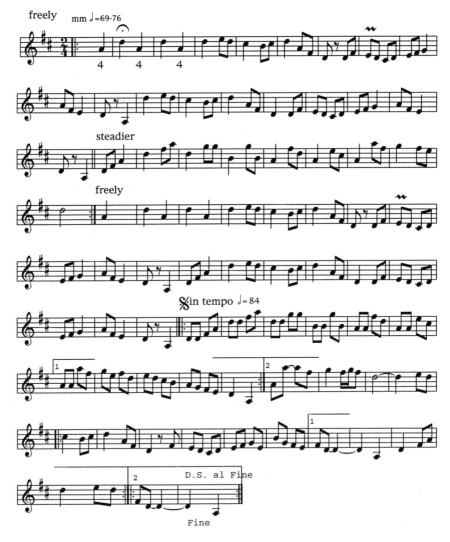

Torbay Jig

This tune, named for the community in which Gerald lives, dates from 1984.

Red Mountain Jig

The "Red Mountain Jig" commemorates Emile's music making with Neil Rosenberg, a banjo player and folklore professor at Memorial University. Gerald suggested the title, a play on Neil's family name. Emile occasionally referred to it as "Neil Rosenberg's."

Fight for Your Rights

This tune remained variable in form, adding and dropping strains at various times along with associated minor changes, and also had "floating" associations for an unusually long time. Sometimes calling it the "Forgotten Reel," in acknowledgment of this state of affairs, Emile also used it as a tune for Wilfred Wareham, a Memorial University folklorist. The first two strains became most stable and solidly attached to Emile's identification with a group of striking workers for whom he performed (letters refer to formal analysis earlier in this chapter).

Lucien Florent's Anniversaire

In 1987 Emile played for the wedding anniversary of Madeleine's parents.

Velvet in the Wind, or Le velours dans le vent

Emile began composing waltzes in the 1980s. These served occasionally as dance accompaniment but like the suites were primarily used in performance for their "change of pace" value. "Velvet in the Wind," a title sometimes misunderstood as "Violets" (or even violence) in the Wind," was composed just before our performance at the Pinewoods dance camp in Massachusetts, where it achieved some popularity.

Gerald Thomas' Burnt Potato Reel

This tune title comments directly on Emile's relationship with Gerald. Its associated narrative pokes fun at both Gerald's habits and Emile's gullibility and, as illustrated by a performance examined in chapter 5, it served to establish an egalitarian footing between them.

Wedding Waltz

The genesis of this 1984 medley is described in chapter 3.

Introduction

Riggydoo

Irish Washerwoman 1

Irish Washerwoman 2

Debbie's Waltz

This waltz was composed in 1986 and named for Debbie Penton, a St. John's musician who plays the Irish harp. Emile felt this melody would "sound good" on that instrument.

Sally's Waltz

This tune was named for an interviewer from the CBC who spoke to him on his birthday in 1987.

Wayne and the Bear

Emile usually followed "Brother's Farewell" and the "Caribou Skin" with this piece that lightens the tone by commemorating a hunting trip with his sons.

Wayne and the Bear that's another story too, that I composed too, and we was in the lumber wood two years ago. We went rabbit catching in the fall and when we got there we set a hundred snares. Next morning we had two rabbits. Very good. Next day we set another fifty snares.

Next morning we had three rabbits. Very good. The afternoon, I took one and I made a pot of soup. We cooked 'till three o'clock, so very good. I had two sons with me, so finest kind. Now my old son . . . he was there too fishing. Now he said, "I'm gonna go up and see my father-in-law," he said. "Is you comin' up?" "Oh yes, you gonna go, sure you goes, I'm goin' too." So all right we went up. . . . And [when we got back] here the camp was flattened down to the ground with the bear. So, at the time it was just dark and my son Wayne got the cramps in the stomach, don't know if the soup done it or what, but anyway he got the cramp in the stomach, he said, "Where you go, here?" They said, "Just down there." Very good he's gone. Yes but one of the guys took a stone and throw, behind him. Holy mack [slaps hand], he turned back and here he comes, looking behind. I said, "What is wrong?" He said, "The bear, the bear's coming." He's coming like that [gestures running while holding up pants]. So I had composed that. So I called it Wayne and the Bear. (Q-tape 17)

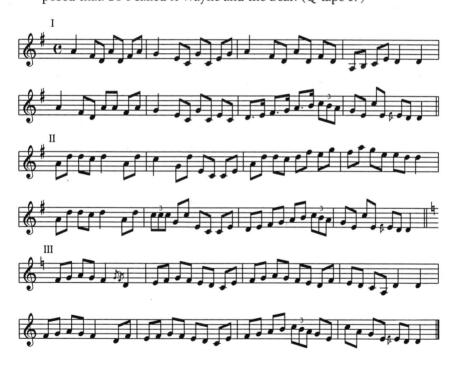

Brother's Farewell and Caribou Skin Nailed Around the Circle

Composed in 1983 on the occasion of his brother Ben's death, this piece takes advantage of the suite form to tell a serious story, recounted in chapter 2. It is invariably followed by its lively rhythmic transposition into the "Caribou Skin Nailed Around the Circle," named for the *bodhrans* Emile encountered among musicians influenced by Irish music; it conveys his attitude toward the inevitable and appropriate passing of the emotions of grief associated with death.

Brother's Farewell

Caribou Skin Nailed Around the Circle

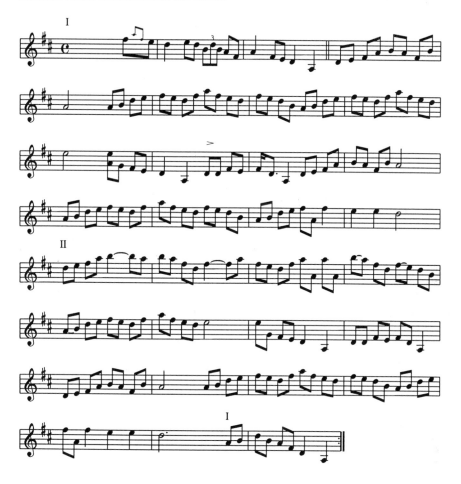

Brother's Answer

Emile's farewell was so compelling that his brother Joachim was uncharacteristically motivated to compose the following tune, which Emile subsequently modified to his liking.

Joachim's Brother's Answer

Emile's Brother's Answer

∿ Manner of Performance

Emile played most often while seated with the fiddle resting against his chest, his bow arm held relatively low and slightly away from the body. His basic bow stroke was articulated primarily from the elbow by the lower arm, extending at most through the upper half of the bow. This position, still relatively common among fiddlers throughout North America, was probably even more typical at one time. It has its roots in the historical development of violin technique but represents an adaptation to the technical demands of the folk tradition (Boyden 1965; Burman-Hall 1984, 165–69).

His playing was both energetic and relaxed. Indeed, he suggested to me several times that I ought to relax my body more when playing to improve both sound and rhythm. One of his first criticisms of my fiddling, for example, was that I should close my mouth. Emile appeared actively engaged with his audience when playing and aware of the impression he created. Employing posture, eye contact, and other gestures, he constantly related to other musicians and members of the audience.

Beating a rhythm with the feet was an essential part of Emile's performance style. He employed the pattern typical of French Canadian fiddlers in my experience, though he claimed to have developed it himself. It is because of the rhythmic pattern used for duple time that I have often chosen to transcribe these tunes in a $\frac{2}{2}$ meter; an accented beat is sounded by the right heel every four subdivisions, but there are only two patterns per measure. Several rhythmic patterns are possible using the same basic movements, but Emile favored the more heavily accented quarter and two eighth note combination, sometimes using continuous eighth notes. Ideally, Emile advocated shifting to the denser and more evenly accented pattern to convey added energy. In practice he did not do this often. Two densities are possible in triple meter rhythms as well; that composed of continuous eighth note triplets seems to be the one most commonly used.

Although his basic fiddling posture was as described above, Emile in fact held his violin in several ways, including on his shoulder, gripped under his chin, and such trick or intentionally unusual manners as behind his back or next to his head. Although he appeared most comfortable with the fiddle held against his chest, he often brought it higher, even all the way up under his chin in an approximation of modern art practice. As Emile explained it, his left hand position, with the neck cradled well down between the thumb and forefinger, necessitated a "supple" wrist to reach the fingers around the neck without shifting the instrument. Although this was his preferred position, he found it difficult when he was older and his wrist stiffer, and holding the instrument under his chin eased this problem. Thus, he explained, he often began to play with the fiddle held high and then, once warmed up, shifted to the other position.

This is a reasonable explanation, and he did often change position in the sequence described, although it does not account for many other occasions when he employed a chin position even though well "warmed up." These situations represent a recent influence from other, more "trained," fiddle players. In fact it appears that he was not merely imitating a playing position but rather trying to incorporate a complex of techniques associated with new influences into some of his more innovative compositions. He associated an under-the-chin position and a straight-wrist left-hand grip on the neck, for example, with the ability to play in higher positions. Although Emile did not play extended pieces in higher positions, he incorporated brief extensions to second and third position on the first (e′) string and glissandi to unison with the string above from first position in some of his compositions and was likely to play these under the chin. He also usually played his slower-tempo, freer rhythmic compositions in this posture. These are pieces also likely to incorporate vibrato, extensive trills, and slurred bowing, none of which are found in his more traditional repertoire. Adopting an under-the-chin playing position is one aspect of his continuing acquisition of new playing techniques, which Emile explained within a framework of technical demands.

Emile referred to left-hand techniques as "the fingers." He usually did not have much to say about this aspect of playing and seemed to consider his technique inferior in this respect to that of many fiddlers, perhaps because of the more extensive use of melodic ornamentation, such as grace notes, and "rolls," a particular Irish ornament (Breathnach 1977, 94–100), in Cape Breton and Irish fiddling, both of which he heard extensively in his later years. He did, however, offer a few observations when I asked him to demonstrate aspects of his technique on videotape.

Emile played almost exclusively in the first position, cradling the instrument neck well down between the thumb and first finger of the left hand, whereas he noted that I and others tended to pinch the neck between the thumb and knuckle. I must say almost here, because although I never saw him actually perform a piece in higher positions or compose one employing such techniques, he acknowledged the possibility and on one occasion gave it a try when asked if he ever did play up the neck (videotape). The result was a somewhat humorous performance but one that indicted he could do it and had probably tried it a few times. This would seem to reflect his willingness to experiment on the instrument and stretch his abilities to their limits. One of his private "practice" tapes contains just such an effort (Q-tape 45).

Emile was aware of and willing to discuss left-hand ornamentation techniques. Although he considered bowing the most distinctive feature of his playing, melodic ornamentation is an important technique that distinguishes style as well: "I makes my squibbles, me, with my fingers" (Q-tape 20). When he played in the dance rhythms these "finger" ornaments were most often single or double grace notes, often with a triplet rhythm. That he conceived of "squibbles" as optional ornamentation of a basic melody is confirmed by his description of them on occasion in French as "des fions" [filigree].

In slower-tempo pieces Emile tended to exaggerate melodic ornaments into extended trills. This practice was common in waltzes, such as "Velvet in the Wind," as well as the slow introductions mentioned above. He also attempted to use vibrato in these pieces, though his hand position limited him to a "finger vibrato." This would seem to be another innovative technique that he imitated from other, more trained fiddlers with whom he came into contact in his revival career. His use of pronounced slides over wide intervals is also an innovative technique he used in his slower pieces. It is found, for example, in "Madeleine's Glass of Lemon Pie." Fourth-finger unisons were likewise not part of his repertoire of techniques until recently.

Emile's compositions are played within a limited number of tonalities, conditioned by the ergonomics of fingering patterns on the instrument, which is how Emile thought of their contrasting "sounds." Emile's compositions include pieces in both major and minor tonalities using tonic notes D, A, G, and C. Melodies on D and G often have a strong pentatonic character, perhaps reflecting a preference for first and third fingering combinations, as is suggested by Peter Cooke for the Shetland Isles repertoire (1986, 101). These "core" notes often form entire melodies or serve as the accented framework for a tune or constituent phrase thereof. The second finger may be placed in either high or low position to create diatonic scales in different modes on these same tonics.

Emile could play in other keys but did so only occasionally. During one interview, for example, he played tunes in F and B flat at my request. They are technically more difficult because they require shifting the first finger toward the nut and offer fewer open string notes, and he performed them with some difficulty. I know of no compositions of his in these keys, although his more recent compositions employed alternations between f''♯ and f'' natural positions of the first finger on the e'' string. While coloring the melody with a "minor" tonality, this technique does not change the patterns of fingering when used. Although all of Emile's compositions are played in standard violin tuning (g d' a' e'') he did know traditional pieces in the common scordatura tuning a e' a' e'', such as the traditional "Hangman's Reel" and "Reel du Demon" (Q-tape 13). This tuning is used for pieces in A tonalities and affords more opportunities for open string drones and third finger unisons than does the standard tuning.

The identification and classification of scales and modes has been a topic of nearly continuous debate since the early days of Anglo-Celtic folk music scholarship.[6] Most previous effort has been largely framed in terms of competing evolutionary theories and differing classificatory goals, and attention to native classification has been surprisingly absent from most of these discussions. This lack may be owing to the broadly comparative goals of most systems and an apparent assumption that the researcher's musical knowledge was superior to that of folk singers and musicians, who were considered to be primarily unconscious practitioners of an inherited art.

Because such abstractions are not commonly discussed by Emile or other fiddlers of his local tradition, one avenue of elicitation I pursued was to ask about his approach to teaching. Emile's teaching practice indicates that he focused first on the open string and octave combinations achieved with the third finger in first position and the accompanying major triads on c', g', and d', which employ the first, third, and second fingers (Q-tape 48). Matthew Guntharp (1980) has likewise noticed the importance of these patterns among traditional fiddlers in Pennsylvania. These core fingering configurations provide patterns and pitch ranges within which he constructed melodies; they are implied by the word "sound" as he often used it.

For Emile, there was a direct and concrete connection between finger position, tones, and melody. He did not appear to think in terms of abstracted scales nor did he ever practice them as such. He did not know the names of the different notes in English or French or the names of scales and keys. He encountered these among younger musicians and learned to identify the G, A, and D notes, which are often used as the tonic, though he asked me on several occasions if he had labeled them correctly. He had similarly encountered the terms *major* and *minor* but created his own interpretation for them. He identified several melodic phrases for me as representing a "minus key." These were framed by the d''- f''-a'' minor triad, distinguished for him by the shift of the first finger from its "normal" f♯'' position on the fingerboard. It is not clear that Emile extended this notion to include the sound of other minor triads, and he did not shift this technique of alteration to adjacent string combinations.

Emile conceived of melodies in terms of their tonic note, identifying tunes as being "on" particular notes. This tone serves as the fundamental tonal center, is usually the final note of the melody, and is clearly the tonic of the scale he is using. Because he thought so much in terms of fingering, however, this tone is identified in terms of finger position, thus creating a potential distinction between phrases "on" c' and c'', for example. The most common tonics he employed are a, a', g, g', and d; c occurs less frequently, f rarely, b flat almost never in common practice but rather only in response to my query whether he could do this. These preferences are, in general, typical of the traditional repertoire at its most widespread (Burman-Hall 1984, 167–68).

Given a particular tonic note, the constraints on possible melody notes are quite limiting, for, as Emile verbalized this all-important criterion for note selection, "the notes got to suit." Notes that suit are chosen from a limited number of scale types, which Emile thought of in terms of fingering positions. This is typical of musically nonliterate fiddlers generally, such as those interviewed by Guntharp in Pennsylvania (1980, 92–101) or Cooke in the Shetland Isles (1986, 100–104). While Emile readily identified the tonic note of his tunes and used this information in reference to them, he did not have a ready terminology with which to distinguish the different scales that might be based on the same tonic. In fact, he did not abstract, nor have I ever heard him play these scales as such.

In his later compositions Emile discovered that he could generate added interest through changing tonality by shifting between major and minor thirds as he does in "Roaming Scott, Welcome to Holiday Inn." This tends to confirm that he did not preconceive of melodies in terms of their scalar frameworks when composing but thought rather in terms of different fingering positions within which melodic phrases are created and explored different possibilities as he went along.

The basic genres of dance fiddling as practiced on the Port-au-Port, as elsewhere, are based on different dance rhythms. Emile's use of the standard terminology applied to traditional dance music, however, was somewhat confusing when I first encountered it. "Jig," "reel," "breakdown," and "quadrille," for example, appear in his tune titles without much reference to whether they describe that tune's particular rhythm or form. They are rather meant as evocative labels equally appropriate for any fiddle tune, and they often appear to be assigned according to their effectiveness as titles per se. "Breakwater Boys Breakdown," for example, is clearly based on assonance. This practice is not unique, however, as such terminology is applied more loosely in titles than descriptive commentary throughout the tradition.

Technical and generic terminology is further obscured by the bilingual environment. A common way to refer to the tunes used to accompany traditional square dances in English, for example, is as *set tunes,* after the dance *set.* These are usually played in a ⁶⁄₈ meter, and Emile sometimes used the term in this way. On one occasion when I asked Emile about different kinds of tunes he mentioned set tunes but speculated on a French etymology for the term, suggesting it might refer to *sept* tunes, that is, tunes with some relationship to the number seven. This interpretation seemed possible by analogy to the use of quatre to identify step-dance tunes in French, known as *fours* in bilingual usage (M-MS 76-491/pp. 3, 7), although *sept* has no such musical connotation. *Eight* often refers to triple meter tunes used for the square dance, this terminology based on the number of dancers. To *gigue* in French usage means to perform a solo step dance; its tune is the *fast four* in duple time rhythms (ibid., 3). A *jig* in typical English usage, however, refers to any triple time rhythm. It is no wonder that the terminology seems confusing when one tries to construct a systematic overview. Individual musicians, however, seem to pick from the variety of terminology available to speak about their music in a relatively consistent manner.

Although Emile did not employ a highly codified, denotative system of verbal labels, he did understand, recognize, and identify the basic rhythmic genres of tunes. Knowledge of the various traditional rhythms is primarily practical. The fiddler knows what rhythms are appropriate for different dances based on the traditional tunes he has learned for them. In Emile's local milieu these were tunes for different parts of the Port-au-Port set, the local version of the quadrille commonly called the *square dance* in Newfoundland, the *old eight, step* dancing, and *waltzes* (Quigley 1985, 15–56).

Within each meter there are a few common rhythmic patterns. Triple meter tunes, with few exceptions ⁶⁄₈ meter, employ a quarter note–eighth note division of the beat or three eighths and sometimes dotted quarter notes to conclude a strain or, less often, a phrase. A particular pattern combining these rhythmic figures often repeats throughout a strain. A reversal of the quarter note–eighth note pattern is occasionally used for emphasis. The "Clode Sound Jig" uses predominantly quarter and eighth note combinations, occasionally reversed for rhythmic emphasis, the phrase ending in a dotted quarter. "Brother's Jig," the "Lightkeeper's," and "Michael T. Wall's" demonstrate typical mixed patterns and the tendency to repeat such patterns. "Emile's Dream" illustrates continuous eighth notes, the most commonly found rhythm. All triple meter dance tunes are usually played at a tempo within a range of MM 130 to 138 for a dotted eighth note in $\frac{6}{8}$ meter.

Among duple meter tunes an even division of the beat into four eighth notes predominates but may be combined with quarter notes to create rhythmic phrases, which generally repeat throughout a particular tune. Once again the end of a strain and sometimes a constituent phrase is usually marked by a note of longer duration. A quarter note followed by two eighths pattern, reminiscent of the Appalachian "shuffle" rhythm, is occasionally found as well. Smaller subdivisions of the beat are used as rhythmic ornaments, especially triplets and sixteenth–dotted eighth note combinations.

The "Bandsaw Reel" is, like so many, played with even divisions throughout. "Le reel de la Pistroli" illustrates possible rhythmic combinations of quarter and eighth notes. The "Forgotten Reel" and "Jim Hodder's" both employ a common combination rhythm of long-short-short. Subdividing the long note of this pattern and slurring the bowing of these notes produces a shuffle effect, as in the "Oil Fields of Newfoundland," a composition modeled along country and western lines.

Waltzes seem to be a more recent interest of Emile's, several having been composed during the time I knew him but none preserved from earlier years. They are considered in some regional traditions, such as the New England contest milieu, to be a test of skill because of their challenge to tone production. Joachim and Emile seemed to consider them "easier" to play because they are less challenging rhythmically. Joachim told me he could never "catch the bow" the way Emile could for jigs and reels, so he played the "slower" songs and waltzes instead. Cornelius Rouzes, a fiddler from Cape St. George, however, seemed to perform his waltzes as show pieces, considering them more "modern" than the traditional jigs and reels (M-tape and MS 78-239/C3584). The dancing preferences that shaped Emile's repertoire and skills were clearly square and step dances to jigs and reels. Waltzes did not appeal to Emile's energizing aesthetic, although in his last years they became appropriate in concert settings and for informal dancing at clubs. The waltzes he played and composed toward the end of his life have a strong dance-influenced character, placing rhythmic stress on the first beat by giving it longer note values and using shorter divisions leading to the next measure to provide a sense of forward rhythmic propulsion.

In all dance rhythms accenting of the primary beats, by sharp attack, slightly increased duration, and louder volume, is an important feature that gives even those tunes with what is notated as continuous even subdivisions of the beat the rhythmic energy characteristic of this dance music. Difficult to represent, it is to be assumed throughout my transcriptions.

Finally, I would note Emile's discovery and use of slow tempos and freer rhythmic performance in introductory sections to several compositions. Such pieces could be played in a manner using stricter meter and tempo but were rendered by Emile much more slowly than his other tunes and often with liberal use of rubato. The "Brother's Farewell" is one of this type in which the first strain of the introduction is rendered in both manners according to Emile's mood and the performance situation.

In keeping with the preeminent place of bowing in his stylistic self-conception, Emile focused immediately on the bow grip when I asked how he might begin to teach someone to play. He placed his little finger under the stick, to control the bow's lateral motion in conjunction with the thumb. The other three fingers laid on top of the stick to apply pressure to the strings, while maintaining the looseness of grip needed to "jig" the bow properly (Q-tape 48).

Emile's basic playing positions, bow and left hand grips, are not unusual compared to those of other fiddlers, though perhaps rather idiosyncratic in his local context. A high degree of individuality in these matters, indeed, seems typical of folk fiddling throughout North America, as does the increasing influence of violinistic art practice (Burman-Hall 1984, 165–69). Among fiddlers on the Port-au-Port today a variety of playing positions can be observed. An on-the-shoulder posture predominates, but the older players I have seen employ the chest position favored by Emile, reflecting the increasing influence of Canadian, Cape Breton, and country fiddlers appearing on television, in photographs, and in person. There is also an ongoing shift from the seated posture preferred by Emile to a standing position as required in most stage bands, which is apparent among the fiddlers at performance events in the area.

Emile's bow-hand grip is relatively idiosyncratic when compared to those documented in historical art tradition and other regional fiddling traditions. It is unlike the thumb and forefinger grip documented in Cape Breton and illustrated by Earl Spielman (Spielman 1972, 46; Garrison 1985, 131). This is the bow grip favored by many of the other fiddlers now playing

Emile's bow grip.

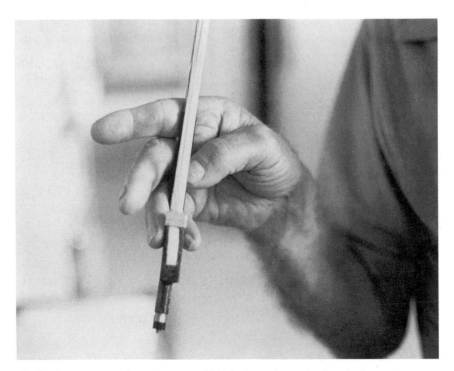

Emile demonstrates the placement of his fingers when gripping the bow.

on the Port-au-Port, including Emile's brother Joachim, reflecting increasing influence from this tradition. Emile's bow grip allows for more pressure to be applied to the strings, by placing all fingers but the pinky on top of the stick in an almost modern art manner. There is, however, historical precedent for his placement of the pinky with the back of the finger pressed against the opposite side of the bow stick (Boyden 1965, 249, 371, Plate 31). Emile's bow grip is reflected in the character of his bowing technique, which also has seventeenth-century historical precedent (Boyden 1965, 159, 401). The left-hand grip of other fiddlers in his area is much the same as Emile's, with the neck cradled well down between the thumb and forefinger. The left wrist is somewhat flexed, allowing the neck to rest on the palm when the fiddle is held against the chest; when the fiddle is held on the shoulder, the wrist straightens somewhat.

Emile expressed what he considered to be the essence of his bowing style as bowing "down" (M-tape 81-045/C5122), an idea mentioned previously in connection with his image of the bow as "like a tongue." When illustrating this idea he usually exaggerated the down-bow motion (Q-tape 48). I tried on many occasions to move from such general statements of the down-bow principle to its realization in actual performances, wondering how accurate his self-perception and conceptualization of bowing technique was.[7] During my first extended visit to Emile's, for instance, he taught me to play several pieces, focusing especially on the bowing. We worked particularly on the "(New) Old Man and Woman," a tune I knew already at the time but which he felt I was not playing well. The bowing pattern he showed me epitomized the effect he was striving to achieve. (See figure 7.) I no longer recall precisely how I formerly bowed the melody, but I employed many more slurs, especially between strings, than did Emile. A later videotape recording showed some variation in the melody from the earlier session but confirms the principle of bowing down on all accented notes.

Transcription and analysis of several other pieces further confirms the principle in practice but also demonstrates its accommodation to the exigencies of particular melodies. The first strain of "Kibitzer's Reel," for example, is very straightforward, an initial up-bow slur on the up-beat leads into simple alternation throughout, though its performance in measures 3 and 4 presents a challenge. The second strain of this tune shows the effect of interpolating ornaments in measures 3 and 4. "Fight for Your Rights" incorporates a typical "rocking" pattern of bowing together with triplet ornaments in measures 2 and 3. "Willie Laney's Wedding Jig" illustrates application of the principle to $\frac{6}{8}$ meter.

Figure 7.

"The (New) Old Man and Woman" bowing patterns, as played by Emile on videotape

Bowing patterns, as originally taught to me

"Ryan's Fancy Arriving" talking bow

Figure 7.

"Kibitzer's Reel" bowing patterns

"Fight for Your Rights" bowing patterns

"Willey Laney's Wedding Jig" bowing patterns

"Madeleine's Glass of Lemon Pie" bowing patterns

"Madeleine's Glass of Lemon Pie" bowing patterns, dance tempo

In addition to this basic bowing technique, Emile also employed several special bowing effects. These epitomize the previously mentioned "dart" or "jump." These terms refer essentially to bowed rhythmic accents or ornaments. The accents when especially pronounced become the "talking bow," while some ornaments are similar to those he considered typical of "Scotch" playing. All provide means to produce some variety of rhythmic accenting that incites the dancers' enthusiasm. The simplest are strongly accented double, that is, eighth-note, divisions of quarter notes in $\frac{2}{2}$ meter tunes, as in measures 3 and 4 of "Kibitzer's Reel." As indicated, these accents may also appear as the more typical triplet or dotted rhythm bowed ornaments of Irish and Scots playing. The same effect is achieved in triple meter tunes by reversing the usual quarter-eighth note rhythmic pattern. The accent is achieved primarily by a change in attack and volume, but the effect verges on a doublet rhythm. A transcription of bowing in the introductory section of "Madeleine's Glass of Lemon Pie" illustrates at indicated points the increased use of slurring which Emile employed in such pieces. Once a dance rhythm was established, he reverted to more usual practice but retained a few atypical slurring patterns.

Although these rhythmic ornaments are similar to those typical of Cape Breton fiddling (Dunlay and Reich 1986, 22–24), they are not as pervasive nor quite the same rhythmic pattern. Neither are they as pervasive as bowed triplets often are in Irish tradition (Breathnach 1977, 94–100). Both of these traditions have much more codified systems of ornamentation shared by most players, as indicated by their well-developed terminology. Emile's terms of reference are of his own devising. His techniques were probably influenced by the Cape Breton style of playing, which he would have heard, but were less refined and contributed to the different rhythmic gestalt or feel of his music. This difference is related to his bow grip, which facilitated a heavy accent on the down bow but inhibited numerous and rapid bow cuts, which originate in the wrist and fingers of the bow arm.

The "talking bow," which I discussed previously as an expression of the conception of music as talk, is distinguished from these techniques that are incorporated into almost all tunes. The talking bow especially serves as a marker of heightened intensity. It is performed much closer to the frog than Emile normally plays, producing a strong, percussive attack on each note. It may actually involve bouncing the bow, similar to the violinistic technique of "chopped" bowing (Green 1976, 59). Emile used this bowing primarily when alternating between notes on adjacent strings, less often in single string phrases, which may, however, be strongly accented to achieve a similar rhythmically expressive result.

Bowing is the technique about which Emile was most explicit, and when asked about his style of playing he singled out bowing as most important (Q-tape 20). His focus on bowing reflects the primary importance of rhythm in this dance accompaniment tradition. Emile often identified "the bow" as the distinguishing feature of his playing and emphasized its appropriateness for dancing.

> Nobody had a bow like me. How many said that, "What a bow you got." Well you gotta go like that [stamps], when I used to play when I was young, eh? . . . Soon [as] I take it, holy gee, everybody on the floor [stamps].
>
> Couldn't sit down.
>
> Yeah, you see, eh? . . . You hear those, nice fiddlers, but . . . not too many gonna give me courage to go dance, eh? But there's some now, they gonna play, holy gee, you gotta get up. You gotta get up [to dance]. . . . You hear my fiddlin', you hears my bow. (M-tape 81-502/ C5311)

5 ～ *So That My Story Will Live On*

Fiddle Performance from House and Hall to Stage and Screen

Within the Newfoundland outport context usually conjured by the term *traditional,* fiddle playing has been used to accompany dances and entertain at the parties known as "times."[1] Investigation of these occasions for fiddling, characterizing their participants, and describing the available "communicative resources" (Herndon and McLeod 1980a, 191) makes it possible to examine particular performances as creative responses to situations within the framework of an expressive system.[2] What are the settings for fiddle performance, how do fiddlers respond to the demands of different situations, what constraints do these settings impose, and what opportunities do they present, are the questions asked in this chapter. The answers will help us to understand the creative choices Emile made as a performer and to discern more clearly the meaning of the musical message he crafted.

～ Hall Times and Dances

Hall times, so called because they usually took place in a public building, were generally public events at which dancing was a primary activity (Quigley 1985, 59). In hall times instrumental dance music was provided by a solo, almost always male, fiddler, a term that continued to refer to the dance musician even when, in later years (ca. 1940 on), he was often as likely to be playing an accordion as a violin. At the hall times the musician's role was filled by a single individual, usually formally hired to play throughout the event, if paid only a token fee. It was a role that carried significant status because his music was a necessary adjunct to the dancing; this function placed him at the center of social activity and in a position of considerable power to control the event.

Emile recalled dances at hall times as the primary setting in which he performed until the 1960s. His comments about playing in such settings echo many of the comments made by other musicians, and he considers that the demands of this milieu were important factors shaping his style of playing.

> The dances that you played for . . . were they mostly . . . house parties, or were there halls that you played at?
> Oh, they were always in the halls. In the halls. Holy gee. Oh, I used to play at Lourdes. I used to play at Campbell's Creek. I used to play at Boswarlis. Dances. Holy, good God yes. (M-tape 81-502/C5311)

> I played fifteen years for the garden party there, [in] Campbell's Creek.
> Every year for fifteen years?
> Yeah, it was once a year, eh? Garden party. And to Boswarlis, it was six seven years I suppose, for their garden party too. Oh I was welcome, oh my God, my god. Yeah welcome. (Q-tape 8)

That Emile consistently recalled these dance events as significant when asked where he used to play is not surprising. The musician's role at the public dances, such as that in Lourdes, and especially the even larger garden parties held by parishes in the area of Campbell's Creek and Boswarlis, carries the greatest prestige among various performance contexts. Such public performances are what define a player's social role as a musician. Indeed, individuals who are able to play but do not perform publicly are not usually identified by others, or by themselves, as musicians (Ashton 1981).

After Emile's first "public" performance he played constantly until the traditional dances declined in popularity during the 1960s. Emile emphasizes that he was considered a public musician even beyond the bounds of his immediate community, that he held this position for good reason, and that this role was significant:

Forty-four years I played for dances. Weddings, garden parties, dances. I was all the time on go, every weekend gone. . . . Forty-four years I play for square dance. Forty-four years now, eh? Used to say, "Who's playin' tonight?" . . . "Emile." "Oh we're goin' we're goin'." "Benoit." "We're goin'. We'll be there."

Yes. Would you play just by yourself?

Oh yes just by myself. No guitar.

Just by yourself.

No guitar nothing.

No piano.

Nothing.

Accordion?

Nothing. It's only since, say, not forty-four years like that . . . I played like that for twenty years like that, by myself.

Did you use a microphone, or?

No microphone, nothing, there was no electricity, there was nothing. And you used to hear me. I used to burn, I used to burn the string. Bow's only [good for] two nights. A bow like that. . . . Now I plays, I play smooth. But them times, hear me, them time. By Jesus cripes . . . used to catch on fire. Sheeew, I played. (M-tape 81-502/C5311)

These themes were often repeated with different emphases in our discussions of his performances at dance events. Playing continuously for hours on end, for example, is an important part of how Emile describes performing at dances as in the following excerpt:

I was the champion of the dancin' there, you know, at home. Yeah, the rest used to play but not like me you know. I used to put something in them, eh? Courage, eh? And a man to his post. Not play one dance and gone two or three hours. Yes. . . . Play all the time. Yes. And I still got that habit. I still got that habit, play all the time. I don't like to see people waitin', eh? Now if somebody take the violin and play, oh ok. But I don't like that break, me. Music should . . .

Should keep going.

Yeah, yeah. I don't like that break. . . . A break sure, for when another person take over, eh?

Yeah, yeah, so that's why you like to play so long.

Well yes, yeah, for to, you know, so like people haven't got to wait or nothing. (Q-tape 8)

Emile explained what the garden parties were like to a small group at a folk festival workshop:

> Well it's almost the same thing like this [festival]. There is a place to go eat . . . and there's a big building, you know. People eats and they goes out and they plays games [as at a fair or carnival]. And when it comes in the night, in the evening, here the spree starts. C'est ça. Going until one o'clock. But before, in my time, it was three or four o'clock in the morning before we stop. And we had a hall. . . . It was a hundred feet long. And I used to play here this end and they used to dance both ends. Dance over here dance over there. I used to play and I used to sing. I guarantee you this, they used to hear me over there too. There was no microphone nothing but they used to hear me. So kept going, kept going, kept going. Now and then I'd drink a home brew, quick, on the sly, you know. Behind the door. Yeah. Yeah, come on again have a seat. "Somebody else want to give me help?" They didn't want to. They want to dance. "Now, come on! You play." They didn't want for the other guy to give me a chance. So I had no pause at all. . . . Didn't want to displease, you know? La. That's my story. And it's a true story. True story. (M-tape 81-502/C5319)

Drinks were an important medium of exchange among the men, and the fiddler usually received plenty from those for whom he played (Quigley 1985, 71–72). Once again, a sign of the musician's status, this is an element one is not surprised to find in Emile's descriptions.

A great deal of interaction with his audience is also characteristic of his descriptions of the social scene at dance events. Emile's activity as a composer received important recognition at these events, the compositions serving as a focus for interaction with his audience. On one occasion when I asked Emile to describe the dances he responded:

> Oh my god, used to go good, boy. . . . I was playing to Boswarlis and I had composed one. From Port-au-Port on Berry Head, that's about five minutes drive, in a car. And when I got on top of the Berry Head I had it composed. I was playin' it. And Harold Hynes, poor, he's dead now, but asked him, I said, "Harold, how you gonna baptize that one?" "Well," he says, Gravel Pond Reel. You heard about it eh?
>
> No, no I didn't hear about that, no.
>
> So, c'est ça, Gravel Pond Reel. So I went to the garden party that night . . . three night I had to play there. They had [a] three night

garden party. Three days you know, three nights. . . . So, that night I played that all night. Every time they used to, "Come on give us Gravel Pond Reel." That's all used to hear, "Gravel Pond Reel." And on the last, after a couple of hours I say, "Now boys I'm gonna play you one you never heard before" [laugh].

Gravel Pond Reel.

Fun eh? They had fun. They had fun with that. (M-tape 81-502/C5311)

Wilfred W. Wareham has characterized the formal hall times as a "testing ground for leadership and dominance positions within the community" (1982, 443). Given the prominent position Emile held in these contexts it is not surprising that he emphasized them when asked about the kinds of events at which he performed. I suspect it is for related reasons that Emile occasionally commented on the absence of fights at dances for which he played. Belligerent behavior at the times, Wareham says, was usually kept in check by a respected member of the community. By making this observation Emile is claiming such status for himself. He went on to explain, for example, that the first performance of the "Gravel Pond Reel" was such a success there were no fights that night.

Everybody enjoyed themselves. No fight or nothing. That's not often. And every time I wasn't there [there was] always a big fight on. That's a funny thing.

I wonder why?

Because me, I keep my music going all the time, you know. (M-tape 81-502/C5311)

Maintaining this role, he often stressed, was an important commitment requiring many sacrifices, a narrative strategy similar to that in his stories of physical hardiness we have already heard.

Oh well, start [at] seven o'clock, my time there. Finish one, two o'clock, sometimes three o'clock in the morning. Going all the time, all the time, stitches in the back. The wrists all tired, and soakin' wet, my son. Then had to walk from Lourdes. I had to walk down home. That's a long ways my son. Seven miles. . . . Oh yes, I used to get here four o'clock in the morning, say like Sunday morning and then I get up seven. . . . Gets a few hours sleep . . . seven [o'clock] to go to mass then, walk up there again. . . . It's a long ways my son. It took a lot of sacrifice. Yes my good boy. But tell that to the young people, they don't want to believe it. They think it happened to me maybe once. No, all the time, all the time. How many soakin' I got? I come here soakin' wet. (M-tape 81-502/C5311)

Emile's performances at a dance event are the least well documented of the situations in which he played because these gatherings essentially stopped just as he was "discovered." The first tape recording of Emile made by collectors from outside his community, however, was made at a dance in the church hall in Lourdes in 1964 (M-tape, 64-15/C115–17). Despite relatively poor sound quality, this recording provides an example of a performance at a fairly large dance event or hall time.

On this occasion he was accompanied on the guitar by his son Mike; both instruments were amplified, resulting in some distortion. Emile does indeed seem to play steadily throughout the recording session; tunes are played in medleys lasting from fifteen to twenty minutes each. When I played this tape for him he explained that these medleys formed the accompaniment for the Port-au-Port set, a version of the Newfoundland square dance in which the first sections are run together continuously. This is the manner of performing the square dance which Emile described as common after World War II (Quigley 1985, 37). Each medley consists of approximately four tunes, each of which is played many times over. Several of the tunes that he played on this occasion were of his own composition and remained prominent in his repertoire. He identified "Tootsie Wootsie," "West Bay Centre," and "Making the Curve to Black Duck Brook," as well as one that was later named "Gerry Squires' Palette" when it resurfaced in his repertoire. There are also tunes I have not heard him play elsewhere, but overall there seems to be a more Scottish character to the rhythms of this repertoire than I hear in more recent performances. Emile taps his feet throughout, he frequently sings along with the tunes, and occasionally he shouts encouragement to the dancers. Between medleys he calls out to the audience with phrases such as "Here we go!", "Get merry!", and "Bring back the old times!" The background noise level is high, and it is clearly a wild scene with yells, shouts, and stamping audible throughout.

It is difficult to convey fully in print the character of Emile's performance for dance events. It is a highly exaggerated, larger-than-life style; all stops are pulled in his effort to generate as much energy as possible. The more he "puts out" the more the dancers respond and he, in turn, is inspired by them. At the heart of the dance event, he provides the musical engine driving this system to higher and higher levels of excitement.

Because of its social significance, performance in this manner is placed at the pinnacle of the traditional, context-sensitive system of aesthetics, and Emile was the best practitioner in his locale.

The preeminence of fiddling as the accompaniment to dance has had an important influence on performance practice. Until quite recently, driven by the demands of playing in relatively large halls without amplification, fiddlers employed various means to increase the volume of sound they produced. The instruments were often tuned higher than standard pitch, increasing tension on the strings and producing a louder tone. As James Martin, a fiddler from the St. John's area, answered when asked if he played for dances alone, "I used to have it tuned up real loud. Wasn't a question of having a nice sound or having a real . . . fine and quiet [sound]. You had to lean on it. . . . You had to play loud with steel strings and tighten up as tight as will go" (M-MS 75-307/p. 13).

He also recalled fiddlers older than he who played and sang at the same time. "Well that was the way the old fiddlers used to play, like for instance Abraham Martin. That was before my time, but my father told me he was a good fiddler. He used to sing and play. He used to make more noise than I did. . . . Could hear him real loud. He had a deep voice. . . . He would go right along with the fiddle. He played just the same thing. When singing, he would be playing exactly the same thing" (M-MS 75-307/p. 7).

This practice has declined with the advent of electronic amplification, although some of the older fiddlers still augment their performance by singing. Emile, for example, can be heard singing in this way on both of his records (Benoit 1979, 1982).

As one can deduce from the above examples and as noted earlier in a broader context, the need to play loudly is another important aspect of playing for dances. Playing for large numbers of dancers without amplification even made it difficult for the fiddler to hear himself. Emile occasionally compensated for this by actually holding the fiddle up next to his ear, commenting that this playing position made the instrument sound almost as if it were amplified.

Foot-tapping was also an integral part of the dance fiddler's performance. Rufus Guinchard, a fiddler of the older generation from the northern peninsula, began playing for dances at age thirteen or fourteen. "After a couple of times out, however, he discovered that he didn't quite have all that it took to play properly for a dance. 'I had to go back and learn how to stamp my feet and keep the time. I used to play either too fast for 'em or too slow'" (Russell 1982, 9).

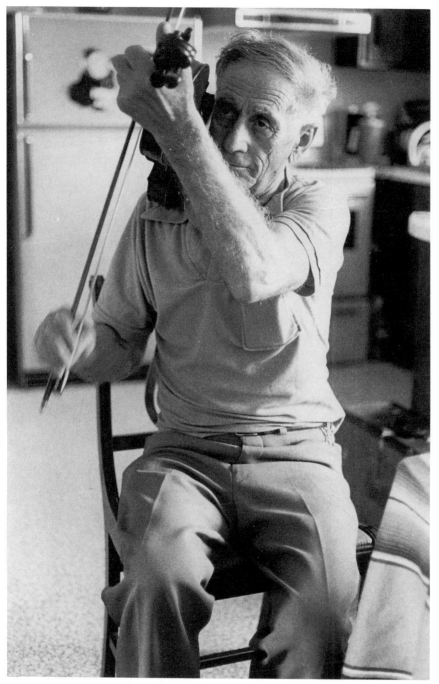
To amplify its sound, Emile plays the fiddle next to his ear.

As Guinchard indicates, "keeping time" was a critical skill for the dance fiddler. So it was for the dancers as well. Another musician indicated this to me as follows: "The old people, they never wanted to miss a beat. Could dance forward or backstep right with the music and never wanted to be off. Now the scattered one that didn't have an ear might make the big stamp when 'twas only half over [the musical phrase] and they might put you out!" (Quigley 1981, 80).

Rhythm is perhaps the key factor in expressed aesthetic judgments. A good musician was one whose rhythm evoked a dance response. Mack Masters, the most respected player in Wareham's community of Harbour Buffet, for example, "had the old time way and 'twas goin' right into the floor out of the accordion. If anybody had any rhythm into 'em at all, they'd have to go with that see, every single thing he played. . . . Real good he could play, he wasn't no fancy player. Herb Reid and Herb Hollet were good players but somehow or another they never had the force behind 'em like Mack. . . . Wasn't the same kind of timing, they put too many notes in there somehow" (Wareham 1982, 339).

∼ House Times

In contrast to the hall time with its focus on the high status of a single musician, most participants at the more informal house times took the role of performer at some point. Instrumental music was thus only one of the performance genres likely to occur. More than one musician might perform during the event, and all musicians present would be expected to perform. Each instrumental performance, however, would be relatively short, consisting of only a few pieces, and serve primarily as listening music rather than as accompaniment for dancing.[3]

Because of its concomitant status, Emile usually presented himself as the preeminent public dance fiddler of his area, yet he was certainly an active performer at more informal house times as well. He recalled for me just how much he used to play in addition to the dances:

And parties, and all that. But they was all after me. How many times they come here, two o'clock, three o'clock in the morning, get me.

To go play, for a party.

For a party, yeah. How many times they come knock to my window since I'm married? I go there and make a little bit of fun then. Play and I made a lot of fun boy. Yes. Should be, you should ask people about me, them Lecour [neighbors of his] and all that, up along . . . how Emile was, what kind of guy he was, right? No good or what? They'll tell you. Made a lot of fun my son. I made a lot of people happy. (M-tape 81-502/C5311)

The demands made upon musicians within the informal house time context are also reflected in the performance practice of many fiddlers. In this setting performances are likely to consist of two or three short selections and often feature devices to gain and retain audience attention and evoke a favorable response from a listening rather than dancing audience. Because the fiddler is not accompanying dancers, there are fewer constraints on his performance. He is free to play in nondance rhythms or forms and to intersperse narratives or otherwise break out of the format imposed by the dance.

Emile's performances at traditional house times in his own community are not well documented on tape. I attended and made recordings at local house party gatherings while visiting him, but behavior at these events was affected by Emile's recent professionalization and my own presence as a result of this same transformation. It seemed that Emile was more the center of attention than probably would have been the case previously, making these gatherings less than ideal examples of typical traditional house times. His performances at these events, however, draw on the repertoire and techniques he developed in earlier years. Furthermore, I have experienced such gatherings without Emile present. By combining my observations with Emile's recollections, his practice in later years, and other published descriptions it is possible to reconstruct a reliable picture of Emile performing in this milieu.

The veillée, as house parties were formerly called by the French of the Port-au-Port, usually occurred on winter evenings beginning about 7:00 P.M. Anywhere from four to twelve people might gather in a kitchen and participate in card playing, storytelling, singing, dancing, drinking, and eating a "lunch" of beans, bread, jam, cookies, and biscuits (Wareham 1982, 93). Before the 1940s it seems that public storytellers were the central performers (Thomas 1983, 52–54). Perhaps like the veillées of Lorraine and Quebec, music was increasingly incorporated as educational and work functions became less important and these gatherings became more and more primarily entertainment events (Marin 1964, and Miner 1939, 159–227).

Gerald Thomas has noted that as a narrator Emile exemplifies the traditional "public" storytelling style employed by performers at *veillées*. It is characterized by active, dramatic presentation, a style that carries over to the narratives Emile incorporated into his musical performances (Thomas 1984, 70–71, 464, 465). This was the style of narration which Emile learned as a youth watching the older generation perform at *veillées*. Though now out of fashion around his home and somewhat ridiculed by the younger generation as typical of the "old Frenchmen" (Thomas 1985, 291–92), it served his performance needs well when adapted to the narration of his own experiences and presentation of his compositions.

The pattern of interaction at a *veillée* was similar to that of the Anglo-Irish house times (Wareham 1982). Whereas a single musician performed for the duration of the public dance, at the house party this status had to be continually negotiated and reinforced by the participants. Coaxing of singers, for example, was expected before they would consent to perform. At least three requests were usual, fended off with standard responses about the condition of the singer's voice and the like. The message that singing was appropriate behavior for that person at that time had to be established (Wareham 1982, 438). During the performance "the audience expresses approval or disapproval by making or withholding comments between the verses such as "'give it to her,' 'come on,' 'that's some song,' or the like" (Wareham 1982, 439). Similar interaction is typical during instrumental performances at such gatherings as well.

Wareham notes that singers might employ the *declamando* (that is, spoken ending to conclude a song, widely recognized as an Irish convention) as a device to cue audience comments. Or they might continue singing through the conclusion, giving them the opportunity to append their own spoken comment to the performance, "challenging or otherwise" (Wareham 1982, 440). I believe that Emile employed other means, appropriate to his medium, to exert similar control over his audience. He often ended a tune with an exaggerated *retardando* and exaggerated gestures, for example, thus eliciting responses. Or he might stop midstream, as it were, with a few strikes of the bow on the strings and cries of enthusiasm, in effect providing his own approbation.

Performances at house times served not only to entertain but also to impress and brought the performer added status and prestige. As one older singer/reciter/dancer said, "And I didn't have much trouble to get a girl at the end of the night either" (Wareham 1982, 447). Gordon Cox has made similar observations in his study of folk singing in Trinity Bay. "Playing the accordion gave added status to a young man, and consequently an accordion player had no trouble in picking up young girls. As one of my informants said, 'You had it made for the rest of the voyage' [i.e., the fishing season]" (Cox 1980, 60).

Group approval was needed in this strongly egalitarian society, perhaps along with a fair bit of liquor, for people to adopt a performance role. Even though all were expected to participate, performance remained an assertive act and there was pressure to do well or look foolish for having imposed oneself on the others. This may explain the emphasis many fiddlers place on their period of solitary practice in accounts of their musical biographies. Premature performance presented too great a risk of being seen as incompetent in the performer's role, for failure meant loss of status rather than the desired approbation.

~ House Time Performance Style

The 1964 prerevival recording already discussed also contains material from a house party that followed the dance discussed previously (M-tapes 64-15/C116, 117). It includes several performances by Emile, as well as others who were present. Emile is only one of the performers and fiddling only one of the performance genres heard. The participants frequently change roles. Requests are boisterously made; some are ignored, some fulfilled, as performances are negotiated by the participants through what only appears to be chaotic social interaction. In this setting Emile sang several songs and fiddled a few pieces, of much shorter duration than at the dance, along with his son Mike on the accordion, in addition to performing both traditional tunes and his own compositions on the fiddle.

Emile developed his characteristic meld of musical and narrative forms in the house party situation. This pattern of performance is not completely idiosyncratic; I have encountered several less flamboyant performers who combined narration with their musical performances in nondance settings. Nor is this pattern limited to Newfoundland. Although such extramusical matters are not well documented, there is evidence that this performance pattern is widespread, perhaps associated with a distinctive repertoire.[4]

Emile performed several of these traditional tune and narrative pairings: the "Hangman's Reel" and its story; the "Devil's Reel" and associated legend; the "Old Man and the Old Woman," and "Les Marionnettes," although these have less-developed narratives. The bulk of Emile's hybrid

Emile "playing the fool" at a party makes fun with a paper moustache. M-84-400, photo CEFT 50. Courtesy Clara Murphy.

repertoire, however, was made up of his own compositions and associated personal experience narratives. These describe the tune's composition or a memorable event it commemorates. These tunes can, of course, be played without their associated story, but usually they are not, especially those with lengthy narratives of importance in themselves rather than merely serving as extended titles. In the later situations in which he performed outside his home locale Emile drew extensively on this repertoire and developed it considerably. This has become the primary format for contemporary presentation of his compositions.

Emile's reputation as a clown was most fully realized in the house party setting. Responding spontaneously to the immediate situation he was likely to do unexpected and incongruous things to "make fun." I can recall him making faces by putting beer-bottle caps in his eye sockets on one occasion, for example, and, although I have forgotten what prompted this particular stunt, the ludicrous image he made was very funny.

As well as interspersing his musical performances with brief narrative comments and introductions, he often augmented them by gestural antics

Emile imitates the "sleepy fiddler."

that usually provoked gales of laughter. This is particularly evident in several of his favorite characterizations, which purport to portray the old fiddlers he heard when a young man. We have already seen Emile's imitation of his Uncle Jean. In a second, more frequently performed characterization, Emile imitates a fiddler afflicted with sleeping sickness.

> The other feller, he used to, there was a disease, a sickness, you know? Some got paralyzed, some more lost their speech, some more used to fall asleep. Now this fella, he could play the violin. And he used to fall asleep. He used to play pretty good. But he take his bow about half-way. And put the leg over the other, and put the violin like this [propped between leg and chest], and then he play. He'd fall asleep then. [Emile mimics falling asleep while playing.]
>
> Gerald Thomas: Wake up old man!
>
> [Emile "wakes up" abruptly and begins to play furiously. He continues to play, then "falls asleep" again.]
>
> GT: Wake up old man!
>
> [Emile "wakes up" and concludes the performance.]
>
> Wok! [laugh]. He sit there, wok!
>
> GT: There'd always be somebody to shout out, to tell him to wake up?
>
> Oh yes. Well they was dancin' you see, so that some see the music was stopping, "Come on boy, wake up old man!" [mimes old man waking with a start]. Then he fall asleep again. Wasn't his fault. Was a sickness you know. And I entertain like him and sometimes I thinks, well gee, I'm gonna be punished some of those days [laughter]. Some time I'm sleepy, that come in my mind. We used to make faces, you know, all kinds, like that. My mother use to say, "Well now, if the tide happen to change, you stay like that." So we used to get frightened eh?
>
> Your face would get stuck, eh?
>
> Yeah, we get frightened so we wouldn't do no more faces eh? (Videotape)

Another example of these imitations is Emile's characterization of a fiddler who became too excited when playing.

> There was a feller. . . . And when he used to play his windpipe used to go like this [pulls at Adam's apple]. Like the jig. . . . The violin music was right in him. Used to take charge, too much, because when he play used to take charge of him, and he used to go ooooo, gone

Emile imitates the fiddler who "went wild."

gone, gone, gone. If he had got a pair of wings he would've fly. He used to play this one here, used to call that the Red Cap. [Emile plays the tune, starting off slowly, becoming progressively faster and faster, until he ends by bowing back and forth on the open d' and a' strings, while hooting, stamping, and laughing with a hysterical screech.] He had to laugh at that because he could do no more, he gone too wild. (Videotape)

These two characterizations underscore the aesthetics of good fiddling through their humor. They are funny precisely because they flaunt basic requirements for fiddling. The dance musician must provide the musical energy to power the dancers; a fiddler who falls asleep is completely ludicrous. A fiddler who cannot control himself and the music enough to maintain a danceable rhythm is equally unsuited to play for dancers. Emile excuses himself from what might be considered unseemly criticism of his neighbors, saying it is all in fun, but this merely points to the implied critique of their musicianship. Although the major focus of these pieces is on characterization, such dramatization is an important feature of Emile's narrative style no matter what the subject. It reflects his acquisition of the public narrating style from the old Frenchmen at *veillées* in his youth (Thomas 1983, 154–57).

∼ A Traditional Fiddler in the Modern World

The constraints of playing at both dances and house parties contributed to the formation of Emile's performance practice. Extensive house party performance gave Emile the opportunity to develop a style that intermingles dramatic narration and fiddling. It shaped his expectations for performer-audience interaction, including the audience's active expression of response, direct interaction with individual listeners, and a looseness of role definition within the situation. Emile's experience in the dance milieu strongly influenced his playing technique. He learned to play loudly, to emphasize rhythmic devices over melodic subtleties, and to employ his feet, his voice, and his movements to project a dominant presence in the midst of raucous activity. In response to the demands of this situation he also acquired the stamina to perform at great length and to appreciate vociferous audience response. He combined aspects of both situated performance styles in a hybrid form that paired tunes and narratives, expanding on traditional precedents to develop a distinctive repertoire of personal

Emile on stage at a festival with his son Mike, daughter Roberta, and Ron
Formanger.

experience narratives and compositions. Public performance offered him
opportunities to assert himself and achieve important status in a socially
approved manner within the traditional value system. It is not surprising
that when new opportunities created by interest in Newfoundland culture
arose, Emile was anxious to pursue them and assume a similar role in a
wider context.

In his later years Emile took the performance style he developed in
these settings into new situations. These placed demands and constraints
on performers to which Emile tried to adapt. His penchant for the dramatic public performance style, however, seems to have suited him well
to succeed in these milieux. A stage performance role is similar to that of
the dance musician, albeit the audience is more passive than the dancers
Emile formerly accompanied. But not only are they less active, they are also
more attentive. Here music is played primarily for listening, as at the house
times. Performances on these stages, however, usually last far longer than
at a party and the performer retains his role throughout. By combining elements of both traditional presentational styles, as well as developing new

techniques, Emile tried to meet the demands of these new performance situations. Although audiences were not always unanimous in their evaluation of his performances, his renewed career as a professional entertainer is testimony to a degree of success.

These new performance contexts are many and varied. They include performances by Emile at folk festivals, in "workshops" or lecture-demonstration settings, in bars, and at schools. Emile also appeared frequently on television and radio and was often interviewed and visited at his home by researchers, younger musicians, folk music aficionados, and students. These varied stage performance and interview situations may be differentiated and grouped according to the nature of the imposed format. Each is characterized by physical variables such as the size of the venue, number and placement of the performers and audience, use of amplification, and the like; social variables such as the kind and degree of interaction between performer and audience; and conceptual variables such as the aesthetic expectations brought to the event by its participants. All combined to influence the way Emile chose to perform.

Despite their many differences, the crucial variable among the new settings is the nature of the relationship between performer and audience, that is, the social (or proxemic) distance between them (Hall 1966), the concomitant degree of audience attention focused on him, and the degree of separation between them. I will consider the range of contemporary performance contexts from those characterized by large audiences, addressed from a "public" distance to smaller, more intimate settings. Situational constraints that affected Emile's performance practice in different settings are noted as they arise.

Performances on stages represent one extreme in which the audience may be large, roles are clearly defined and quite separate, and the degree of focus may be high, although sometimes of a relatively short span. Folk festivals are one such event in which Emile appeared many times. At one extreme of audience "distance" I would place those events in which he appears amplified on a stage well removed from a large audience to whom he may speak, for whom he may play, but with whom he cannot converse. Audience response in such situations is limited to public gestures such as clapping, shouting, or the like. In some concertlike situations the audience focus may be very high, in others interaction among members of the audience may predominate. Although such an audience may employ the performance to facilitate more intimate interaction among themselves, such as dancing, this action does not evoke much response from the stage.

Emile on stage at Une Longue Veillée at Cape St. George.

Performance formats in the festival setting may vary. At the large yearly provincial festival in St. John's, for example, Emile often participated as one of a group of performers, brought together around a theme such as fiddling or storytelling, who took turns at the invitation of a "presenter." The presenter serves primarily to introduce the performers and regulate the proceedings by directing performers to certain items in their repertoire. The presenter's presence is also intended to make the "folk" performers, presumably more accustomed to intimate performance in their homes, more at ease on stage. They are also meant to serve as a bridge between the performer's experience and repertoire and the expectations of the audience by providing, in their introductions, background helpful to appreciate the performer's artistry fully.

In this circumstance Emile has been seen as difficult to control from the presenter's and audience's point of view. He occasionally monopolized the performance time, spinning one of his tune introductions out into a lengthy narration, leaving little time for other performers. Or he became somewhat carried away, playing more than his allotted number of tunes. Such tension between the imposed format and Emile's practice may be partially blamed on a presenter who was unfamiliar with Emile's repertoire or narrative style and asked for an inappropriate item. But it is also attributable to some extent, I believe, to the similarity between this format and the public, hall time performances in which Emile developed his public stage persona and performance style. Emile was used to being the sole performer and filling lots of time. He found it difficult to compress his performances into a shorter time span and take a back seat to others in a stage context of this type. A response that brought him more success in these situations was to interact with other performers on stage, bringing some of the character of his performances in more intimate settings to the stage.

Whereas the large-audience stage setting somewhat constrained Emile's preferred performance style, he found smaller-scale performances at which he was the center of attention for periods upward of twenty minutes more conducive to achieving his communicative goals. This view is supported by his greater success when given an entire "set" to himself. In this format he could weave together stories and tunes into a twenty-minute, half-hour, or forty-minute sequence, becoming his own presenter. Many of the statements I have employed for the information they contain about his life history, for example, were taken from such performances.

In so-called workshops, performances for smaller audiences within a folk festival environment, Emile might be the sole performer, as at the Pinewoods camp performances which I arranged, or one of a group, as at the Sound Symposium in St. John's. The distinguishing feature is the more intimate relationship to the audience, which allows more direct conversation. In such settings performers are physically separated from the audience and their roles clearly established, yet their closer proximity allows for more intimate interaction. Eye contact can be made with particular individuals, and his use of gestures, including dancing, here evokes an immediate kinesthetic response at this "personal" distance, communicating much more effectively than as the mere visual spectacles they become on a "public" stage. Emile also tended to perform many more and longer narratives and relatively less music. This created some conflict at Pinewoods, as several audience members, whose expectations were conditioned by concert performances of folk-revival groups, wished he had been more serious and played more music.

Performances of the lecture-demonstration variety, which he often gave at Memorial University, are similar, although the situation is usually somewhat more formal because it occurs in an educational institution. These audiences are likely to be more attentive and respectful, allowing him to perform more extended narratives. They are also less exuberant and spontaneous in their reactions, lending a more serious tone to his performances than is typical elsewhere.

Various cultural festivals were the first of the nontraditional performance settings Emile encountered, but bars, or clubs as they are known in St. John's, became his predominant venue during the early 1980s. The club scene is quite different from the traditional dance, the house party, or the festival stage, and Emile's performances changed accordingly. Emile tried both to bring the setting closer to that of the house party and to adapt his performance to the club's particular demands.[5]

Emile's style of performance met many of these demands well, and he was hired frequently to play at Bridgett's, often for engagements of a week or more. This continued until the owner decided to change the club's format, eliminating live performance and installing video games in the former listening area, apparently intending to attract a more regular, neighborhood-based clientele. Another bar soon opened, however, which hoped to capitalize on the combination of traditional music and party atmosphere. This was Kibitzer's, also now defunct. I spent a week at Emile's house along with its owner, Jerry McDonald, and the three of us had several discussions about performing at his club. Jerry echoed the sentiments of other bar owners, and Emile explained some of his strategies for dealing with the demands of this situation.

Jerry explained that he likes to hire traditional musicians because they work harder. From the barman's viewpoint, "you get more for your dollar." It is cheaper than a modern group who will do "forty and twenty"; a typical gig format is forty minutes on and twenty off, sometimes thirty and thirty. Performances usually begin at 9:30 P.M. and go until the last set ends between 12:30 and 1:00. The bar closes by 1:30 (Fraser 1981, 167). Jerry contrasted Emile's practice as follows: "On Friday, for example, [Emile] played till a quarter to eleven—that was his first set! He loves to play, you know. Traditional musicians play because they love the music" (field notes).

Emile explained that he would keep playing "because he doesn't like to see people waiting." This is the same way he felt about playing for dances and is an attitude that made Emile somewhat vulnerable to economic exploitation. Because of his background, he was unfamiliar with the "set" format and typical standards of payment for club performance when he began to play in bars. Aware of this risk, however, he often asked others close to him to help negotiate with prospective employers. Gerald Thomas became, in effect, his manager (Thomas 1984, 9).

The arrangement under which Emile played at Kibitzer's was to perform once a month as the "headliner." He earned $100 a night—more than the $50 to $75 less well-known musicians were paid. Travel and living expenses were absorbed by Emile. This is the reverse of the typical arrangements for festival appearances in which travel and subsistence costs are paid for, but performing fees are minimal or nonexistent. One hundred dollars a night is, of course, a great deal more than traditional musicians were ever paid around Black Duck Brook and was significant in Emile's economic picture. Although by many professional standards it is not high, for Emile it was a level he worked to achieve.

Emile considered the frequently low level of pay for which he performed to be a necessary sacrifice to achieve the success he gained. For his first trip to St. John's, he recalled, only travel expenses were paid. Emile had asked an accordion player to come with him who would not go without his girlfriend, a friend, and his friend's girlfriend as well. Emile went alone. He explains that "you can't expect to get paid every time." If the accordion player had come, "well then in a little while he could be going around, be on TV. You got to build it up" (field notes).

Emile seemed to be well aware of the special demands of the club scene, although he did not always succeed in matching his performance to the audience's desires and expectations. While discussing Kibitzer's with Jerry and me, he noted some of the special requirements of this setting, commenting that his rendition of the Newfoundland song "I's the B'y" was successful because it satisfied them:

> There's a little fun it and you know it goes fast, and then some music with it and things goin'. Because people is fast now, eh? They're fast. You know, oui?
>
> Everything moves fast.
>
> You got to go, because there're so many things goin' they got no time to wait there. You gonna tell a story, they got no time to wait half an hour, three-quarters of an hour for a story. They're too much in a hurry. They want to hear, there's so many things to hear, so when you tells jokes, something, they got to be right short and funny and play your music again.
>
> So you got to keep the show moving along fast.
>
> Oh yes. Got to move fast. You can't, you can't go too long with it. Change, change, change so fast. But the world is fast. One time it'd take you about ten minutes for to make a mile, eh? Oui? Now you're six hundred miles an hour. Yeah, and still it's not goin' fast enough yet. (Q-tape 9)

My own observations support Emile's perceptions. I recorded at least one occasion on which one table of audience members asked to hear a lengthy wonder tale. Emile began to tell it, but others in the crowd quickly lost interest, and it was difficult for anyone to follow the story closely in the noisy situation. After a short time Emile abandoned the narration because most of the audience had ceased to listen.

It is significant that when there was little or no audience with whom to relate, as at the beginning of a slow night for the club, his performance was entirely different. This may seem obvious, yet one need only think of professional entertainers whose stage shows vary very little to find a striking contrast. At such times, Emile, contractually obligated to perform, played in an introspective manner, as he reported doing when alone. He made no introductions or comments but simply played tune after tune, often recalling pieces he did not usually perform. Once the audience arrived, he reverted to his more usual fare of recent compositions, old favorites, and their stories.

An important situation in which Emile was the center of attention for a small audience with whom he could easily converse and who were happy to do so was provided by the house parties he hosted when admirers, students, fellow musicians, and the like came to visit him at home. Gerald Thomas, for example, brought many groups of students from Memorial University to visit Emile after 1980. Emile's hospitality and extroverted nature led to an almost continuous stream of visitors throughout the year. Such visits invariably occasioned parties at his house, and often those of his children and close relatives as well, attended by members of his family and other local residents.[6] These events closely resembled the traditional house times, but Emile's special status distorted them somewhat, placing him more at the center of attention for at least some of the evening.

At the other extreme of performer-audience distance from the stage of a large folk festival is the intimacy of a private interview. This context became familiar to Emile after many years of interest in his music on the part of collectors, musicians, and others. Achieving fully engaged interaction is not usually a problem in this situation, but "breaking through" to performance often is (Hymes 1975). Ever the public performer, Emile found it difficult to perform repertoire items designed for party and stage in a one-on-one conversational setting, especially if he knew the interviewer was already familiar with the piece. Why bother to do that again, he seemed to wonder. Yet when asked, he did his best to comply. The resulting performances were, of course, never as fully realized as those for an enthusiastic audience. He had a repertoire of narratives, geared to such more intimate conversation situations, which I discovered through my own mistakes as a public presenter of Emile. These stories were told less for their entertainment value as public performance pieces, and they revealed the more private man. The interview situation was therefore somewhat artificial, in that Emile was usually asked to perform public repertoire items in his public presentation manner for an inappropriately small audience.

Media performances represent a special case. Like interviews, media performances are usually highly controlled by another party, perhaps an interviewer, producer, or director. The people in charge usually had some idea of Emile's abilities and a particular product in mind. The quality of the results vary, of course, with the knowlege and sensitivity of the producers as well as their own talents. His appearance on Peter Gzowski's CBC television program, *90 Minutes Live,* was an example of an ill-prepared "host" who was taken by surprise when Emile initiated his own performances rather than be controlled and directed by him.[7] Emile was quite as comfortable before a camera as on a stage and generally achieved a high level of performance if the producers created a framework that could accommodate his presentational style. The Memorial University Educational Television productions made with the advice and assistance of Gerald Thomas are an example of such successful presentation (*Emile Benoit: Fiddler* 1980; *Ça Vient du Tchoeur* 1980; Benoit 1985).

The tune-narrative combinations that were developed in the house party setting were best suited to this situation. In fact, further development of this form was encouraged by many of the newer performance settings. The major difference, of course, is that media performances are no longer "spontaneous," emerging from natural, ongoing social interaction, but rather produced on demand in a situation created solely for this purpose. As among interview contexts, the more closely these settings approximated the house party the more successful was Emile's performance.

It is difficult to evaluate fully such performances from the finished product alone, but I was able to participate in the making of several media performances in which the dynamics of this process could be observed. During the summer of 1985 Emile was filmed by Disney Productions for a film on life in Canada which they were making for the Vancouver EXPO 86 fair. Emile was the centerpiece of a brief scene meant to convey the sense of a festive "old-time" community gathering. A fish store, storage building for fishing gear, was used as the setting, people from the community were grouped around the room, Emile was placed prominently in the middle, his accompanists around him, and the cameras, which shot a 360-degree, "in the round," picture, tracked slowly toward him as he played, or rather pretended to play. To get a good sound quality, the music had to be recorded separately. It was then played back during the actual shooting and the musicians played along with themselves on tape. In my view, Emile's performance suffered from the necessary imposition of this unfamiliar technique because he found it difficult to synchronize with his earlier recording and perform with his usual abandon at the same time. Several viewers of the film who knew him agreed with me that he appeared more self-conscious than usual.

His commercial records represent another special context that had an important impact on his performing style (Benoit 1979, 1982). The first, *Emile's Dream,* was recorded in a commercial studio and its character largely determined by its producer, Kelly Russell. He chose the guitar accompanist, Ron Hynes, who performed together with Kelly in the Wonderful Grand Band but who had not previously played with Emile nor been particularly interested in traditional fiddle music. The result was a style of rhythmic accompaniment unfamiliar to Emile, featuring continuous strumming rather than the alternating bass-strum style derived from country music with which he was acquainted from the playing of his sons, a style Emile would have preferred. The choice to have an accompanist at all reflects Kelly's commercial vision of the record rather than an accurate representation of Emile's normal performance style. Similarly, Kelly's arrangements of Emile's compositions in medley reflected his experience in presenting such music arranged for a rock band ensemble in concert format.

Emile internalized these values, however, as evidenced by his preference for this first album over his second, *Ça Vient du Tchoeur/It Comes from the Heart* (1982), produced by Gerald Thomas following a different agenda. Gerald wanted to showcase Emile's narrating talents as well as his compositions (Thomas 1982, 7).[8] As a result, on this record Emile plays unaccompanied and introduces his stories as he would in a live performance. It was recorded in Gerald's home in an effort to reproduce an informal atmosphere and evoke natural narrative performances and was largely successful in achieving these goals. Emile, however, did not consider it is as "good" a record as the first. As he observed to me on several occasions, the stories might be nice the first time, but who would want to hear them repeated with each playing of the record? Emile did not want to document his style of performance; he preferred to produce a record successful as such, which meant a greater emphasis on the music alone. His expression of this attitude shows increasing acceptance of a new set of musical values which views the music as product.

By both drawing upon the traditional performance models for fiddling, which he mastered in his youth, and adapting their elements, Emile developed a highly individual style of performance. It is distinguished especially by the combination of narration and fiddling through which he attempts to present himself to audiences who do not know him: life-story anecdotes are told in conjunction with compositions that commemorate experiences, and these associated tunes evoke the world to which they refer. As I suggested in the preceding descriptions of different performance contexts, Emile was best able to realize this performance model in relatively intimate settings at which he was the undisputed center of attention for an audience with whom he could easily converse. He often combined the tune-narrative items of repertoire, which he developed as relatively independent entities in house party settings, into loosely structured sets. Grouped in this way they become a powerful distillation and presentation of his particular life experience, worldview, and values. Emile's whole performance personifies an idealized image of that world.

He may introduce himself with personal anecdotes about his childhood or learning to play, such as those quoted previously. Several frequently performed tune-title narratives, such as the "Skeleton Reel" and "Brother's Farewell," embody his spiritual beliefs; others, such as "Wayne and the Bear," his sense of humor. Humorous stories are often told at his own expense, serving to "level" participants' roles in the social situation and reinforcing his "common man" persona. The story of "Gerald Thomas' Burnt Potato Reel," for example, which he performed regularly, and especially whenever Gerald was present in the audience, does this at the same time that it pokes fun at Gerald. The following narration was recorded at a lecture-demonstration performance for folklore students at Memorial University in 1984 following a lengthy introduction of Emile by Gerald Thomas recounting his life and emphasizing his unique talents. It seemed as though Emile were using this story in response to Thomas's lavish praise, pointing out his own gullibility and Thomas's less than ideal culinary habits.

Another time I was to his place. Oh about a nice little ten years I know him. Oh I find him a good fellow, all right [chuckles]. I like that. And I went there to his place and when I got there, well it was in the evening. Went up to the door and I come in. So fine. "Oh," he said, "Emile, oh come in." So I stayed there, I stayed there that night. Next day, I believe this was my first time there, I'm not sure, or my second time, whatever. So anyway when it got around ten, eleven o'clock I said, "Gerald, I'm gettin' hungry mon homme." Had no breakfast. He said, "Yes." He was readin' in his book, he was there and the book he was reading [imitates reading while lying down]. First time he didn't hear me too good, but second time he heard me. He said, "Go look in the fridge, you might find something there. You might find something. We can eat it." So I goes and open the fridge door. I look. A can of corn beef hash in the corner. *Nothing else!* Not a, not a, not even a bottle of pickle or mustard or *nothing*. That's all. Only [a] can, left there. I said, "Gerald, but," I said, "you got only a can of bully beef there." Said, "*Gerald!*" "What?" I said, "You got only a can of bully beef there." "Oh yes." He keep reading. I said, "You got any spuds? Any potatoes?" "There should be some," he said, "in the cupboard." So I goes up, cheee, four potatoes, four. Four potatoes, and they were,

So That My Story Will Live On   193

well [indicates they were getting old]. So I said, "Now I'm gonna peel them," I said, "And cook them, and we're gonna keep, that, that can of stuff, corned beef hash it was, I said, that's all right, makes no difference. So I said we're gonna make a hash out of it and we're gonna have something to eat." "Oh yes," he said, "sure." He kept readin'. So I peeled the potatoes, got a saucepan. And I was composin' a reel at the time. I had start the day before. I had practiced it for to get everything on the move, eh? And all right, put the potatoes, four potatoes in. And put a cover on, start to boil. So I went back on the Chesterfield and I, I was there jiggin' [fiddling] that. Jiggin' an' jiggin' an' jiggin'. Here he was there, shhh [gestures reading]. But now, but he was abreast the stove, but me I was back on over there. I kinda forgot about the potatoes [laughter]. I said, "Gerald," it come in my mind, I said, "Gerald, is the potatoes cook?" "By gosh," he said, "they should be cook." But he never made no move or nothing. So I got up. Put the violin out of sight. I got up. I went over, rose the cover of the pot. The four, four potatoes was right black. I said, "Gerald come here." He said, "What? What?" I said, "Come here, come here," I said. Sweet God he knowed, but me I didn't know he knowed. I said, "Look a there. You ever see that before, you?" [laughter]. He said, "What?" I said, "Look. Them four potatoes is right black. They burned [stamps] in water. That's the first time I seen that" [laughter]. Potatoes burned in water!"

As Emile first began telling the story, this was its conclusion (M-tape 78-239/C3581, for example). The tune title commemorated this strange event, something never before seen. Thomas confirmed the essential accuracy of this narrative and Emile's genuine surprise at his discovery (Q-tapes 57 and 58). Subsequently, however, Emile learned, as he indicates in this telling, that Gerald was having a joke on him.

> So I went up to Massachusetts, there was six or seven thousand people on the field, now it seemed like it was so true, 'cause me I don't like to tell a lie, you know, it's only in a story. So anyway after the show was finished I asked them. . . . I told them that story. I say, "Anybody seen a potato burned in water please rise up your hand. So you come along we'll have a chat." Well I look, nobody rose up their hand, sheeew. So I came back with nothing. So, came here and that's three years ago eh? Or four years ago.
> GT: Seven years ago.
> Yeah that's right, more'n that. And you know what? He let me

go with that, until last summer. He said, La, I was playin'. The pot went dry, and the potatoes burned in the bottom, and they was right cooked and [he] fill up the pot, pheew. Put water again! [laughter]. So don't believe him, what he tells you [laughter]. So then with that I had no name for the reel I composed. So now I says I'm gonna call it Gerald Thomas' Burnt Potato Reel. But it's a long story, but there's something on the end. You bad [Gerald, that is. Laughter]. (M-tape 84-562/C7275)

"Gerald Thomas' Burnt Potato Reel" was played whenever Gerald was present in the audience, its request, often prompted by Gerald, and announcement providing an opportunity for the kind of repartee Emile loved. The tune-title narrative was told whenever the proxemic distance was personal enough, the audience attention focused enough, and the time available sufficient.

Although Emile was familiar with at least some traditional titles for traditional tunes he played, he rarely used them in performance. His own compositions, which formed the bulk of presented material in almost every contemporary performance, however, were almost always announced as such and titled. The titles of his compositions served in many cases as an encapsulation of the associated anecdote he would narrate. At a minimum he would shout out the title.

No one has addressed the function and significance of tune titling or examined their use in performance contexts within a musical community at any length. This is unfortunate because I have found that the process of naming a tune can be an important meaning-giving act through which the musician and his audience connect the musical experience of the fiddle tune with their other individual and shared worlds of experience. In performance, tune titles serve to facilitate performer-audience interaction. Recalling the first of his compositions to be titled, "Tootsie Wootsie," Emile explains why it seemed important:

So you made up tunes, before "Tootsie Wootsie." You made up tunes . . . but you didn't put names on them?
  Didn't put names on them.
  How come?
  Oh it's just like that [pause]. . . . Then I seen that, you know, it was important to have a name on it, oui? Well, you hear, say, "Play Tootsie Wootsie. Well I had to play that all the time for maybe a year because everybody loved it eh. So, I had to play it. They'd say, "Come

on play Tootsie Wootsie." Well c'est ça, come Tootsie Wootsie. But if there hadn't been no name, well they would [say], "Play the other one you used to play, I heard you play." But now which one I plays? Eh? But with a name, well you knows. So you learns the name with the piece that you compose, right? So like that, when you mention the name, same like a note, same thing like you be playing it on the violin . . . the sound, brings to your attention, eh? That's how it works. (Q-tape 8)

In an earlier conversation, Emile had described to me how a particular individual had enjoyed this tune and dubbed it "Tootsie Wootsie." It would seem that because the give-and-take he describes between himself and the audience was so central to his performances Emile was highly motivated to title his compositions. He continued to involve his audience in this process, and frequently asked those present what he should call a new piece when he first began to play it.

Making fun with tune titles is an important use to which they are put. In an interview conducted by a Memorial University folklore student from Black Duck Brook, we can see how Emile begins using the tune titles, diligently requested by the student for each piece, as a part of his performance. Because this interviewer was known to Emile's family and viewed as a member of their community, the ambience at this recording session was relatively relaxed and conducive to the spontaneous humor for which Emile was well-known and in which tune titling often figured.

As the student wrote, at one point during the interview Emile finished a tune and said,

> "I don't know what I'm going to call that one. I think I'm going to call that one The Crazy Woman in the Kitchen." His wife had been laughing at him because she has never heard the names of the tunes before. She says that he's making them up, but he says they are the real names.
>
> After the next tune Emile says, "That one calls The Crooked Knee." The family find that very funny. Apparently the tune is called after a bow-legged man that they know. The next tune Emile calls The Friction Nose. This is because he cut his nose that day and is wearing a bandage over it. After some more conversation, when asked the name of the final tune he played, Emile answered, You'll Never Get Drunk Enough. (M-MS 72-10/p. 8)

In this brief account we see Emile using tune titles to make fun by alluding to humorous characters and incidents familiar to those present. He also uses the titles to refer to the immediate situation in a humorous way, teasing his wife, joking about himself, and, finally, commenting in general on the social situation.

Tune titles are a crucial means for giving his compositions extramusical associations. Once so "baptized," compositions serve to carry the meaning of their associated narratives. Emile's choice of tune in performance, for example, was significantly affected by his ability to use it in this manner. He played tunes named for people present, such as "Gerald Thomas' Burnt Potato," whenever possible; he played tunes requested by name; and he played tunes that incorporate narratives he wished to relate. Primarily those tunes with communicatively useful titles remained in active use. Others dropped gradually from his repertoire, although they might be recalled in appropriate circumstances. Thus titles are an important part of a tune's performance identity and significantly affect its role within his repertoire.[9] The rest of his musical performance was much less loaded communicatively. Rather than making specific reference to the immediate situation, or carrying a statement he wished to make, untitled tunes served primarily to convey to the audience the impression of "old-time, Newfoundland music."

Certainly some compositions are less striking than others, yet given the right circumstances he played them in preference to more musically interesting pieces. Such is the case for the "Motorcycle Club Rally Reel," which commemorates a performance we shared together. As far as I can ascertain, Emile played this tune only when I was present and he wished to evoke this experience. Above a certain level of sophistication, however, it would seem that all tunes were functionally interchangeable. Although one can elicit musical value judgments, these are not particularly relevant to the choice of performed repertoire.[10] The tune-title complex together was the meaningful communicative unit in Emile's performances. His melodic innovations were not truly "compositions" until they were titled, after which they could function as public statements.

The tune-title narrative complex was the basic unit of Emile's later performances, which he strung together as means of self-presentation and in response to the immediate environment, but a lack of fit between the ideal performance model and the imposed formats of different situations could result in various tensions. Emile continually adjusted the balance of components according to different settings and audiences, within limits set by his own expectations and values. In a variety of situations, for example, I occasionally observed audiences that were neither attentive to his stories nor appeared to appreciate them. These stories were an important part of his performance, however, which he seemed reluctant to give up. Given the opportunity, he did a lot of narrating. This practice could lead at times to some confusion, tension, and negative response, especially in club performance settings.

The audience in bars, as at the dances he used to play for, wanted continuous music. They were unwilling, however, to give him the level of attention required to follow a lengthy narrative. For performing in clubs Emile developed a new repertoire of very short items that he could throw in when his energy lagged to "keep things going." He used these "one-liners" to punctuate his performance, to fill what would otherwise be "dead air," give himself a respite from continuous playing, keep his audience laughing, and often to evoke a response from them. This new genre helped solve the problem created by having to be the only performer. Gaps had to be filled because Emile's repertoire of tune and narrative pairings was meant to fill a certain length of time and end, allowing another party participant to perform. As the only performer, Emile was compelled to keep going and "go fast."

Many of the short performance items are drawn from that paragon of condensed drama, the television commercial. This was a recent influence for Emile as for other narrators. Emile's adaptation of television commercials for narrative use can be seen as an aspect of the pervasive influence of television on narrative practices on the Port-au-Port which Thomas observed, in this case affecting the contemporary manifestation of the "public" tradition (Thomas 1980, 1983, 64–66).

One of these is the line, "What am I going to do with my hair?" or "I don't know what I'm gonna do with my hair," spoken in his whining falsetto voice while brushing his thinning gray hair over a bald spot with his hand and making a humorous face. I prompted discussion of these devices by asking him if this was an example of the "short jokes" to which he referred. "Yes, yes, something like that yeah. . . . Well [I] seen that on television. . . . Get Smart and Ninety-nine [the characters], they was makin' a show and now . . . she was supposed to say that, 'What I'm gonna do with my hair.' Well I seen that on television" (Q-tape 9).

Though drawn from the television program *Get Smart,* the image Emile creates is humorous in a self-referential manner. For me it refers to the

Emile gestures, "What am I going to do with my hair?" Courtesy of
Christine Tixier.

performer's self-conscious awareness of his appearance, mocking this preoccupation, bringing Emile down a notch as he makes it clear that no matter
what he did with his hair it would not make much difference. Another
favorite line is "I'm good lookin' but not pretty," supposedly spoken of him
by a woman and often presented as a question, "What do you think? Good
lookin' but not pretty, eh?" Or, "Sometimes I say, 'You got it Pontiac.' Well
they seen that lady come, she does that, 'You got it Pontiac!'" Or another
line comes from the ad in which a "fellow comes in, he said, "That Sucret
[Sucrets breath mint], that Sucret, I know it's expensive, lots more expensive than candy, but you never knows what time you're gonna be caught
with your breath" [laughter] (Q-tape 9).

Here again he refers to concern about appearance and then describes
the use of such lines: "So it makes a laugh you know? They heard it, maybe
not everybody, but a good many people, heard it. . . . Another one . . . she's
there holding a cup, tea, advertising the tea, eh? And she's there, she's got
a hat on the head, 'What a nice cup of tea' [in whining falsetto]. Well you
gotta laugh eh? It looks uh, it looks foolish and looks cute [and] you gotta
laugh" (Q-tape 9).

One of his most frequently heard quips is the question, "Are you married?" This does not come from television but represents a distillation of a

personal experience. As Emile explains it, he had finished performing for a group of elderly people when two women came up to him and asked this question. He found it very funny and made it more so in the telling by imitating the old ladies' efforts at demonstrating a coy interest in him. In performance context, however, Emile merely uses the question. He might, for example, ask this of people as they come in the door of Kibitzer's. The victim, male or female, may rise to the occasion and respond. If not, Emile might provide his own answer, "Say, 'No, but my wife is!'" The whole audience would laugh with him. This phrase is so effective because of its reference to the sexual energy that pervades socialization within the bar context. And as a question it challenges audience members to respond vocally. It is of interest that other examples are in question form as well.

Emile did his best to transform the bar scene into something like a house party by devices such as these questions. His strategies to redefine some of the typical aspects of club performance might seem refreshing to some audience members and provide part of his appeal as a performer, but they could create problems if patrons wanted him to fulfill more usual expectations for bar performance, especially if they wanted the musician to provide background for their own social pursuits. In this case they resisted focusing attention on Emile to the degree necessary for the fully engaged interaction he tried to provoke. Some audience members, however, have expressed attitudes closer to those of concert-goers who expect the focus of attention to be the presentation of music "for its own sake." These people might resent Emile's constant efforts to involve them in more than a listening role.

Emile's desire to have other musicians familiar with his music, such as me, play with him at these clubs was another strategy to bring the situation closer to that of a house party. Although those who came to join him seemed to prefer playing along with Emile, which he enjoyed as well, he seemed to prefer that we take over during his breaks. Two dynamics were at work here. When playing together, the other musicians represented a fully engaged audience with whom he could interact intimately. When he was tired of fulfilling the demands of the performer's role, he could depend on others to take over, as he would at a party.

Successful spontaneous embellishments of repertoire items tended to become standardized. On one occasion, for example, Gerald Thomas began clapping along with one of Emile's tunes, "Jim Hodder's," to encourage audience response. Emile began to conduct the clapping, leaving out several notes of the melody for the clapping to happen (Q-tape 57). It worked well, and in subsequent performances he often tried to recreate this moment of rapport with his audience.

Standardization of his repertoire was an important response to the newer performance settings. In most of these contexts Emile's performances did not emerge naturally from ongoing socialization but had to be called up on demand. This accounts for the large number of recordings of the same narratives that were available to me. Moreover, these stories themselves became rather standardized through so much repetition.

Emile also commonly used visual or physical effects while performing, providing an element of antic humor. When playing the "Flying Reel," for example, he often raised and lowered his elbows, in effect "flapping his wings." Emile played "close to the floor," by lying down, thus rendering this phrase commonly used to evoke lively dance music as a visual pun (Quigley 1985, 3, 19–21). Such antics served as a means to elicit laughter from an audience, grabbing their attention if it began to flag or rewarding it with humor.

Emile commanded a large repertoire of performance pieces, drawn from a variety of performance genres. He knew different sorts of stories,

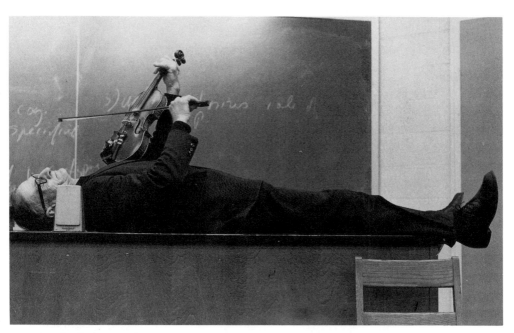

Emile plays one "close to the floor" for a folklore class at Memorial University. Courtesy Peter Gard.

tunes, and songs, which he deemed appropriate to different situations. Thomas, for example, includes examples of wonder tales, anecdotes, legends, memorates, and personal experience narratives in his collection of Emile's narratives (1984, 295–371). Whatever the genre of performance, however, he employed a style of presentation characteristically his own.

Characterization was one of the prominent features of Emile's narrative style. To this end he employed especially vocal effects, gestures, and facial expressions (Thomas 1983, 175, 178–79). When playing the violin, Emile was equally animated. It is a performance style that sprang from his own extroverted personality but was conditioned by the interpersonal dynamics of the situations in which he had the opportunity to perform. He conveyed an impression of total commitment to the task of entertaining and communicating with his auditors, a commitment rooted in his values and musical worldview. Emile's more recent patterns of performance, shaped in response to the constraints of the performance contexts described above, departed from those of the dances and times in which he first learned to perform. Emile took the performance skills developed in those contexts and adapted them to suit a new milieu, one in which his role as a composer had more significance and the presentation of his compositions as tune-tale conglomerates became the focus of his performances.

The sudden upsurge of opportunity and activity after the late 1960s introduced Emile to new performance situations for which he adapted his repertoire and manner of performance. He was confronted with new sets of audience expectations and immersed in a changed world of musical values, which Peter Narvaez (1982) characterizes as "reflective" and activist. These he experienced through the networks of musicians, sponsors, and even researchers with whom he worked closely. As Gerald Thomas has noted, Emile was "well placed to take advantage of the opportunities presented to perform outside his home context" when "new government policies emerged in the sixties and seventies promoting the growth and development of ethnic minorities in Canada" (1985, 298). One of the most prominent effects of these policies in Newfoundland was the promotion of highly visible forms of expressive culture, especially music and song.

Some have viewed this new performance milieu as a manifestation of "folklorismus," emphasizing its differences and discontinuities from older "traditional" performance settings (Thomas 1984). For Emile, however, the transition was a natural one, representing the continuity of his motivation to perform wherever and whenever he could. He took advantage of opportunities provided by new media in the past as well, for example, playing

Emile playing in his
usual animated manner.

accompaniment on several occasions for silent films shown in Stephenville (field notes 1987).

But self-conscious attempts both to revive traditional Newfoundland music and to direct it and audiences' tastes into distinctive channels reflecting a nostalgic "vision of the Newfoundland experience" were significant in influencing Emile's development (Narvaez 1982). Perhaps most important in its impact on Emile's musical values is the emphasis on regional identity that permeated this milieu in Newfoundland. This is an aspect of self-perception that had not been of much significance in the local setting previously. The social and political context of the Newfoundland cultural "revival," however, resulted in a high value being placed on distinctive Newfoundland traits and characteristics.

That Emile adopted this view of his compositions is clear from the following comments he made during our informal performance for the motorcycle club. The two of us had been invited there particularly to present some representative Newfoundland music for out-of-province visitors. We spent Saturday afternoon playing at a local bar whose proprietor enjoyed country and western music. There was a small audience, only about five men seated at the tables around us, and a few young people playing pinball across the room. Emile and I played our fiddles anyway, and the other patrons seemed to enjoy it, one of them joining us by playing spoons. Emile performed familiar pieces, "Over the Waves," "Tennessee Waltz," "Star of Logy Bay," "I'se the B'y," "The Irish Washerwoman," often clowning and "playing the fool." I took the lead for a while, playing some of the fiddle tunes I knew well, including his composition "Bridgett's Reel." Emile stopped me after the first notes to introduce it.

> Bridgett's Reel. Ça va bien. It goes good. I compose that in the first of July when I was up to St. John's in Bridgett's club there, I was there for fifteen days. An' when I got there I compose it. An' I calls it the Bridgett's Reel. And it goes like this.
> [EB and CQ play tune.]
> Audience members: Way to go. All right. Pretty good.
> Right on, eh? That's Newfoundland work! Eh? That's right. That's from this place, Newfoundland. If we compose our own . . . we just have as much right to compose our own, as some other foreign country, eh? We're entitled to that.
> Audience member: You, you compose that one?
> I compose that one, yeah. . . . So I got twenty-four of this here

[shows record], twenty-four on it that's all my compose. Don't belong to nobody. Mine. (M-tape 81-502/C5316)

Many young revival musicians have taken advantage of the opportunities provided by this phenomenon. Almost all those active in the early 1980s used some of Emile's repertoire in their own performances, featured arrangements of his tunes on their recordings, and most performed with him on various occasions (Thomas 1981; Figgy Duff 1983; Payne and Russell 1983; Tickle Harbour 1979; Red Island 1978; Wonderful Grand Band 1978). Part of the explanation for the enthusiastic adoption of Emile's compositions by revival musicians is their claim to Newfoundland origin. There are, for example, many other fine fiddlers and accordionists on the Port-au-Port, but their tunes have not been much taken up by the outsiders (*Music from French Newfoundland* 1980). One reason, I suspect, is that Scots, Irish, and French Canadian sources and influence are easily identified in their playing. Such repertory did not satisfy the need for distinctive material they could identify as belonging to Newfoundland.[11] In fact, I can recall Noel Dinn, leader of the locally preeminent folk group Figgy Duff, rejecting some of Emile's tunes because they sounded too "American."

Emile's compositions have achieved a prominent status in the emerging mythology of Newfoundland music, and he is presented as one of this newly constructed tradition's leading exponents. In this final transposition from its original milieu, through high-profile appearances as a cultural representative and especially his media exposure, Emile's music has come to epitomize traditional Newfoundland fiddling for many people. Several of his compositions, for example, were presented in an orchestral setting, the "Fiddle Concerto," composed by a prominent local violinist, Peter Gardner (Q-tape 43). Somewhat ironically, while the orchestra performed this piece for the CBC, featuring Kelly Russell as the fiddler in a rather "highbrow" event, Emile himself was performing at Kibitzer's club. His music served such a symbolic function as the introductory music for episodes of the nostalgic dramatic radio program *The Newfie Bullet* (Narvaez 1986, 71). Photographs of Emile have been used to evoke an image of the province in advertisements directed at tourists, such as that for "Newfoundland Days" held at a hotel in Halifax (*Chronicle-Herald/Mail Star* May 30, 1985).

The potential impact of this role is exemplified by Emile's appearance in the Disney film, along with Kelly Russell, Christina Smith, and Noel Dinn, all revival players from St. John's. There was, in fact, a local fiddler in the host community who had hoped to appear with his sons in the segment, but the director felt that Emile's music sounded stronger and found his image as a performer more compelling, repeating Emile's phrase that it "came from the heart" to explain his choice. The decision to bring Emile and his support musicians from St. John's to create an essentially false yet powerful image of tradition in Newfoundland reveals the degree to which Emile has come to play the role of cultural symbol.

But no more than he was merely a carrier of tradition, Emile was a passive victim of manipulation by the agents of cultural hegemony. As we have seen, he strove actively to make a place for himself, his art, and his message in a changing world, indeed through such activities as his collaboration in this project, and by so doing to affect the course of these changes.

Conclusion ~ *Everybody Got a Sound*

At the beginning of this book I indicated that innovation has generally been considered anomalous in traditional forms marked by re-creative performance. Continuity, conservatism, and allowable, minor variation have long been considered the hallmarks of such traditions. When the importance of individual creators has been acknowledged, they have often been portrayed as at odds with this norm, perhaps exhibiting extraordinary talents or neuroses. If not exceptions to the traditional norm, traditional creators have been portrayed alternatively as exhibiting such distinctive behavior only on the surface. It is hypothesized that they draw upon traditional models at a "deeper" level, from which underlying continuities may be realized in differing but merely surface manifestations. In either view the individual creator is distinctly subordinate to the tradition. This perspective on the relationship of creator to tradition has been reversed in this study by focusing instead on how a particular musician used his tradition for intentionally innovative expression within the context of a changing musical milieu.

Close examination of Emile's personality, as it emerged in our relationship and was reported by others, reveals a man of strongly held opinions and values of a traditional character, such as religious faith, fidelity, self-reliance, hardiness, and courage. He lived his life within the framework of institutions provided by his society—church, marriage, small farm/fishing economy—adopting its values as his own, fulfilling its expectations, and achieving a measure of success in its terms. He was not a misfit or a marginal character, except insofar as he valued his own creative expression through music more than most. He did, however, exhibit the flirtation with the limits of permissible behavior in performance which Arden King has associated with innovation (1980). His willingness to go beyond the bounds of learned behavior no doubt contributed to his ability to innovate in music.

Emile's apprenticeship as a fiddler was not atypical but was marked by intense involvement from the very beginning. Encouraged and enabled to play by family tradition and rudimentary tutelage, he was early thrown on his own devices because there were so few "master" fiddlers in the community. This fostered a reliance on his own musical intuition, talent, and concomitant confidence which found expression in his willingness to experiment. Such early "immersion and exploration" have been found to "characterize the early stages of development of the creative young person" (John-Steiner 1985, 206). This is especially true of musicians, the "musical intelligence" often seeming to develop in early childhood (Gardner 1982, 108). Family encouragement and tutelage also seem to be crucial in fostering musical development, and such response to demonstrated interest and ability appears to be a particularly successful pattern (John-Steiner 1985, 142–45). Emile's family provided such encouragement as was within their means, and he clearly recalled their response to his enthusiasm as a crucial formative experience.

Social acceptance and approbation, moreover, reinforced his commitment to musical expression. Long, intense hours spent with others in a mutual pursuit and setting of communitas, such as is characteristic of the dance events in which Emile apprenticed as a performer, have also been identified as providing a crucial opportunity for the developing artist. It is in these situations that young people often move from the acquisition of "raw materials for later accomplishment" to establishing a pattern of sustained effort (Wilson 1977, as cited in John-Steiner 1985, 208). This was certainly so in Emile's case.

Emile incorporated attitudes toward music making into his belief and value systems as he matured, combining culturally shared attitudes with his own unique perspectives. These I examined under the analytical rubric of his musical worldview. Scholarly interest in musical worldview, I noted earlier, has not been much focused on Western folk traditions, perhaps because of the researchers' assumption that the conceptions of music held by informants were not sufficiently different from their own, usually those elaborated within Western art music traditions, to demand such treatment. What studies there have been indicate, however, that although western

European and their derived North American folk traditions may share common tonal and rhythmic norms in practice, the conceptual frameworks within which these musics are created, performed, and heard are different enough to warrant investigation. Folk music has attracted researchers' interest since its emergence as a field of inquiry in large part because such differences are intuitively apparent. Indeed, as Ellen Koskoff suggests, even musicians from the same local tradition may evince a variety of musical worldviews (1982, 352–70). In Emile's case, knowledge of the particular confluence of traditional attitudes with personal beliefs and values is necessary for an understanding of why he stands out from among the many other musicians of his community and for an appreciation of the meaning of his musical message.[1] Such examination of the connections between the patterns of peoples' lives and the music they make is what John Blacking has called for in commenting on an important examination of the closely related Irish traditional instrumental music (1972–73, 57).

If one acknowledges the cognitive nature of music, along with the rest of culture, systematic study of how all musics, including our own folk traditions, are conceived by their makers and listeners becomes essential for our understanding not only of its meanings (Blacking 1981, 184–94) but of its very nature (Herndon and Mcleod 1980a, 59–60; 1980b, 181, 184). As this study illustrates, a particular musical worldview not only gives meaning to musical products but serves to define the music maker's understanding of his own musical experience. The fundamental ideas of Emile's musical worldview, that music is a spiritually inspired voice to be discovered within oneself and "spoken" in composition and performance, are realized in his methods of composing, in the form and content of his compositions, as well as in the style of his performances and the playing techniques he employs. All aspects of his musical activity are thus imbued with meaning drawn from his network of musical associations, both personal and culturally shared.

Emile made a strong impression as a performer. Though his style of performance attracted me when I first met him, I was most impressed by the large number of his own compositions which he played and the "folk" background he seemed to personify. Here, I felt, was a musician who had learned to play in an almost archetypal traditional environment and had internalized the spirit and logic of this music to such an extent that he was utterly fluent within the idiom. Fiddle music of authoritative style seemed to gush spontaneously from some wellspring within him. I had never encountered such a prolific composer of fiddle music before and felt, along with most of the other "revival" musicians in St. John's, that Emile was a very special musician from whom to learn something of the essence of traditional music. Study and analysis of his compositions and compositional processes from an ethnomusicological perspective revealed early on the importance of a strongly rooted musical worldview of a particular cast for understanding the intensity of feeling which Emile communicated through his music. He drew energy from strongly held beliefs and values to fuel the creative process and give voice to spiritual experience through the language of music. Although the formulation of music as language may seem commonplace (Nketia 1986, 13), this study shows that it is one with strong roots in western European folklore and holds great power for individual self-actualization.

The first chapters of this book provide a picture of dynamic interactions among aspects of Emile's life experience, personality, and musical worldview, which help to account for the character of his musical behavior. Music making was a primary focus for Emile's sense of identity since childhood and early adolescence. Experiences related to this activity formed a positive complex that counterbalanced the struggles of life in a harsh environment. I have suggested that Emile responded to its challenges through the assertive act of composition, creating a musical chronicle of his life experience. As he matured, Emile came to see his compositions as a medium through which to make a lasting mark on the world and, especially as he found his formative experiences to be at odds with a changing environment, to perpetuate his legacy.

His commitment to composing was reinforced by the impact of national and local cultural policy as well as an upsurge in the importance of Newfoundland regional identity and its cultural representation. The occurrence of a cultural revival at a fortuitous moment in Emile's life clearly provided opportunities for the flowering of tendencies that were already inherent. Many values promoted by the revival complemented his own and facilitated his development as a composer.

Underlying Emile's unusual level of creative output were particular personality traits, beliefs, values, and life experiences that combined to energize his musical identity. Recent studies of creative thinkers have concluded that it is the intensity of commitment to a creative life that is distinctive about them and "central to their being." Moreover, such intense involvement regenerates itself, allowing for the continuity of application over time that distinguishes extraordinary creators (John-Steiner 1985, 219–

21). Emile exhibited both of these traits, clearly deriving enough pleasure from the process of composing itself to continue in the face of declining interest in the early 1960s, or negative audience response as in the case of the "Roaming Scott," even while relishing and working for audience approbation. Immersion in the social milieu of music making helped to make him such a successful composer of traditional music, for his creative energy was nourished by his role as a performer.

The expressive means and skills at his disposal were learned and honed within traditional situations and from the internalization of traditional models. The constraints imposed by performance situations shaped his musical style and manner of performance, helping to define the range of possibilities with which he experimented as a composer. Although the basic musical knowledge on which he drew was acquired within traditional contexts, as his revitalized career developed he was exposed to new influences to which he responded with enthusiasm.

Examination of his repertoire and musical ethnotheory reveal that the specifics of musical materials at his disposal consisted of a limited number of rhythmic and fingering patterns within a few tonalities which nevertheless could generate a seemingly endless melodic variety within what is essentially a single musical form of repeating, contrastive strains. Variety was generated within these bounds by alteration and recombination of musical schemata drawn from his repertoire in the service of melodic experimentation as guided by evaluation based on the norms of the tradition. Sustained compositional activity and active performance of those compositions in preference to traditional tunes over many years, however, meant that a large portion of the reservoir of musical ideas from which new compositions emerged and against which they were measured consisted of his previous compositions. This resulted in a dense web of interrelationships among items in Emile's active repertoire.

While employing musical materials of a "formulaic" character, the process of composition itself is not essentially one in which a repertoire of melodic units is conjoined within frameworks provided by traditional tune models, as would be suggested by the term *formulaic composition*. Rather, Emile, while recognizing and often consciously manipulating relationships among his compositions, viewed them as distinct entities and intended to generate novel melodies with the materials at his disposal. These materials include knowledge of schemata for musical building blocks at different structural levels which he might choose to incorporate whole or modify in some way. "Models" thus operate at all levels, as do "formulas." The tools with which he worked include ideas about how melodies are put together, notes must "suit" one another; how their component phrases may be generated, notes are "taken off" other melodies and "changed in a different direction"; and how phrases and tunes are constructed, they must "balance" and "rhyme."

Melodic tradition, however, does not exist in pristine cognitive isolation, nor can it productively be analytically so isolated if we wish to understand how musicians use their traditions to "relate themselves coherently to the past while offering something of themselves as individuals for the present and future," as Cowdery suggests is their goal (1990, 123). The perspective developed in this analysis, embedding the compositional process within the frameworks that imbue it with meaning, is more apt particularly for consideration of the processes of change.

This perspective takes fuller account of individual musical action than previous scholarship on related material, an emphasis still recent in ethnomusicology and increasingly at the center of attention in many humanistic sciences (Rice 1987; and respondents Harwood 1987; Koskoff 1987; and especially A. Seeger 1987). A too limited focus on the relationships among musical materials abstracted from their context of use risks overlooking the lived experience of music making which gives it meaning. A perspective emphasizing musical process and practice, messy and encumbered as these are, offers more potential as a means to assess and appreciate the value of music in society and culture in terms of the human experiences involved in its creation (Blacking 1973, 50, 53).

Emile's musical knowledge and skill were fairly typical of his musical peers. Creation of new strains and entire tunes is not uncommon or atypical, and most musicians have a few such pieces in their repertoires. Emile's intense level of commitment to the continuing search for creative musical expression, however, transformed his musical abilities into a powerful tool for composition. As an unusually prolific composer, he was not at odds with his tradition. Rather, he internalized its essential characteristics and actualized its inherent potential as a generative system of musical expression. Emile recognized this himself in explaining his compositional activity and exhorting others to do likewise.

While melodizing seemed to some extent to be its own reward for Emile, the fixing of compositions as titled tunes and their subsequent performance were motivated by intense desires for self-expression and self-perpetuation. Such goal-directed motivation, combined with pleasure in the creative activity itself, is typically behind the sustained effort that marks high levels of creative activity. Indeed, recent researchers have concluded that it is the very essence of creativity because the cognitive acts involved in creative thinking appear to be much the same as those required in everyday activities. Creativity is not so much a special skill as a way, or combination of ways, of using universal skills (Perkins 1981, 285). As one writer concluded, the "tools and skills" used in the process of ordinary thinking "may not be so different from the tools and skills used by individuals engaged in creative endeavors. But their sustained commitment to their queries transforms the power of the tools and the magnitude of their achievement" (John-Steiner 1985, 221).

Creative individuals are often aided in maintaining long-term commitments to their pursuits by what have been called "images of wide scope" (Gruber 1978). These are dominant metaphors, rich in associations and "susceptible to considerable exploration" (Gardner 1982, 108), which help to direct their thinking back to issues perhaps only partially understood but fundamental to their quest. Emile's metaphorical understanding of the nature of music and composition partake of this character, sustaining a continuing search for his unique "sound."

I have found my own growing understanding of the nature of creativity in this idiom of traditional music to be likewise conceptualized in terms of recurring metaphors, which have occasionally colored the prose of this study. I can trace them back to some of my first intimate associations with fiddlers who personified their tradition in the same way as Emile. Listening to Paddy Reynolds, a master Irish fiddler, playing at a bar in New York City in the early 1970s, I was overwhelmed by his endless repertoire. Surely, I thought, no one could have learned all these tunes as I taught myself, by tedious repeated listening and note-by-note emulation. Some other process must be at work. And indeed there was, for internalized schemata facilitate "perception" and "apprehension" for learning as well as "action" (Perkins 1981, 173; Adler 1980, 176–88).

It seemed to me that Paddy's repertoire was like a great ocean of melody with currents constantly welling up from the depths, within and through which the fiddler swam or sailed. As I described Emile's process of composition and the dynamics of his repertoire while writing, I found myself picturing it as an organic system of growth, decay, and regrowth from the fertile soil of "decomposed" repertoire. Both images somehow capture, for me, the character of traditional music as played by one who fully internalized its generative principles.

There is no end to the repertoire of such traditional musicians. Their creativity provides the vitality to sustain a tradition. Their musical world-view, musical knowledge, and technical skill, acquired from predecessors but modified by their own experience and talent, are what give their reper-toire and the tradition to which they belong and to which they contribute its character, shaping, in turn, the musical creations of those who fol-low them.

Emile stands revealed in this study as a model of creativity within tradition, offering testimony to the tenacity with which human beings pur-sue the urge to make a distinctive mark on their worlds. Thus his most significant legacy may be the inspiration he gave to others to find the cour-age to search their hearts for their own sound. "Everybody got a sound, my son. That's the reason they're here, [to] give us the sound of music, eh? . . . To put that in our head, what it means, the sound of music, eh? Yes" (Q-tape 20).

~ Notes

Preface

1. These resources are reviewed in the bibliographical essay.

2. Emile generally presented himself on a first-name basis in his public performances, and I follow that practice in my references to him.

3. Timothy Rice makes this observation (1987, 475). His respondents agree on this point in particular (A. Seeger 1987, 494; Koskoff 1987, 502; Harwood 1987, 507–8).

1. My Son, I Had a Hard Life Story: Emile Benoit, the Man and the Musician

1. To bring Emile's voice into the foreground and to convey the character of our exchanges, I have employed transcriptions from recorded interviews. For methodological consistency I have usually kept my questions and responses together with Emile's statements of analytical interest. Scene-setting information, crucial to interpretation (Briggs 1986), is provided either in the text or in conjunction with the archival sources listed among the works cited. I have edited the transcriptions to improve their readability. Because performance aspects per se are not generally the subject of my analysis and interpretation, I have not employed the various typographical devices available to convey them. Comments in brackets provide supplementary information. Increasing awareness of the situated nature of the ethnographic process and the misleading claim to "objectivity" implicit in much ethnographic writing has led to increasing interest, especially among anthropologists, in exploring alternative formats in which to present research (Clifford 1988; Sanjek 1990, 404–9). Information that makes researchers' preoccupations,

expectations, and background explicit, as well as the social matrix from which the data have been extracted, are needed to allow readers to assess research findings properly. Moreover, because ethnographic "findings" are constructed mutually in the encounter between researcher and subject, explicit acknowledgment and scrutiny of interpersonal context, which lies behind fieldwork in all the social sciences, becomes an important part of ethnographic studies, the more so in a work such as this, with a psychological focus.

Although this focus on the methodological and literary implications of literary style is a recent anthropological preoccupation, there are related precedents in both folklore and ethnomusicology. Gottfried Henssen's *Uberlieferung und Personlichkeit* (1951) is one of the first examples of overt concern with the effects of interpersonal context. In American folklore studies Ellen Stekert's "Two Voices of Tradition: The Influence of Personality and Collecting Environment upon the Songs of Two Traditional Singers" (1965) was one of the first studies to incorporate such self-scrutiny as a critical tool in assessing just how representative of tradition a collection might be. As she demonstrates, the collecting environment, and especially the participants' perceptions of one another, is a crucial variable affecting the character of material collected. Kenneth Gourlay has argued for a "dialectic" approach in ethnomusicological study that would emphasize the intersubjectivity of the research process. Previous scholarship, he observes, treats performers as "*external* to the recording ethnomusicologist and bear the relation of object (of study) to subject (investigator), yet the fact that both are human beings necessitates a 'partial identity.' The methods of the 'hard' sciences are applicable only on the assumption that musical sound is made an object in its own right and that the human beings who produce it are down-graded to the status of things or the ethnomusicologist deprived of the humanity he shares with them through elevation to omniscience or reduction to non-existence" (1978, 12).

I have adopted an overtly subjectively directed analysis throughout this study, rather than pretending to the "objective" omniscient nonexistence against which Gourlay so rightly declaims. I present, then, an interpretive account, not of Emile's life and personality but of the relationship within which this interpretation has been framed. At the same time, I have tried to avoid the pitfalls of an overly myopic view by drawing upon additional material available in the Memorial University of Newfoundland Folklore and Language Archive which has been gathered by a varied group of researchers.

2. Butler (1985) provides a thorough history of Black Duck Brook.

3. Thomas gives the story in French, using phonetic spelling he employs throughout his published transcriptions, which approximates the spoken dialect (1983, 187–93). Because this style is at odds with my editing of Emile's speech into a more easily readable format, I generally paraphrase Thomas's renderings when quoting them and do not enclose them in quotation marks.

4. Chronicling their musical careers by focusing on when instruments were acquired is a typical pattern in folk musicians' life stories.

5. I tried with varying degrees of success to move beyond this standard narrative response, which, like the others examined earlier is strongly shaped toward self-presentation, to elicit more information about his learning process. I have arranged his recollections in a roughly chronological fashion and taken quotes freely from many conversations to provide as complete a picture as possible. His own ordering and emphases, which should be apparent in what follows, are acknowledged and used as information in themselves.

6. Virginia Garrison, in a study of learning practices among Cape Breton fiddlers (1985), reports, for example, that "would-be fiddlers" could "join in" by "playing two kindlings" and "jigging" tunes, much as Emile described his early exposure to fiddling. The young learner usually "got ahold" of his first violin between the ages of twelve and fifteen years, again like Emile, proceeding to experiment with those tunes already "in his head." They then tried to expand their repertoire by listening to the radio, at parties and dances, and to records and tapes. Performance opportunities provided motivation through increased status and occasional financial earnings. The primary motivation, however, appears to be "aesthetic gratification" and a sense of accomplishment. After the initial learning stage, some fiddlers received limited help from relatives and neighbors, but a good many, like Emile, continued to be self-taught. Indeed, Garrison found that the sense of responsibility for one's own learning along with an awareness of and determination to develop one's "natural talent" were typical of successful learners (1985, 273–80). Bayard points out that most American fiddlers are vague about the instruction they received from older players. Three of his informants said they had "learned 'how to play' from one person, but went on to others to amass their repertoires" (1956, 16–17). Marion Thede found in a survey of traditional fiddlers that almost all learned early in life, between the ages of six and eighteen years. Most said that no one had taught them. Learning their first tune took less than a month and often less than a week (1962, 19–24). Emile's narrative fits this pattern, but the extreme speed with which he claimed to have learned his first tune serves to confirm his "gift." This also seems to be true of another respected public performer from nearby Cape St. George. Like Emile, Victor Cormier first learned by and from singing.

> Mark Cormier: What are your first recollections of music? Eh, I mean, how did you get into playing music?
>
> Victor Cormier: Well when I was a young fellow you know, going to school, eh, grandmother used to be always singing tunes and so, eh, I used to do a bit of singing myself. So finally decided well, buy a cordeen accordion and eh, see if I could learn to play. And, eh, I did.
>
> MC: Did you have anybody teaching you to play now or?
>
> VC: No, I took it all by myself.

MC: Had you seen anybody playing the accordion before?

VC: Well [laughs] Dad used to play a little bit of accordion and eh, some of the older guys used to come home and they used to do the same thing. But eh, oh, it didn't take me long anyway. First time, when I first, I got the accordion was, this was during Christmas I think then. And eh, I got the accordion about four o'clock in the evening and I, of course I didn't eat any supper because interested, hey. So eh, I started to play, I tried it anyway and by ten o'clock I could pick out four or five tunes.

MC: How old were you then?

VC: About eight, eight years old. Yeah. (M-MS 76-491/p. 2)

Learning pieces "by ear" and reworking them in a personal style is also typical. Bayard observed that "fiddlers learn by absorbing the bowings and fingerings of each melody, mastering one tune at a time, in a sort of graded series" (1956, 16–17; 1966, 54). After this period the novice player will try to expand repertoire in preference to improving technique deliberately. The resulting wide gradient of skill among players produced "marked and sometimes highly personalized individual styles beyond habitual regional tendencies" (Burman-Hall 1973, 30).

7. Adler identifies an aesthetic level in his study of competence acquisition among bluegrass banjo players which is "psychologically the most central and therefore the first level to coalesce" (1980, 137–38, 177).

8. This step represents acquisition of a basic "articulatory" level of competence, "a general term for the physical actions and strategies through which any type of instrument is made an agency of expression" (Adler 1980, 95). This level consists of rules and units based on the physical movements producing the musical sound. David Sudnow, who traces his jazz learning process in *Ways of the Hand* (1978), underscores the importance of this level by emphasizing the physicality of piano improvisation. Achieving a competent level of performance, he concludes, is based on the development of a "hand-to-key" relationship he compares to typing. The "singing fingers" of successful improvisation employ fluid, constantly reconfigured positions which his hand would maintain over the keyboard and from which it could instantly take direction to the melodic tones lying at hand (1978, 78–80, 92–93). This competence is achieved through much listening, watching, and experimentation. The memorization of scales, chords, and patterns, though common, is not necessarily a part of the process. "One does not have to learn about places by their names to become an improviser" (1978, 143).

In acquiring these skills the player also learns to control basic units akin to the formulas employed by the orally composing poet (Lord [1960] 1970, Adler 1980, 121). Emile would have acquired familiarity with the melodic formulas of his fiddling idiom in the process of learning his repertoire. Along with the tunes he would have learned in the graded manner suggested by Bayard (1956, 16–17; 1966, 54), fiddlers are also absorbing their often unrecognized and unacknowledged components. Nevertheless, as Adler found among banjo players, such an articulatory competence is required of fiddlers at this level even if it remains unacknowledged or inaccessible to their conscious control. This may represent an important distinction between improvisatory traditions and musical idioms similar to fiddling, in which musicians are not required to invent new melodies to perform competently. In my experience of learning to play in this idiom, growing familiarity with common melodic formulas was an important aid in learning new repertoire. Similar musical phrases, formulaic expressions if you will, became more easily recognized as such. These could thus be learned as a "chunk," speeding the process of learning a tune, which could be learned in such larger units rather than note by individual note. As a competent player but not a composer, I was able to perform in an acceptable manner without ever extending my conscious control of these formulaic units to their intentional recombination in new patterns. This would have been the next level of competence which Adler identifies, that of "syntactics," an operational level of competence in which "certain selected and transformed units of composition . . . are reordered and combined in patterns that characterize whole tunes" (1980, 133). It is at this level that fiddling tradition seems to depart from the overtly improvisatory musical idioms discussed by Adler and Smith (1983), for most fiddlers do not exercise this recombinative level of competence actively. Rather than generating new "tunes," which is the unit of musical discourse in fiddling as well as bluegrass banjo playing (Adler 1980, 135), fiddlers use this competence more passively. In my experience, good fiddlers develop the skill of learning "new" tunes quickly. Those fiddlers who do compose, such as Emile, must learn to exercise a more active control of this competence.

9. These stages follow an outline typical for performers in many other oral traditions, parallel to those identified by Lord in his study of epic singers: "first the period of listening and absorbing; then the period of application; and finally, that of singing before a critical audience" (Lord [1960] 1970, 21). Gregory Smith cites much corroborating evidence from other discussion of jazz learning and pedagogy (Smith 1983, 62, 85).

10. James Hornby has noted the influence these same Cape Breton fiddlers had in nearby Prince Edward Island (1983, 138). Bill Lamey, for example, hosted a short weekly program in the early 1940s which had a big audience in Prince Edward Island. Many of the fiddlers who were heard on the radio, among them Winston "Scotty" Fitzgerald, to whom Emile refers in the preceding quote, also began making records in the mid-1930s and exerted a widespread influence through this medium as well (136).

11. Emile often reiterated his frustration with the repetition required by the limited traditional repertoire available to him. Blanton Owen (1980) has posited a similar source of creativity in his brief study of Manco Sneed, a fiddler who moved away from the community in which he learned to play and developed his own unique and idiosyncratic renditions of the traditional tunes he knew in relative isolation from other players.

12. This attitude is akin to that noted among traditional singers, who think of songs as belonging to the performers who frequently sing them.

13. A similar pattern may be seen in the careers of other folk fiddlers, such as Tommy Jarrell of North Carolina and Tom Anderson of the Shetland Islands, who found the folk revival milieu conducive to renewed musical activity and prominence.

14. The oldest recording I have of his playing was made in 1964 by John Widdowson, one of Herbert Halpert's first folklore students at Memorial University (M-tapes 64-15/C115–C117). He brought his recorder to a "time" at a hall in Lourdes for which Emile played. The sound quality is generally poor because of extraneous noise, but the tunes are discernible, as are a few of Emile's comments from the stage. From 1972 on, many more sources become available. Various folklorists and students associated with Memorial University visited Emile and deposited their tapes in the archive: Michael Taft and Shelley Posen, both then graduate students in folklore, investigating country music in Newfoundland; Don Gale, an undergraduate folklore student from the Port-au-Port; Kenneth Goldstein, the well-known folk song scholar; and, most prominently in later years, Gerald Thomas, a folklorist at Memorial University specializing in folk narrative. Kelly Russell, a fiddler from St. John's who has been instrumental in popularizing Emile's music through his own performances as well as by producing Emile's LP record albums (M-tape 82-095/C5674; Benoit 1979, 1982), recorded several tapes with Emile and other fiddlers in the area dating from April 1977, which he made available to me along with other recordings of fiddlers he has made throughout the province (Q tapes 32–40). Gerald Thomas, who began visiting Emile regularly at this time as well, continued to record Emile's new compositions on a regular basis during Emile's visits to St. John's. Christina Smith's 1990 recordings are my most recent. Furthermore, many of the festivals Emile appeared in were recorded for the archive and some of his many radio, film, and video performances were available to me. A variety of performance situations are represented among these recordings, and each of the many collectors had different interests, personal styles, and techniques of interviewing, thus evoking a different performance from Emile. The result is a much more complete picture of Emile as a performer than I could have achieved alone.

15. Emile often described Gordon as his preferred accompanist, and a copy of the tape I made of this concert was one of Emile's favorite recordings of himself performing despite its poor quality (they played together rarely because Gordon lived so far away) (M-tapes 81-271/C5257–5259).

2. There's a Spirit in the Violin: A Musical Worldview

1. My usage of the term closely parallels its application in folklore and anthropology in which, stated concisely and essentially, worldview refers to "a holistic

view on nature, society, and man" (Pentikainen 1978, 38). Pentikainen (1978, 337, n. 111) provides further references on the concept of worldview in general. In 1951 Robert Redfield contrasted worldview with other anthropological concepts employed for the description and comparison of ways of life as follows: " 'World view' differs from culture, ethos, mode of thought, and national character. It is the picture the members of a society have of the properties and characters upon their stage of action. While 'national character' refers to the way these people look to the outsider looking in on them, 'world view' refers to the way the world looks to that people looking out. Of all that is connoted by 'culture,' 'worldview' attends especially to the way a man, in a particular society, sees himself in relation to all else. It is the properties of existence distinguished from and relating to the self. It is, in short, a man's idea of the universe" (Redfield 1952, 30).

Any individual's worldview is shaped by a process of enculturation and will reflect both shared and particularistic features (Pentikainen 1978, 28–35). A musical worldview is similarly formed by the specifics of a musician's particular talents, experiences, and opportunities, as well as the sounds, behaviors, and ideas found within his or her musical community which constitute a shared musical culture. Thomas Adler (1980) examines this acquisition process in a folk musical tradition.

2. Timothy Rice (1980) has considered Bulgarian concepts of music, inspired, however, by semantic misunderstandings between himself and his informants.

3. This approach is taken by Burt Feintuch and Erkki Pekkila (Feintuch 1975, 113–91; Pekkila 1983). Both use ethnoscientific methodology to construct taxonomies of musical terminology which are essentially hierarchical in structure. Ellen Koskoff has improved upon their methodology by organizing concepts into heterarchies, clusters of categories which an informant associates with one another (Koskoff 1982, 356), an idea she draws from Hofstadter (1979, 134).

4. The examples of informants' "music networks" which Ellen Koskoff presents demonstrate the richness of individuals' musical conceptualizations, which "ordinary language alone cannot exhaust" but are limited by her dependence on a single interview with each informant, an artificial recording context that would certainly affect the data (Fabian 1975, 194).

5. See, for example, Pentikainen (1978, 13–19) and Ellen Stekert's examination of two folk singers' personalities and repertoire (Stekert 1965) for summary reviews of this literature.

6. An exception is James Porter's (1976) study of changes over time in Jeannie Robertson's performance of the song "My Son David." In a more recent article (1986) he continues to argue for attention to the complex ways in which singers confer meaning on their songs, a lack that is even greater in studies of instrumental folk music.

7. Hugo Zemp observed in an early ethnomusicological study of cognition that direct interviewing of his informants among the Are'are of the Solomon Islands about their musical concepts was not very productive. Rather, he noted the termi-

nology on which his study was based in conversations which he encountered while learning to play. By placing terminology in its habitual context, this procedure helped him to connect the semantic analysis of language with performance practice, amplifying his understanding of underlying concepts (Zemp 1979, 32–33). Kaeppler (1971, 171) makes a similar point. Such a participant-observer role also allows for recording and use of much situational information and nonverbal data, as Zemp notes is suggested by Marcia Herndon (Herndon and Brunyate 1976, 221). Hiromi Sakata (1983) has made a related point by demonstrating the importance of sociolinguistic variables, such as the speaker's language community, status, sex, occupation, and level of sophistication, among others, for semantic analyses of musical terminology.

8. A recording of this performance was privately issued on cassette (*Sound Symposium* 1984).

9. This is a widespread distinction which I have encountered in Irish and Anglo-American tradition. Rice reports it from Bulgaria (1980).

10. Similar strategies have been employed by David Such (1981), for example, who has observed the use of metaphors among avant-garde jazz musicians, identifying those relating to the concept of "outside" as central to their shared philosophy of musical expression. Steven Feld has examined Kaluli theory through the metaphoric language in which they speak about music (1981), and interpretation of myth plays a central role in his larger ethnography of Kaluli singing (1982). Aesthetics is another realm of musical conception amenable to verbal analysis, as for example, Jihad Racy's (1982) study among musicians in Cairo shows, being largely based on examination of the language in which musical performance is evaluated. He has also investigated attitudes toward music in Beirut through various linguistic forms, such as specialized jargon, music-related words, idiomatic phrases, old images, and proverbs, applied to it by the population in general and professional musicians in particular (1986).

11. This expression is, of course, not limited to Newfoundland but is widespread in the English-speaking world. Southern blacks, for example, use the same expression when referring to instrumental proficiency. A comparative examination of the range of this expression, however, is beyond the scope of this study.

12. In a classic case of serendipity, I came across David Spalding's note in an advice column for songwriters that several Shetland fiddlers report dream compositions as well (Spalding 1985, 9–10).

13. The importance of dreams also represents an interesting parallel to Bernard Lortat-Jacob's observation that dreams hold a special place in the musical life of the launeddas maker Attilio Cannargiu. "If he hears a piece of music on the radio, he says he dreams of it at night and is capable of playing it the following day" (Lortat-Jacob 1982, 48). Like Emile, he sees himself as having "learned from none" and so has "come to regard his natural gifts . . . as the source of his knowledge."

14. It has likewise appeared in the title of his second LP recording *It Comes from the Heart/Ça Vient du Tchoeur* (Benoit 1982).

15. As Thomas observes, "He recognized very early that he wished to devote himself to his first love, the violin" (1983, 122).

16. Feintuch (1983) has also briefly investigated a fiddler's musical motivation.

3. *Catching Rhymes: Compositional Processes*

1. Improvisation has been defined in a variety of ways, but common to most uses of the term is the concept of music composed during performance; scholarly investigations of the topic are discussed in the bibliographical essay.

2. Nettl (1974) places these at the far ends of a spectrum ranging between rapid and slow composition.

3. These perspectives are particularly predominant in scholarship on fiddling such as Burman-Hall (1968, 1973, 1975, 1978), Goertzen (1983, 1985), and Spielman (1972, 1975).

4. This is true even of studies that acknowledge the active role of particular musicians in giving the tradition its character and take more account of performance context such as Blaustein (1975), Burman-Hall (1984), Cowdery (1990), Feintuch (1975, and 1983a), Feldman and O'Doherty (1979), Joyal (1980), and O'Súilleabháin (1987).

5. Burman-Hall comments: "The difficulties of establishing boundaries to a tune family . . . demonstrate the high degree of cross-influence exerted from within the tradition. This cross-influence has caused convergence as well as divergence in the repertory" (1973, 754). Goertzen explains changes in versions of the tune "Billy in the Low Ground" in Britain and America since the eighteenth century largely in terms of variation in patterns of performance occasion, concluding that the adequacy of the tune family concept for describing the relationships among the tunes in this repertoire has not been demonstrated and suggesting that further study of the processes of variation is needed (Goertzen 1983, 191). Most recently Cowdery challenges its applicability to the sean-nós songs and dance tunes, i.e., the melodic tradition, of Ireland (1984; 1990, 93).

6. My impression from other conversations is that the insistent rhythm of the truck's engine was also significant. Other examples of rhythmic mechanical sounds are among the few examples of similar accounts in the literature. Peter Cooke describes "some monotonous rhythm" as an important source of inspiration for tune composition in the Shetland Isles, citing the instance of an "old BMB single cylinder six-horse engine" (Cooke 1986, 94). Rhythmic sounds found in nature are mentioned by Irish fiddler John Doherty as an important source of inspiration. "The old musicians in them days, they would take the music from anything.

They would take music from the sound of the sea, or they would go alongside of the river at the time of the flood and they would take music from that" (Feldman and O'Doherty 1979, 50). A longer narrative follows in which the sound of a galloping horse's hooves, occasioned by an otherworldly encounter, inspired a reel that commemorated the experience. Accounts of natural sounds and supernatural experiences as the inspirations for tune creation are typical in Irish tradition (Jardine 1981). Such accounts of musical inspiration drawn from the environmental soundscape are found in other musical genres as well. Titon cites cases from blues performers, interpreting this as part of their role in giving voice to universal "truths" and shared "human patterns" that "affect" the singer who "translates" the experience in a public manner (1992, 139–40).

7. Composition from preexisting elements in liturgical chant has been called centonization and the presence of such units seen as evidence of oral composition (Chew 1980). My work with Emile would suggest that use of preexisting melodic units is only one strategy for oral composition. The recurrent musical motifs which Emile drew on, for example, served primarily as a starting place for imaginative transformation, rather than as restrictive constraints on where he might go and what he might use. Indeed, the constraints imposed by traditional aesthetic norms must be temporarily lifted to allow imaginative freedom for the generation of new compositions.

8. I use Titon's (1978) term *preform* because it can encompass preexisting musical units of varying size and type, whereas I have used *phrase* and *motif* here to suggest the components of a strain.

9. A. B. Lord ([1960] 1970) has demonstrated that the oral composers of epic narratives were able to achieve their fluency through the use of formulaic language and larger stereotyped units. David Buchan's (1972) hypothetical "oral" performer of ballads similarly employs guiding principles of character, plot, and stanzaic structuring. Sloboda argues that "what distinguishes improvisation from composition is primarily the preexistence of a large set of formal constraints which comprise a 'blueprint' or 'skeleton' for the improvisation" (Sloboda 1985, 139), while "the keynote of the compositional process seems to be the moulding and perfecting of musical ideas. Although an idea may come spontaneously, unbidden, and instantaneously, its subsequent development may take years" (138).

10. I recognize that this is not the usage of the term *soundscape* as coined by R. Murray Schafer (1977), who applies it to environmental sounds, but I nevertheless find it apt here to describe possible musical routes suggested by compositional moves.

11. "One might adequately summarize the situation once and for all, I think, by simply saying that any tune-title may become a floater, and that any traditional player could give any tune he knew any title he wished, at any time" (Bayard 1982, 5).

12. I have modified Thomas's phonetic transcription style, meant to convey

the language as spoken, while remaining true to the content as it is somewhat inconsistent with my own practice (Thomas 1983, 187–93).

13. Gerald Thomas commented, for example, that while he and Emile were in France Emile responded to all music in this manner, often quite inappropriately for some more "serious" performances such as arrangements of medieval French songs, reflecting an idea of what music is supposed to do for one and how to express one's approbation (Q-tape 57).

4. Fingers and Bow: Repertoire and Style

1. I have examined Emile's process of composition throughout this book in the general frameworks of social and cognitive psychological models (Amabile 1983; Sloboda 1985). Amabile describes three "components" of creativity: task motivation, domain-relevant skills, and creativity-relevant skills (1983, 68). The preceding discussions of Emile's personality, values, and attitudes toward music revealed much about his task motivation and personality-related components of his creativity-relevant skills. I examined heuristic components of the latter as part of his compositional processes (Amabile 1983, 72–74). In this section I focus on Emile's domain-relevant skills, that is, the knowledge and skills with which an individual can both synthesize a response and evaluate that product (Amabile 1983, 69). These channel creative effort by both providing the means and constraining the possibilities for expression. This knowledge has been aptly described as delimiting a creator's "network of possible wanderings" (Newell and Simon 1972, 82; Amabile 1983, 69).

2. Adler refers to this technical knowledge as the articulatory level of competence (1980, 95).

3. Two studies of Western folk fiddling traditions which move in this direction are Jos. Koning's discussion of concepts of tonality in Irish fiddling tradition and Pandora Hopkins's experiment in cross-cultural musical perception of a rhythmic pattern found in Norwegian fiddling (Koning 1979; Hopkins 1982 and 1985, 188–210). Philip Donner's essay suggestively titled "Tuuso Lempinen: A Fiddler from Lammi and His Concepts of Music" (1978) was unavailable to me.

4. According to Nattiez, Sandra Smith, for example, identifies "mythical and historical explanations of the origin and function of music," such as those considered in relation to Emile's musical worldview, along with semantic fields applied to musical elements and activities, nonverbal "patterns of sound and motion," and "interrelationships between music theory and the theories of other expressive forms" as possible "levels" in which music theory may be articulated (Smith in press, cited in Nattiez 1981, 49). The investigator must systematize data from these varied sources, often inferring concepts from observed behavior which may remain out of the informant's conscious awareness to discover and articulate an appropriate ethnotheory (Nattiez 1981, 50; Pekkila 1983, 210–11, 217).

5. To avoid redundancy I have not reproduced associated narratives which appear elsewhere in the text, but rather refer the reader to the sections in which they may be found.

6. This literature was reviewed by Jack Bevil in his dissertation study of Southern Uplands folk song melody (1984, 8–80) and by Cowdery in relation to the tune family concept (1990, 82–87).

7. I found that a combination of methods was needed to provide an answer. Playing pieces which I knew well together with Emile proved to be an effective way to absorb his method of bowing. In this situation I was able to focus my attention on his bowing and could often imitate his bowing patterns closely; as the tunes were repeated many times I could slowly refine my perceptions, drawing especially on a kinesthetic response, while trying to match my entire posture and movement style to his as we sat next to each other, in addition to using aural and visual information. The pitfall, of course, is that my own natural bowing style might reassert itself when I subsequently reflected upon what I was doing in order to record it.

On other occasions Emile attempted to teach me specific bowing patterns for a tune. This approach was useful but further removed from the reality of his playing. As he slowed enough to isolate his own perceptions of bowing patterns and demonstrate portion of them to me, I found that the melodies and bowing inevitably changed slightly, not enough to invalidate the demonstration of the principle but enough that the demonstration was somewhat removed from reality, usually somewhat more regularized and systematized, no doubt by his self-conception of the underlying principle.

Analysis of videotape recordings, which provides evidence for this problem with the intentional demonstrations, would seem to be an ideal technique, but I found the primarily visual transcription method more difficult, and I would suspect less reliable, than I had anticipated. Video playback at normal speed was too fast to observe, retain, and record more than a few moments, or a few crucial highlights, of a bowing pattern. Repeated viewing of the same sequence allowed for reevaluation and filling in, but some patterns were simply too quick to see clearly. Slow-motion playback, to my great frustration, was unavailable with sound, necessitating aural recall of the melody, checked against the visible fingering, to be mentally matched with the now observable bowing. Once again, too much information had to be supplied by the viewer. More sophisticated equipment might have facilitated my analysis, but in any case, I found that the video transcription process lacked the sense of kinesthetic confirmation available in mutual performance. I believe that by combining all of these methods, however, I was able to develop a reliable analysis of Emile's bowing technique.

5. So That My Story Will Live On: Fiddle Performance from House and Hall to Stage and Screen

1. A time is a festive gathering of a community, family, or other group, characterized by dancing, singing, drinking, and fun-making (Wareham 1982, 1).

2. This approach is drawn from a conception of folklore as "performance and communication," a research perspective that emerged as a major concern within the field in the late 1960s (Ben-Amos and Goldstein 1975, 1). Its scholarly development is discussed in the bibliographical essay. It seems an especially apt perspective from which to examine creativity in the performance of folk musicians who draw upon a traditional repertoire because it emphasizes the unique qualities inherent in the performance of even the most timeworn traditional items.

3. One of Wareham's informants recalls such events as follows: "Like go to some fella's house to have a drink and then he'd spend the night singin'. Singin' and drinkin'. That was mostly moonshine then or beer. Never dance there. If they had a cordeen there, Mack might play two or three fast tunes or something on the accordion just for listening, just for entertainment. . . . Could be somebody step dance but not very often, 'bout 50/50 chance I'd say, that this bar would be played without anybody movin' a foot, just listenin', mostly drinking and songs" (Wareham 1982, 224–25).

4. The Irish musician Johnny Dougherty, for example, seems to interweave stories and tunes in a similar manner (Feldman and O'Doherty 1979). Not surprisingly, he performed often at small kitchen gatherings, without dancers. Judith McCulloh (1975) reports a number of historical narratives tied to traditional tunes by an Arkansas fiddler. The "Hangmans's Reel," studied by D. K. Wilgus, is usually presented with an accompanying legend, as is Emile's "Devil's Reel" (Wilgus 1965, 1980). The "Old Man and Old Woman" is also clearly not for dance accompaniment as described by Bayard (1982, 200). Burman-Hall describes an entire portion of the southern fiddle repertoire as follows: "Besides the tradition of dance music, the fiddler will usually know one or more British-American instrumental airs of the same form and meter as the dance tunes. These tunes are not played at dance tempo (MM 112–132) however, but in a stately tempo of MM 60–84, with a freer and more lyrical manner of rendition, and often with a special story or tradition associated, and programmatic effects" (Burman-Hall 1984, 158). A few of Emile's compositions fit this model although most are played in a danceable manner and many can be presented with an accompanying narrative. Further removed from the Anglo-Celtic world, Pandora Hopkins notes the importance of listening genres and tune-legend complexes in the Hardanger fiddle traditions of Norway (Hopkins 1985, 153–57).

5. Ingrid Fraser (1981) has described how performers and audiences interact in this setting. She applies previous studies of bar interaction to the St. John's scene and finds relatively mixed patterns of use. Important for its impact on performers is

the result that though focus on the performance is evident, "individuals or groups may be present for a variety of reasons. They might have come to meet friends, to 'pick up' someone, or to drink and forget their problems" (52). Performers would develop strategies for controlling the situation so as to satisfy their goals at the same time they were beholden to the bar owner and audience. The bar is, after all, primarily a business, presenting a potential conflict between the service aspects of the performer's occupation and its artistic values (72).

One business strategy which several bar owners in St. John's have tried with varying success is to create an informal, partylike ambience to draw customers. Fraser interviewed Paul Kelly, the owner of Bridgett's, the first St. John's club at which Emile appeared as a regular attraction. Kelly, she concludes, wants musicians to "meet the clientele on their own terms," reduce the "social distance," and "heighten the relaxed, party-like atmosphere" (76). He therefore preferred not to hire "serious" musicians, who would demand a high degree of focused attention on themselves and their music. Such a pattern of performance, he felt, decreased the patrons' alcohol consumption by inhibiting their behavior. He also expected musicians to socialize with the patrons for similar reasons. "We don't make it a rule, but it's sort of an informal rule that it is part of the job for the musician to be friendly during breaks. And if they have any sense, they will know that this is how they will establish a following. And if you establish a following then you get rehired" (74).

6. Jos. Koning (1980) noted a similar phenomenon during his fieldwork in Ireland.

7. This observation was confirmed by many people, including experienced folklorists and media observers Peter Narváez and Neil Rosenberg.

8. Emile's creativity was not confined to his extraordinary ability at composition. He was also a fine storyteller. He neglected this talent to a certain extent because of his love of the fiddle, but he was capable of telling lengthy folktales or *Märchen*. On stage or in a club or party, of course, his narrative abilities were limited to short tales, humorous anecdotes, and his specialty, which, in a sense, is the raison d'être for this record: his explanatory tales with which he prefaces his tunes (Thomas 1982, 7).

9. Casey, Rosenberg, and Wareham (1972) have commented on the importance of extramusical associations for folk singers' repertoire categorization.

10. This is the converse of the situation described by Christopher Goertzen in his study of the widely known tune "Billy in the Low Ground" (1983). He seems to suggest that of two tunes he found in competition for this title in the American South, the more unusual and striking, and thus the more memorable, melody won out (Goertzen 1983, 158–62, 185–91). Melody is seen here as the dominant aspect of fiddle-tune identity.

11. The only other Newfoundland fiddler whose tunes have achieved province-wide exposure of the type given Emile is Rufus Guinchard, who plays in a style

easily distinguished from the mainstream of fiddling tradition (Guinchard ca. 1978, ca. 1982). In his collection of Guinchard's tunes Kelly Russell, one of the leaders of the music revival, separates tunes "composed by Rufus," "those which are believed to be unique, not heard anywhere else as far as can be determined," and "more common tunes heard elsewhere" (Russell 1982, 27), reflecting his interest in finding a distinctive Newfoundland repertoire. In his own performances and on the recordings he has produced, Kelly features only those pieces he considers to be unique or newly composed (Payne and Russell 1983; Wonderful Grand Band 1978).

Conclusion. Everybody Got a Sound

1. Porter (1980, 120). He cites D'Andrade (1984, 103) and Hofstadter (1979, 158) on the important distinction between meaning and message.

∿ Works Cited

Books and Articles

Abrahams, Roger, ed. 1970a. *A singer and her songs: Almeda Riddle's book of ballads.* Baton Rouge: Louisiana State University Press.

————. 1970b. Creativity, individuality and the traditional singer. *Studies in the Literary Imagination* 3, no. 1:5–34.

Adler, Thomas Albert. 1980. *The acquisition of a traditional competence: Folk-musical and folk-cultural learning among bluegrass banjo players.* Ph.D. diss., Indiana University.

Amabile, Teresa M. 1983. *The social psychology of creativity.* New York: Springer-Verlag.

Andersson, Flemming G., and Thomas Pettit. 1979. Mrs. Brown of Falkland: A singer of tales? *Journal of American Folklore* 92:1–24.

Ashton, John. 1981. Some thoughts on the role of musician in outport Newfoundland. Paper read at the Folklore Studies Association of Canada meeting, Halifax.

————. 1985. A study of the lumbercamp song tradition in Newfoundland. Ph.D. diss., Memorial University of Newfoundland.

Atlantic Fiddling. 1980. Canadian Broadcasting Corporation (CBC), LP recording LM 47.

Azadowski, Mark. 1974. *A Siberian tale teller.* Center for Intercultural Studies in Folklore and Ethnomusicology Monograph Series No. 2. Translated by James R. Dow. Austin: University of Texas.

Barry, Phillips. 1933. Communal re-creation. *Bulletin of the Folk Song Society of the Northeast* 5:4–6.

———. 1936. The psychopathology of ballad singing. *Bulletin of the Folk Song Society of the Northeast* 11:16–18.

———. 1939. *Folk music in America.* National Service Bureau Folk-Song and Folklore Department American Folk-Song Publications 4, edited by George Herzog and Herbert Halpert. New York: Works Progress Administration, National Service Bureau.

———. 1961. The part of the folksinger in the making of folk balladry. In *The critics and the ballad,* edited by MacEdward Leach and Tristram Coffin, 59–76. Carbondale: Southern Illinois University Press.

Bayard, Samuel. 1950. Prolegomena to a study of the principal melodic families of British-American folk song. *Journal of American Folklore* 58:1–44.

———. 1956. Some folk fiddlers' habits and styles in western Pennsylvania. *Journal of the International Folk Music Council* 8:15–18.

———. 1966. Scales and ranges in Anglo-American fiddle tunes: Report on a desultory experiment. In *Two penny ballads and four dollar whiskey: A Pennsylvania folklore miscellany,* edited by Kenneth Goldstein and Robert Byington, 51–60. Hatboro, Pa.: Folklore Associates.

———. 1982. *Dance to the fiddle, march to the fife: Instrumental folk tunes in Pennsylvania.* University Park: Pennsylvania State University Press.

Bégin, Carmelle. 1981. *La musique traditionelle pour violon: Jean Carrignan.* Ottawa: National Museums of Canada.

Ben-Amos, Dan. 1976. "Introduction." In *Folklore genres,* edited by Dan-Ben Amos, ix–xlv. Austin: University of Texas.

Ben-Amos, Dan, and Kenneth S. Goldstein. 1975. "Introduction." In *Folklore: Peformance and communication,* edited by Dan Ben-Amos and Kenneth S. Goldstein, 1–10. The Hague: Mouton.

Bennett, John. 1985. "The fiddler's heritage at Pangnirtung." *Canadian Folk Music Bulletin* 19, no. 3:32–35.

Benoit, Emile. 1979. *Emile's dream.* Pigeon Inlet Productions PIP 732. First issued as Quay CS7932 by the Newfoundland Fiddle Association (= Kelly Russell).

———. 1982. *Ça vient du tchoeur/It comes from the heart.* Pigeon Inlet Productions PIP 7311.

———. 1985. *Black mountain.* Videorecording produced by Robert Pitt and Gerald Thomas. St. John's: Memorial University Television.

Bevil, Jack Marshall. 1984. Centonization and concordance in the American southern Uplands folksong melody: A study of the musical generative and transmittive process of an oral tradition." Ph.D. diss., North Texas State University.

Blacking, John. 1972–73. Review of *Folk music and dances of Ireland. Irish Folk Music Studies* 1:56–58.

———. 1973. *How musical is man.* Seattle: University of Washington Press.

———. 1981. The problem of "ethnic" perceptions in the semiotics of music. In

The sign in music and literature, edited by Wendy Steiner, 184–94. Austin: University of Texas Press.

————. 1986. *Identifying processes of musical change. World of Music* 28:3–13.

Blaustein, Richard J. 1975. Traditional music and social change: The old time fiddlers association movement in the United States. Ph.D. diss., Indiana University.

Blumenthal, Arthur L. 1977. *The process of cognition.* Englewood Cliffs, N.J.: Prentice-Hall.

Boyden, David D. 1965. *The history of violin playing from its origins to 1761 and its relationship to the violin and violin music.* London: Oxford University Press.

Brailoiu, Constantin. [1959] 1984. "Reflections on collective musical creation." In *Problems of ethnomusicology,* edited and translated by A. L. Lloyd, 102–9. Cambridge: Cambridge University Press.

Breathnach, Breandan. 1977. *Folk music and dances of Ireland.* Rev. ed. Dublin: Mercier Press.

Briggs, Charles. 1986. *Learning how to ask: A sociolinguistic appraisal of the role of the interview in social science research.* Cambridge: Cambridge University Press.

Bronson, Bertrand. 1969. *The ballad as song.* Berkeley and Los Angeles: University of California.

Buchan, David. 1972. *The ballad and the folk.* London: Routledge & Kegan Paul.

Burman-Hall, Linda. 1968. The technique of variation in an American fiddle tune: A study of "Sail Away Lady" as performed in 1926 by Uncle Bunt Stephens. *Ethnomusicology* 12:49–71.

————. 1973. Southern American folk fiddling: Context and style. Ph.D. diss., Princeton University.

————. 1975. Southern American folk fiddle styles. *Ethnomusicology* 19:47–68.

————. 1978. Tune identity and performance style: The case of "Bonaparte's Retreat." *Selected Reports in Ethnomusicology* 3, no. 1:77–98.

————. 1984. American traditional fiddling: Performance contexts and techniques. In *Performance practice: Ethnomusicological perspectives,* edited by Gerard Behague, 149–221. Westport, Conn.: Greenwood Press.

Butler, Gary Reginald. 1985. Supernatural folk belief expression in a French-Newfoundland community: A study of expressive form, communication process, and social function in L'Anse-a-canards. Ph.D. diss., Memorial University of Newfoundland.

————. 1990. *Saying isn't believing: Conversational narrative and the discourse of tradition in a French-Newfoundland community.* St. John's: Institute of Social and Economic Research, Memorial University of Newfoundland.

Ça vient du tchoeur: Emile Benoit, musicien et raconteur francoterreneuvien. 1980. Video, 29 min. St. John's: Memorial University of Newfoundland Educational Television Centre (ETV).

Casey, George, Neil V. Rosenberg, and Wilfred W. Wareham. 1972. Repertoire categorization and performer audience relationships: Some Newfoundland folksong examples. *Ethnomusicology* 16:397–403.

Chew, Geoffrey. 1980. Centonization. In *New Grove dictionary of music and musicians*, Vol. 4, edited by Stanley Sadie, 56–58. London: Macmillan.

Clifford, James. 1988. "On ethnographic authority." In *The predicament of culture: Twentieth century ethnography, literature, and art*, 21–54. Cambridge: Harvard University Press.

Cohen, Anne, and Norm. 1973. Tune evolution as an indicator of traditional musical norms. *Journal of American Folklore* 86:37–47.

Cooke, Peter. 1978. Album jacket notes to *Calum Ruadh: Bard of Skye*. Scottish Tradition 7. LP disc. Edinburgh: School of Scottish Studies.

––––––. 1986. *The fiddle tradition of the Shetland Isles*. Cambridge Studies in Ethnomusicology. Cambridge: Cambridge University Press.

Cowdery, James R. 1984. A fresh look at the concept of tune family. *Ethnomusicology* 28:495–504.

––––––. 1990. *The melodic tradition of Ireland*. Kent, Ohio: Kent State University Press.

Cox, Gordon. 1980. *Folk music in a Newfoundland outport*. National Museum of Man Mercury Series, Canadian Centre for Folk Cultural Studies Paper 32. Ottawa: National Museums of Canada.

D'Andrade, Roy G. 1984. Cultural meaning systems. In *Culture theory: Essays on mind, self, and emotion*, edited by Richard A. Schweder and Robert A. Levine, 88–122. Cambridge: Cambridge University Press.

Dégh, Linda. 1969. *Folktales and society: Story-telling in a Hungarian peasant community*. Translated by Emily Schossberger. Bloomington: Indiana University Press.

Donner, Philip. 1978. Tuuso Lempinen: A fiddler from Lammi and his concepts of music. *Antropologiska Studier* 25–26:142–47.

Dunlay, K. E., and D. L. Reich. 1986. *Traditional Celtic fiddle music of Cape Breton*. Wayland, Mass.: K. E. Dunlay and D. L. Reich.

Elschek, Oskar. 1981. Die musikalische Individualitat der slowakischen Primgeiger. In *Studia Instrumentorum Musicae Popularis* 7, edited by Erich Stockmann, 70–85. Stockholm: Musikhistoriska Museet.

Emile Benoit: Fiddler. 1980. Video, 28 min. St. John's: Memorial University of Newfoundland Educational Television Centre (ETV).

Ericsson, K. A., and H. A. Simon. 1980. Verbal reports as data. *Psychology Review* 87:215–51.

Fabian, Johannes. 1975. Taxonomy and ideology: On the boundaries of concept classification. In *Linguistics and anthropology: In honor of C. F. Voeglin*, edited by M. Dale Kinkade, Kenneth L. Hale, and Oswald Werner, 183–97. Lisse: Peter de Ridder Press.

Feintuch, Burt. 1975. Pop Ziegler fiddler: A study of folkloric communication. Ph.D. diss., University of Pennsylvania.

———. 1983a. Examining musical motivation: Why does Sammie play the fiddle. *Western Folklore* 42: 208–15.

———. 1983b. "The fiddle in the United States: An historical overview." *Kentucky Folklore Record* 29, nos. 1–2:30–38.

———. 1984–85. A fiddler's life. *Pennsylvania Folklife* 34, no. 2:50–60.

Feld, Steven. 1974. Linguistic models and ethnomusicology. *Ethnomusicology* 18:197–217.

———. 1981. Flow like a waterfall: The metaphors of Kaluli musical theory. *Yearbook for Traditional Music* 13:22–47.

———. 1982. *Sound and sentiment: Birds, weeping, poetics, and song in Kaluli expression.* Philadelphia: University of Pennsylvania, Publications of the American Folklore Society, New Series, vol. 5.

———. 1984. Communication, music, and speech about music. *Yearbook for Traditional Music* 16:1–18.

Feldman, Allen, and Eamonn O'Doherty. 1979. *The northern fiddler.* Belfast: Blackstaff Press.

Figgy Duff. 1980. *Figgy Duff.* LP disc. Posterity Records PTR 13014.

———. 1983. *After the tempest.* LP disc. Boot Records BOS 7243.

Fraser, Ingrid. 1981. Public tradition in an urban context: An occupational folklore study of musicians in St. John's. M.A. thesis, Memorial University of Newfoundland.

Friedman, Albert B. 1983. The oral-formulaic theory of balladry a re-rebuttal. In *The ballad image,* edited by James Porter, 215–40. Los Angeles: Center for the Study of Comparative Folklore and Mythology, University of California.

Gardner, Howard. 1982. *Art, mind, and brain: A cognitive approach to creativity.* New York: Basic Books.

———. 1983. *Frames of mind: The theory of multiple intelligences.* New York: Basic Books.

Garrison, Virginia Hope. 1985. Traditional and non-traditional teaching and learning practices in folk music: An ethnographic field study of Cape Breton fiddling. Ph.D. diss., University of Wisconsin, Madison.

George, Marcus E., and Dick Cushman. 1982. Ethnographies as texts. *Annual Review of Anthropology* 11:25–69.

Georges, Robert A. 1980. Toward a resolution of the text/context controversy. *Western Folklore* 39:34–40.

Giannattasio, F., and B. Lortat-Jacob. 1982. Modalita di improvvisazione nella musica sarda: Due modelli. *Culture Musicali: Quaderni di Etnomusicologia* 1:3–36.

Glassie, Henry. 1970. "Take That Night Train to Selma": An excursion to the outskirts of scholarship. In *Folksongs and their makers,* edited by Henry Glassie,

Edward D. Ives, and John Szwed, 1–70. Bowling Green: Bowling Green University Popular Press.

Goertzen, Christopher Jack. 1983. "Billy in the Low Ground": History of an American instrumental folk tune. Ph.D. diss., University of Illinois.

———. 1985. American fiddle tunes and the historic-geographic method. *Ethnomusicology* 29:448–73.

Goldstein, Kenneth S. 1971. On the application of the concepts of active and inactive tradition to the study of repertoire. *Journal of American Folklore* 84:62–67.

Gourlay, Kenneth A. 1978. Towards a reassessment of the ethnomusicologist's role in research. *Ethnomusicology* 22:1–36.

Gower, Herschel. 1973. Wanted: the singer's autobiography and critical reflections. *Tennessee Folklore Society Bulletin* 39:1–3.

Grainger, Percy. 1908. The impress of personality in traditional singing. *Journal of the Folk-Song Society* 12:163–66.

———. 1915. The impress of personality in unwritten music. *Musical Quarterly* 1:416–35.

Green, Elizabeth. 1976. *Orchestral bowings and routines.* Ann Arbor: Campus Publishers.

Greenfield, Vernie. 1986. *Making do or making art? A study of American recycling.* Ann Arbor: UMI Research Press.

Gruber, H. E. 1978. Darwin's tree of nature and other images of wide scope. In *On aesthetics in science,* edited by J. Wechsler, 121–40. Cambridge, Mass.: MIT Press.

Guinchard, Rufus. ca. 1978. *Newfoundland fiddler.* Breakwater Recording No. 1002.

———. ca. 1982. Step dances and doubles. Pigeon Inlet Productions PIP 737.

Guntharp, Matthew. 1980. *Learning the fiddler's ways.* University Park: Pennsylvania State University Press.

Hall, Edward T. 1966. *The hidden dimension.* Garden City, N.Y.: Doubleday.

Halpert, Herbert. 1943. The devil and the fiddle. *Hoosier Folklore Bulletin* 2:39–43.

Harwood, Dane. 1987. Interpretive activity: A response to Rice's "Toward the remodelling of ethnomusicology." *Ethnomusicology* 31:503–10.

Henssen, Gottfreid. 1951. *Uberlieferung und Personlichkeit: Die Erzahlungen und Lieder des Egbert Gerrits.* Münster: Aschendorffsche Verlagsbuchhandlung.

Herndon, Marcia, and Roger Brunyate, eds. 1975. *Proceedings of a symposium on form in performance, hard-core ethnography.* Austin: University of Texas, Office of the College of Fine Arts.

———. 1976. Reply to Kolinski: Taurus omicida. *Ethnomusicology* 20:217–31.

Herndon, Marcia, and Norma Mcleod. 1980a. Conclusions. In *The ethnography of musical performance,* edited by Norma Mcleod and Marcia Herndon, 176–98. Darby, Pa.: Norwood.

———. 1980b. *Music as culture.* Darby, Pa.: Norwood.

Hickerson, Joseph C., and Maggie Holzberg. 1974. *A bibliography of fiddling, fiddle tunes, and related dance tune collections in North America including representative materials from the British Isles and Scandinavia.* Washington, D.C.: Archive of Folk Culture, American Folklife Center, Library of Congress.

Hofstadter, Douglas. 1979. *Gödel, Escher, Bach: An eternal golden braid.* New York: Basic Books.

———. 1985. *Metamagical themas: Questing for the essence of mind and pattern.* New York: Basic Books.

Hogan, Dorothy, and Homer Hogan. 1977. Canadian fiddle culture. *Canadian Studies* 3, no. 4:72–100.

Hood, Mantle. 1960. The challenge of bi-musicality. *Ethnomusicology* 4:55–59.

Hopkins, Pandora. 1976. Individual choice and the control of musical change. *Journal of American Folklore* 89:449–62.

———. 1982. Aural thinking. In *Cross cultural perspectives on music,* edited by Robert Falk and Timothy Rice, 143–61. Toronto: University of Toronto Press.

———. 1985. *Aural thinking in Norway: The transmission of history through the musical codes of the hardingfele.* New York: Human Sciences Press.

Hornby, James John. 1983. The fiddle on the island: Fiddling tradition on Prince Edward Island. M.A. thesis, Memorial University of Newfoundland.

Hymes, Dell. 1975. Breakthrough into performance. In *Folklore: Performance and communication,* edited by Dan Ben-Amos and Kenneth S. Goldstein, 11–74. The Hague: Mouton.

Ives, Edward D. 1964. *Larry Gorman: The man who made the songs.* Bloomington: Indiana University Press.

———. 1970a. A man and his song: Joe Scott and "The Plain Golden Band." In *Folksongs and their makers,* edited by Henry Glassie, Edward D. Ives, and John F. Szwed, 71–148. Bowling Green: Bowling Green University Popular Press.

———. 1970b. *Lawrence Doyle, the farmer poet of Prince Edward Island: A study in local songmaking.* University of Maine Studies, No. 92. Orono: University of Maine Press.

———. 1979. *Joe Scott: The woodsman songmaker.* Urbana: University of Illinois Press.

Jabbour, Alan. 1971. *American fiddle tunes from the Archive of Folksong.* Booklet accompanying Library of Congress LP No. AFS L62, Washington, D.C.: Archive of Folk Culture, Library of Congress.

Jardine, Stephen C. 1981. A study of the composition of tunes and airs and their assimilation into Irish traditional dance music. Ph.D. diss., University College Cork.

John-Steiner, Vera. 1985. *Notebooks of the mind: Explorations of thinking.* Albuquerque: University of New Mexico Press.

Jones, Michael Owen. 1975. *The handmade object and its maker.* Berkeley and Los Angeles: University of California Press.

———. 1989. *Craftsmen of the Cumberlands: Tradition and Creativity.* Lexington: University Press of Kentucky.

Joyal, Jean-Pierre. 1980. Le processus de composition dans la musique instrumen-tae du Québec. *Canadian Folk Music Journal* 8:49–54.

Joyce, Patrick W. 1873. *Ancient Irish music.* Dublin: McGlasham and Gill.

Kaeppler, Adrienne. 1971. Aesthetics of Tongan dance. *Ethnomusicology* 15:175–85.

King, Arden. 1980. Innovation, creativity, and performance. In *The ethnography of musical performance,* edited by Norma McLeod and Marcia Herndon, 167–75. Norwood, Pa.: Norwood.

Knudsen, Thorkild. 1978. LP disc and liner notes to *Calum Ruadh: Bard of Skye.* Scottish Tradition 7. Edinburgh: School of Scottish Studies.

Koning, Jos. 1979. "That old plaintive touch": On the relation between tonality in Irish traditional dance-music and the left hand technique of fiddlers in east C. Clare, Ireland. In *Studia instrumentorum musicae popularis VI,* edited by Erich Stockmann, 80–84. Stockholm: Musikhistoriska museet.

———. 1980. The fieldworker as performer: Fieldwork objectives and social roles in county Clare, Ireland. *Ethnomusicology* 24:417–29.

Koskoff, Ellen. 1982. The music network. *Ethnomusicology* 20:353–70.

———. 1987. Response to Rice. *Ethnomusicology* 31:497–502.

Krell, Roberta. 1986. Folklore and the elderly: Aging, creativity, and community. Ph.D. diss., University of California, Los Angeles.

Laforte, Conrad. 1976. *Poetiques de la chanson traditionelle française.* Les archives de folklore no. 17. Quebec: Les Presses de l'Universite Laval.

Lederman, Anne, ed. 1985. Special issue: Fiddling in Canada. *Canadian Folk Music Bulletin* 19, no. 3.

———. 1987. *Old native and métis fiddling in Manitoba.* Vols. 1 and 2. Booklets accompanying LPs Falcon FP 187 and FP 287. Toronto: Falcon Productions for Manitoba Culture, Heritage and Recreation.

LeVine, Robert A. 1982. *Culture, behavior, and personality: An introduction to the comparative study of psychosocial adaptation.* 2d. ed. New York: Aldine.

Long, Eleanor. 1973. Ballad singers, ballad makers, and ballad etiology. *Western Folklore* 32:225–36.

Lord, Albert. [1960] 1970. *The singer of tales.* Reprint. New York: Atheneum.

Lortat-Jacob, Bernard. 1982. Theory and "bricolage": Attilio Cannargiu's tempera-ment. *Yearbook for Traditional Music* 14:45–54.

———. 1987. Improvisation: Le modèle et ses réalisations. In *L'improvisation dans les musiques de tradition orale,* edited by Bernard Lortat-Jacob, 45–59. Paris: SELAF, Ethnomusicologie 4.

Macdonald, Graham, and Philip Pettit. 1981. *Semantics and social science.* London: Routledge & Kegan Paul.

McCulloh, Judith. 1975. Uncle Absie Morrison's historical tunes. *Mid-South Folklore* 3:95–104.

McCullough, Larry. 1979. Some brief analytical remarks about Ed Reavy's compositional style in *Where the Shannon Rises.* In booklet accompanying *Ed Reavy* LP, Rounder 6008. Somerville, Mass.: Rounder Records.

McKinnon, Ian Francis. 1989. Fiddling to fortune: The role of commercial recordings made by Cape Breton fiddlers in the fiddle music tradition of Cape Breton Island. M.A. thesis, Memorial University of Newfoundland.

Marin, Louis. 1964. *Les contes traditionnels en Lorraine.* Paris: Geuthner.

Marshall, Christopher. 1982. Towards a comparative aesthetics of music. In *Cross-cultural perspectives on music,* edited by Robert Falck and Timothy Rice, 162–73. Toronto: University of Toronto Press.

Mendelson, Michael. 1975–77. A bibliography of fiddling in North America, parts 1–5. *John Edwards Memorial Foundation Quarterly* 11:104–11, 153–60, 201–14; 12:9–14, 158–64; 13:88–95.

Merriam, Alan P. 1964. *The anthropology of music.* Evanston: Northwestern University Press.

Miller, Terry E. 1986. *Folk music in America: A reference guide.* New York: Garland.

Miner, Horace. 1939. *St. Denis: A French-Canadian parish.* Chicago: University of Chicago.

Monahan, Gordon. 1983. Two fiddlers. *Musicworks* 24:10–11.

———. 1986. A half hour behind means they're slightly ahead: A report on the 1986 Newfoundland Sound Symposium. *Musicworks* 36:10–12.

Music from French Newfoundland/Musique de la Terre-Neuve Française. 1980. LP disc. Pigeon Inlet Productions PIP 734.

Narvaez, Peter. 1982. On Rovers and Ron, reflex and revival: Preserving culture in Newfoundland. *This Magazine* 16, no. 2:9–12.

———. 1986. "The Newfie Bullet"—The nostalgic use of folklore. In *Media Sense: The folklore-popular culture continuum,* edited by Peter Narvaez and Martin Laba, 65–76. Bowling Green: Bowling Green State University Popular Press.

Nash, Dennison. 1961. The role of the composer (parts 1 and 2). *Ethnomusicology* 5:81–94, 187–201.

Nattiez, Jean-Jacques. 1981. Paroles d'informateurs et propos de musiciens: Quelques remarques sur la place du discours dans la connaissance de la musique. *Yearbook for Traditional Music* 13:48–59.

Nettl, Bruno. 1954. Notes on musical composition in primitive cultures. *Anthropological Quarterly* 27, n.s. 2:81–90.

———. 1974. Thoughts on improvisation, a comparative approach. *Musical Quarterly* 60:1–19.

————. 1982. Types of tradition and transmission. In *Cross cultural perspectives on music,* edited by Robert Falk and Timothy Rice, 3–19. Toronto: University of Toronto Press.

————. 1983. *The study of ethnomusicology.* Urbana: University of Illinois Press.

————, ed. 1991. New perspectives on improvisation. *World of Music* 33:no. 3.

Newell, Allen, and Herbert Simon. 1972. *Human problem solving.* Englewood Cliffs, N.J.: Prentice-Hall.

Nielsen, Svend. 1982. *Stability in musical improvisation: A repertoire of icelandic epic songs.* Acta Ethnomusicologica Danica No. 3. Copenhagen: Forlaget Kragen.

Nisbet, R. E., and J. D. Wilson. 1977. Telling more than we can know: Verbal reports on mental processes. *Psychology Review* 84:231–59.

Nketia, J. H. Kwabena. 1981. Juncture of the social and the musical: The methodology of cultural analysis. *World of Music* 23:23–37.

————. 1986. Integrating objectivity and experience in ethnomusicological studies. *World of Music* 23:3–21.

No Strings Attached. N.d. *Traditional music of the future.* Turquoise Records. Whitestone, Ky.

Ornstein, Lisa. 1982. Instrumental folk music of Quebec: An introduction. *Canadian Folk Music Journal* 10:3–11.

Osborne, Harold. 1977. Inspiration. *British Journal of Aesthetics* 17, no. 3:242–53.

O'Súilleabháin, Micheál. 1987. "Tourner" un air: L'improvisation dans la musique traditionelle irlandaise. In *L'improvisation dans les musiques de tradition orale,* edited by Bernard Lortat-Jacob, 211–20. Paris: SELAF, *Ethnomusicologie* 4.

Otto, Herbert A. 1967. The Minerva experience: Initial report. In *Challenges of humanistic psychology,* edited by James F. T. Bugental, 119–24. New York: McGraw-Hill.

Owen, Blanton. 1980. Manco Sneed and the Indians: These Cherokee don't make much music. *North Carolina Folklore Journal* 28:59–65.

Payne, Jim, and Kelly Russell. 1983. *Jim Payne & Kelly Russell.* Pigeon Inlet Productions PIP 7314.

Pekkila, Erkki. 1983. "Musiikki" and "Kappalevalikoima": Aspects of the ethnotheory of a Finnish folk musician. *Suomen Antropologi* 4:209–17.

Pentikainen, Juha. 1978. *Oral repertoire and world view: An anthropological study of Marina Takalo's life history.* FF Communications no. 19. Helsinki: Suomalainen Tiedeakatemia, Academia Scientiarum Fennica.

Perkins, D. N. 1981. *The mind's best work.* Cambridge, Mass.: Harvard University Press.

Piaget, Jean. 1964. Developmental psychology: A theory of development. In *International encyclopedia of the social sciences,* edited by David Sills, 140–47. New York: Macmillan.

Porter, James. 1976. Jeannie Robertson's "My Son David," a conceptual performance model. *Journal of American Folklore* 89:7–26.

———. 1980. Principles of ballad classification: A suggestion for regional cata-
logues of ballad style. *Jahrbuch fur Volksliedforschung* 25:11–26.

———. 1986. Ballad explanations, ballad reality, and the singer's epistemics.
Western Folklore 45:110–25.

———. 1989. *The traditional music of Britain and Ireland: A research and information guide.* New York: Garland.

Profile. 1978. *Newfoundland Herald TV Week,* March 15, pp. 6–7.

Quigley, Colin. 1982. Folk dance and dance events in rural Newfoundland. M.A.
thesis, Memorial University of Newfoundland.

———. 1985. *Close to the floor: Folk dance in Newfoundland.* St. John's: Memorial
University of Newfoundland Folklore Department.

———. 1987. Creative processes in musical composition: French-Newfoundland
fiddler Emile Benoit. Ph.D. diss., University of California, Los Angeles.

———. 1988. A French-Canadian fiddler's worldview: The violin is "master of the
world." *Selected Reports in Ethnomusicology* 7:99–122.

———. 1990. Melodizing as generative process: A case study of fiddle tune composition. In *Ethnomusicology in Canada,* edited by Robert Witmer, 166–75.
Toronto: Institute for Canadian Music.

Racy, Ali Jihad. 1982. Musical aesthetics in present day Cairo. *Ethnomusicology*
26:391–406.

———. 1986. Words and music in Beirut: A study of attitudes. *Ethnomusicology*
30:413–27.

Rahn, Jay. 1983. *A theory for all music: Problems and solutions in the analysis of
non-western forms.* Toronto: University of Toronto Press.

Randolph, Vance. 1954. The names of Ozark fiddle tunes. *Midwest Folklore* 4,
no. 2:81–86.

Redfield, Robert. 1952. The primitive world view. *Proceedings of the American
Philosophical Society* 96:30–36.

Red Island. 1978. *In pursuit of the wild bologna.* LP recording Quay CS-7803.

Rice, Timothy. 1980. Aspects of Bulgarian musical thought. *Yearbook of the International Folk Music Council* 12:42–66.

———. 1987. Toward the remodelling of ethnomusicology. *Ethnomusicology*
31:469–89.

Rosenberg, Neil V. 1980. A preliminary bibliography of Canadian old time instrumental music books. *Canadian Folk Music Journal* 8:20–22.

———. 1984. Review of *Rufus Guinchard: The man and his music. Newfoundland
Quarterly* 79:45.

———. 1985. Newfoundland fiddle recordings: An annotated discography. *Canadian Folk Music Bulletin* 19, no. 3:5–7.

Russell, Kelly. 1979. Liner notes for LP disc *Emile's Dream*. Pigeon Inlet Productions PIP 732. First issued as Quay CS7932 by the Newfoundland Fiddle Association.

——. 1982. *Rufus Guinchard: The man and his music.* St. John's: Harry Cuff.

Sakata, Hiromi Lorraine. 1983. *Music in the mind: The concepts of music and musician in Afghanistan.* Kent, Ohio: Kent State University Press.

Sanjek, Roger. 1990. "On ethnographic validity." In *Fieldnotes: The makings of anthropology*. Ithaca: Cornell University Press.

Schafer, R. Murray. 1977. The Tuning of the World. New York: Knopf.

Scott, John Roper. 1975. The function of folklore in the interrelationship of the Newfoundland seal fishery and the home communities of the sealers. M.A. thesis, Memorial University of Newfoundland.

Seeger, Anthony. 1987. Do we need to remodel ethnomusicology? *Ethnomusicology* 31:491–95.

Seeger, Charles. 1971. Reflections on a given topic: Music in universal perspective. *Ethnomusicology* 15:385–98.

——. 1977. *Studies in musicology, 1935–1975.* Berkeley and Los Angeles: University of California Press.

Sharp, Cecil. [1907] 1965. *English folk song: Some conclusions.* London: Methuen.

Shaw, John. 1978. *Cape Breton Scottish violin.* Booklet accompanying Topic LP disc 12TS354.

Skinner, Chesley John. 1984. Drama in Newfoundland society: The community concert. Ph.D. diss., Michigan State University.

Sloboda, John A. 1985. *The musical mind: The cognitive psychology of music.* Oxford: Clarendon Press.

Smith, Gregory Eugene. 1983. Homer, Gregory, and Bill Evans? The theory of formulaic composition in the context of jazz piano improvisation. Ph.D. diss., Harvard University.

——. 1991. In quest of a new perspective on improvised jazz: A view from the Balkans. *World of Music* 33, no. 3:29–53.

Smith, S. Forthcoming. The constituents of music ethnotheory: An example from the Kuna of Panama. In *Ethnotheory,* edited by M. Herndon. Darby, Pa.: Norwood.

Sound Symposium. 1984. Cassette tape. Edited by Don Wherry. Sound Symposium, St. John's.

Spalding, David. 1985. You and I and nobody knows: Singing our dreams. *Canadian Folk Music Bulletin* 19, no. 4:8–10.

Sparks, Hugh Cullen. 1984. Stylistic development and compositional processes of selected solo singer/songwriters in Austin Texas. Ph.D. diss., University of Texas at Austin.

Spielman, Earl V. 1972. The fiddling traditions of Cape Breton and Texas: A study in parallels and contrasts. *Anuario Interamicano de investigacion musical* 8:39–48.

———. 1975. Traditional North American fiddling: A methodology for the historical and comparative analytical style study of instrumental music. Ph.D. diss., University of Wisconsin.

Stekert, Ellen. 1965. Two voices of tradition: The influence of personality and collecting environment upon the songs of two traditional singers. Ph.D. diss., Indiana University.

Such, David G. 1981. "Out There": A metaphor of transcendence among New York City avant-garde jazz musicians. *New York Folklore* 7:83–93.

Sudnow, David. 1978. *Ways of the hand: The organization of improvised conduct.* Cambridge, Mass.: Harvard University Press.

Swackhammer, Robert McBeth. 1979. "I'm a professional, but I'm not on records": The reflection of a performer's self image in his repertoire. M.A. thesis, Memorial University of Newfoundland.

Szwed, John F. 1970. Paul E. Hall: A Newfoundland song-maker and his community of song. In *Folksongs and their makers,* edited by Henry Glassie, Edward D. Ives, and John F. Szwed, 149–67. Bowling Green: Bowling Green University Popular Press.

Taylor, Irving A. 1975. A retrospective view of creativity investigation. In *Perspectives in creativity,* edited by Irving A. Taylor and J. W. Getzels, 1–36. Chicago: Aldine.

Thede, Marion. 1962. Traditional fiddling. *Ethnomusicology* 6:19–24.

Thomas, Gerald. 1980. Other worlds: The folktale and soap opera in Newfoundland's French tradition. In *Folklore Studies in Honour of Herbert Halpert,* edited by K. S. Goldstein and N. V. Rosenberg, 343–51. St. John's: Memorial University of Newfoundland, Folklore Department.

———. 1981. Contemporary traditional music in Newfoundland. *Bulletin, Canadian Folk Music Society* 15:3–6.

———. 1982. Booklet accompanying *Ça vient du tchoeur/It comes from the heart.* LP disc PIP 7311. Pigeon Inlet Productions.

———. 1983. *Les deux traditions: Le conte populaire chez les Franco-Terreneuviens.* Montreal: Les Editions Bellarmin.

———. 1985. Emile Benoit, Franco-Newfoundland storyteller: Individual and ethnic identity. In *Papers IV: The eighth congress for the International Society for Folk Narrative Research, Bergen, June 12th–17th 1984,* edited by Reimund Kvideland and Tarunn Selberg, 287–98. Bergen: Forlaget Folkekultur.

Tickle Harbour. 1979. *The hare's ears.* Quay CS 7955.

Titon, Jeff Todd. 1978. Every day I have the blues: Improvisation and daily life. *Southern Folklore Quarterly* 42, no. 1:85–98.

———. 1980. The life story. *Journal of American Folklore* 93:276–92.

————. 1992. North America/Black America. In *Worlds of music: An introduction to the music of the world's peoples,* edited by Jeff Todd Titon, 105–65. New York: Schirmer Books.

Treitler, Leo. 1974. Homer and Gregory: The transmission of epic poetry and plainchant. *Musical Quarterly* 60:333–72.

————. 1975. "Centonate" chant: Or E pluribus unus? *Journal of the American Musicological Society* 28:1–23.

————. 1981. Oral, written, and literate process in the transmission of medieval music. *Speculum* 56:471–91.

————. 1991. Medieval improvisation. *World of Music* 33, no. 3:66–91.

Trimillos, Ricardo D. 1987. Guest editor's preface. *Yearbook for Traditional Music* 19:xi.

Wareham, Wilfred W. 1982. Towards an ethnography of "times": Newfoundland party traditions, past and present. Ph.D. diss., University of Pennsylvania.

Wegenast, David. 1979. Finger quick fiddling. *Decks Awash* 8, no. 4:25–26.

Wells, Paul. 1978. *New England traditional fiddling: An anthology of recordings, 1926–1975.* LP record album and booklet, JEMF-105. John Edwards Memorial Foundation.

Wilgus, D. K. 1965. Fiddler's farewell: The legend of the hanged fiddler. *Studia Musicologica* 7:195–209.

————. 1980. The hanged fiddler legend in Anglo-American tradition. In *Folklore on two continents: Essays in honor of Linda Degh,* edited by Nikolai Burlakoff and Carl Lindahl, with Harry Gammerdinger, 120–40. Bloomington: Trickster Press.

————. 1981. Andrew Jenkins, folk composer: An overview. *Lore and Language* 3:109–28.

Wilson, Marjorie. 1977. Passage-through-communitas: An interpretive analysis of enculturation in art education. Ph.D. diss., University of Pennsylvania.

Wolf, John Quincy. 1967. Folksingers and the re-creation of folk song. *Western Folklore* 26:101–11.

Wonderful Grand Band. 1978. *The Wonderful Grand Band.* Quay CS 014.

Zemp, Hugo. 1978. Are'are classification of musical types and instruments. *Ethnomusicology* 22:37–67.

————. 1979. Aspects of Are'are musical theory. *Ethnomusicology* 23:5–48.

Zenger, Dixie Robinson. 1980. "Violin techniques and traditions useful in identifying and playing North American fiddle styles." M.A. thesis. Stanford University.

Zuckerkandl, Victor. 1976. *Man the musician: Sound and symbol.* Vol. 2. Translated by Norbert Guterman. Bollingen Series 44:2. Princeton: Princeton University Press.

Newspapers

Selections from the St. John's *Evening Telegram,* Toronto *Globe and Mail,* and other newspapers cited in the text are held in the Centre d'Etudes Franco-Terreneuviens (CEFT) collections.

Archival Sources

Because much of the archival information I have employed is taken from collections made by other researchers I have provided recording and collector data for these sources here as well as briefly contexting my own materials.

M-tapes, 64-15/C115–17. Recorded on August 15, 1964, by John A. Widdowson in Lourdes and Black Duck Brook. Emile Benoit performed along with friends and family at a dance and later party.

M-MS 72-10. Manuscript transcription of an interview conducted by Donald A. Gale at Emile Benoit's home in Black Duck Brook written December 16, 1971. Don was an acquaintance of Emile's family and a student in an undergraduate folklore class at Memorial University. Though the directed interview was set up, Emile behaves quite naturally, entertaining the assembled family members.

M-tape 73-45/C1424–25. Recorded by I. Shelly Posen and Michael Taft in Aguathuna, September 29, 1972, an interview with Gerry Formanger (Reeves), a musician from Black Duck Brook.

M-tape 73-45/C1426. Recorded by I. Shelly Posen and Michael Taft at Emile Benoit's home in Black Duck Brook on September 30, 1972, an informal, but induced social setting in which Shelley plays guitar with Emile and others present participate to a lesser extent.

M-tape 73-45/C1430. Recorded by I. Shelley Posen and Michael Taft in Stephenville on October 1, 1972, an interview with Neil Shepard about music history in the area.

M-MS 75-307. Transcript of interviews conducted by Earl Spielman with fiddlers in the St. John's area.

M-tape and MS 76-491/C2583–2585. Essay and transcript of recording by Mark Cormier interviewing his brother Victor Cormier, an accordian player, on October 26–27, 1976, at home in Cape St. George.

M-tape and MS 78-239/C3581. Recorded at Black Duck Brook, July 25, 1978, by Kenneth S. Goldstein and Gerald Thomas. Emile, Joachim, and Benjamin Benoit play fiddle separately and together.

M-tape and MS 78-239/C3584. Recorded at Degras, Cape St. George, by Kenneth S. Goldstein and Gerald Thomas, an interview with Cornelius Rouzes, who plays the fiddle and sings.

M-MS 80-406. "'Le Reel du Squelette': Analysis of a Personal Experience Narrative of Emile Benoit of l'Anse-a-Canards, Port-au-Port Peninsula" submitted by Gary Butler. Stored at CEFT.

M-tape 81-045/C5122. Recorded on July 26–27, 1981, by Gerald Thomas, at his home in St. John's, with Wilfred Wareham also present.

M-tapes 81-271/C5257–59. Recorded August 1979 in St. Fintan's by Colin Quigley. Emile is performing with his son Gordon on guitar for a dance and concert.

M-tape 81-502/C5309. Recorded August 21, 1979, at Emile Benoit's home in Black Duck Brook by Colin Quigley. We "trade" tunes and discuss his bowing technique, and he begins to teach me several tunes.

M-tape 81-502/C5310. Recorded August 21, 1979, at Emile Benoit's home in Black Duck Brook by Colin Quigley. Emile teaches more bowing, especially for "St. Anne's Reel" and a third strain of his composition and discusses and demonstrates his singing of fiddle tunes.

M-tape 81-502/C5311. Recorded August 21, 1979, at Emile Benoit's home in Black Duck Brook by Colin Quigley, an interview and fiddle lesson during which Emile and I talked about his life as a musician.

M-tape 81-502/C5312. Recorded August 1979 at Joachim Benoit's home in Black Duck Brook by Colin Quigley with Joachim Benoit. It contains playing of traditional tunes and pieces of his and Emile's composition as well as discussion of their father's and grandfather's fiddling.

M-tape 81-502/C5313. Recorded August 1979 at Emile Benoit's home in Black Duck Brook by Colin Quigley. Just the two of us were present, and Emile plays tunes with little interruption.

M-tape 81-502/C5314. As above, but the next day.

M-tape 81-502/C5315. As above, the next day again. Discussion of "where they come from."

M-tape 81-502/C5316. Recorded in August 1979 at Town and Country Hotel in Grand Falls by Colin Quigley. At first privately in our room, Emile works on his new composition, the "Motorcycle Club Rally Reel." Later in Ed's Lounge, Emile and I perform, Emile clowns and describes his compositions as "Newfoundland work."

M-tape 81-502/C5317–18. Our performance at Ed's Lounge continues from previous tape, then moves to evening concert performance.

M-tape 81-502/C5319. Recorded at Pinewoods Music Camp in Massachusetts on August 25, 1980, Emile is performing informally for a small audience. I occasionally prompt him to tell a particular story, and audience members ask him questions about his life.

M-tape 81-502/C5319. As above on August 24. Emile plays for dance classes.

M-tape 81-502/C5320. As above on August 26. Emile tells stories and plays for dance class.

M-tape 81-502/C5321–24. As above on August 27. Emile tells the "Black Mountain," plays his compositions, and then accompanies a dance class.

M-tape 81-502/C5325. As above on August 28.

M-tape 81-502/C5326. As above on August 29.

M-tape 82-091/C5676. Recorded by Neil V. Rosenberg on April 2, 1982, an interview with Don Randall, well-known fiddler originally from Port Rexton, Trinity Bay.

M-tape 82-095/C5674 with transcript. Recorded by Neil V. Rosenberg at Memorial University April 16, 1982, an interview with Kelly Russell concerning his career and involvement in producing Emile's record albums.

M-photograph 84-400. Color print taken by Clara Murphy of Emile Benoit during March 1983; #50, held in CEFT collections.

M-photograph 84-416. Color print taken by Barry Rowe of Emile Benoit during March 1984; #35, held in CEFT collections.

M-tape 84-562/C7275. Recorded by K. Kimiecik, October 17, 1984, at Memorial University of Newfoundland in St. John's. Emile speaks to a Folklore Department "brown bag lunch," introduced by Gerald Thomas.

M-MS 86-139. Transcript of interview with Emile Benoit recorded in March 1986 at his home in Black Duck Brook by Elaine C. Pelley and unnumbered tapes, housed in CEFT collection.

M-MS 86-143. Transcript of interview with Emile Benoit recorded at his home in Black Duck Brook on March 11, 1986, by Tod Saunders and unnumbered tapes, housed in CEFT collection.

Q-tape 1. Kevin and Ronnie Cornect recorded June 15, 1984, at Kevin's home in Mainland, mostly bluegrass songs but some "jigs" on mandolin and general conversation about music in their family. Songs also recorded on Nagra IV.

Q-tape 2. Kevin and Ronnie Cornect as above. Side B: Vincent Cornect recorded June 17, 1984, at his home in Mainland. Accordion music and general conversation. Some pieces of his own composition. Also recorded on Nagra.

Q-tape 3. Vincent Cornect, as above.

Q-tape 8. Emile Benoit interviewed July 2, 1984, in my car on the way to Black Duck Brook.

Q-tape 9. Recorded on July 3, 1985, at Emile Benoit's home in Black Duck Brook, Quigley, Emile, and Jerry McDonald talking.

Q-tape 14. A copy of Emile's practice tape from June 1984, which he made during a visit to his daughter's home in Massachussetts. It contains his newest compositions, as well as some old pieces he remembered and "protopieces."

Q-tapes 15 and 16. Copy, recorded during July 1984 through speaker of home stereo system, of "party" tapes recorded by Terry Chaisson (from Mainland) of local musicians: Bernie Felix, Vincent Cornect, Robert Felix, Mattis Benoit, and Harry Chaisson.

Q-tape 17. Recorded at the Sound Symposium in St. John's on July 16, 1984, Emile performing for a small audience with other musicians taking turns in a workshop format.

Q-tape 20. Recorded July 18, 1984, at Gerald Thomas's home in Torbay, a directed interview of several hours' length in which I pressed Emile to elaborate on the concepts of balance and rhyme.

Q-tape 30. Recorded December 22, 1983, at Gerald Thomas's home in Torbay. It contains tunes and discussion of composition technique.

Q-tape 32. Emile Benoit recorded by Kelly Russell in April 1977. It contains six tunes in response to Kelly's request for French tunes. Side B, Newfoundland Old Time Fiddle Music by the Shamrocks.

Q-tape 33. Emile Benoit recorded by Kelly Russell.

Q-tape 34. Recorded by Kelly Russell. Side A: Emile Benoit November 12, 13, 1977, at the Good Entertainment I Festival held in the community arts center (formerly the Longshoreman's Protective Union Hall). Side B: Emile in January 1978.

Q-tape 35. Recorded by Kelly Russell. Emile Benoit tells "The Beast with Seven Heads" and "Jack and the Seven Skins" on November 12, 1977, at the Good Entertainment I Festival.

Q-tape 36. Recorded by Kelly Russell, n.d. Side A: Ron Formanger, Ivan White, Ed Doucette. Side B: Ed Doucette.

Q-tape 37. Recorded by Kelly Russell, January 1979. Side A: Cornelius Rouzes, Ron Formanger. Side B: Emile Benoit.

Q-tape 38. Recorded by Kelly Russell. Emile Benoit, April 1979 (tunes for *Emile's Dream*); July 1979 at Bridgett's Club in St. John's.

Q-tape 39. Recorded by Kelly Russell, Ed Doucette performs.

Q-tape 40. Recorded by Kelly Russell, his #23. Ed Doucette with Gerry Formanger, guitar.

Q-tape 45. Recorded on March 10, 1985, at Emile Benoit's home in Black Duck Brook. An interview and copy of his then current practice tape.

Q-tape 46. An interview recorded on March 10, 1985, at Emile Benoit's home in Black Duck Brook.

Q-tape 47. An interview recorded on March 11, 1985, at Emile Benoit's home in Black Duck Brook.

Q-tape 48. An interview recorded on March 11, 1985, at Emile Benoit's home in Black Duck Brook.

Q-tape 49. Recorded March 22, 1985, at Gerald Thomas's home in Torbay while videotaping.

Q-tape 51. Recorded on August 4, 1985, at Emile Benoit's home in Black Duck Brook during a visit by my wife, another couple, and me. After an afternoon helping Emile bring in his hay, we spent a few hours in the evening chatting and playing music. I took advantage of the visit to ask about several tunes and topics I felt were not well documented.

Q-tape 54. Recorded on August 14, 1987, at Emile Benoit's home in Black Duck Brook by Isabelle Peere. Emile, and his son Mike Benoit (on accordion), and I were playing music in the evening. Mike reacted critically to Emile's slow compositions.

Q-tapes 57 and 58. Recorded June 1987 at Memorial University. Gerald Thomas discussed his recent trip with Emile to France and answered my questions about their relationship.

Q-tapes 67 and 68. Recorded at Gerald Thomas's home July 18, 1984, on the Nagra IV. Emile plays recent compositions at my request.

Q-tapes 69 and 70. Recorded at Emile Benoit's home in Black Duck Brook on March 10, 1985, on the Nagra IV. Emile plays recent compositions at my request.

Videotape. Recorded at Gerald Thomas's home in St. John's on March 22, 1985. In an interview I requested Emile to illustrate playing techniques and perform particular tunes and narratives. Gerald and Wilfred Wareham, also present, assisted.

∼ Bibliographical Essay

Fiddle Tunes, Fiddlers, and Fiddling

Traditional fiddling as found in Newfoundland has only recently begun to receive some attention through LP album releases, regional folk festivals, archival collection, and graduate research at Memorial University of Newfoundland, but the resources available for its study are not insignificant. The early collectors of folk song in this province left several tune transcriptions and descriptions of the dance events that provided the primary venue for public performance. The Memorial University of Newfoundland Folklore and Language Archive (MUNFLA) contains rich contextual documentation of dance events. This has been summarized and incorporated into my study of traditional dancing in Newfoundland, *Close to the Floor: Folk Dance in Newfoundland* (1985). MUNFLA holds, as well, recordings of many fiddlers, representing much of the province. Supplemented by the personal recordings of Kelly Russell, who has made collecting trips on the west coast of the island and along the Labrador coast with the financial support of the Canada Council (Q-tapes 32–40), a good sample of actual playing can be assembled. Russell is also responsible, through his company Pigeon Inlet Productions, for several LP discs which include other unique documents of Newfoundland fiddling (Rosenberg 1985). Interviews with fiddlers from throughout the province have been particularly useful in discerning typical patterns of individual response to historical developments affecting this tradition (M-tapes 73-45/C1424–25, C1426, C1430; MS 75-307; tape 82-091/C5676; tape 82-095/C5674 transcript).

Important background for this study has been provided by previous academic studies of North American fiddle music. The most ambitious of these have included several dissertations, of which Linda Burman-Hall's "Southern American Folk Fiddling: Context and Style" (1973) was the first. Although extramusical features of

fiddling tradition are largely excluded from her analysis, Burman-Hall does acknowledge their importance and suggests that her "music-based analysis of regional
sub-styles of the South within the British-American tradition may eventually be
correlated with . . . [different] sociological and ethnomusicological approaches"
(113). Her most recent publication on fiddling is perhaps the best condensed treatment of the American tradition as a whole in print, integrating observations from
several of her earlier studies (Burman-Hall 1984). While providing a valuable overview, Burman-Hall's perspective remains largely historical and does not attempt to
penetrate into the concepts of its practitioners. Earl V. Spielman has also addressed
the issue of what factors should be considered in a comparative stylistic study of
fiddle music (1975). Spielman extended the geographical range of his comparisons beyond the South to include Canada and the northeastern and midwestern
United States. Style areas in Canada which he identifies are Scottish, Irish, and
French, along with an "Old-Time" rubric for more modern contest-style fiddling.
Burman-Hall's Blue Ridge and southern Appalachian areas are conflated into an
Appalachian/southern region. He also conducted interviews with fiddlers in New-
foundland, the texts of which are held by the Memorial University Folklore and
Language Archive, but has never published any of this material (M-MS 75-307).
I found these interviews useful in gaining a broader picture of fiddling traditions
throughout Newfoundland.

Delimitation of North American fiddling styles is a continuing process (Goertzen 1983, 11–12). Dixie Zenger, for example, has distinguished some of the same
styles but adds Cajun to the list (Zenger 1980). Certainly, many more might be
considered, such as those of various Scandinavian groups or the native peoples of
Canada who have adopted the fiddle as their own (Lederman 1987; Bennett 1985).
Of greater interest in the present context than the different stylistic boundaries
drawn is that most writers address the explanation of the differences they discover
only as a secondary question. When it is considered, a combination of cultural heritage and constraints imposed by different settings for performance is presented as
sufficient to account for stylistic variation. The individuals' dynamic role in bringing these influences together in the framework of their own values, experience, and
aspirations is largely overlooked.

Fiddling traditions in the northern and eastern regions of North America are
less well covered by scholars than those of the American South. Paul Wells offers
a useful social history of fiddling in New England, along with recorded examples
of various styles that have influenced fiddling in this area (1978). Some of these
same influences have been felt as far away as Newfoundland, especially those of
Cape Breton and Quebec. The great wealth of Quebecois fiddling has not been adequately surveyed in print, although Lisa Ornstein (1982) provides a brief overview
of its study, history, and repertoire. Cape Breton fiddling has only recently begun
to receive much scholarly attention. The notes accompanying the Topic LP disc
Cape Breton Scottish Violin and K. E. Dunlay's introduction to her tune collection

incorporate stylistic descriptions (Shaw 1978; Dunlay and Reich 1986). Virginia Garrison (1985) provides more information about the social aspects of fiddling in Cape Breton. The commercial recording of Cape Breton fiddling has been thoroughly examined by Ian McKinnon (1989), who provides extensive discography and tune annotations along with a narrative history of this recording genre and consideration of its effect on tradition. Fiddling on Prince Edward Island has been studied by James Hornby of Memorial University (1983). Though strongly influenced by Cape Breton, Prince Edward Island fiddlers retain a degree of regional identity. Irish and Scottish traditions, both important influences in the Northeast, are better represented in academic literature as well as in popular collections and on recordings. James Porter (1989) provides an up-to-date and comprehensive bibliographic guide.

Following the surveys of Burman-Hall and Spielman, which identified major style areas, at least in the American South, several academic studies appeared which address extramusical elements of fiddling tradition. Richard Blaustein (1975) has examined the social context of the so-called revival of traditional fiddling that swept the United States in the late 1960s. He argues that the establishment of "old time fiddlers associations" across the country represents a revitalization movement in response to radical social change. Illustrating the ways in which the social history of fiddling in North America fits anthropological models of social change, he provides perhaps the best overview of this tradition in its social context. Burt Feintuch (1983b) covers much the same ground in a very condensed manner. While Blaustein primarily addresses issues of social context, Feintuch (1975) focuses on an individual musician. He demonstrates that his informant's fiddling represents a particular mode of communication through performance which Feintuch identifies as folkloric; such performance employs a number of modalities, including oral-aural, kinesic, tactile, thermal, and proxemic subsystems. Although he presents many useful observations of his informants' performance practice and a few comments on his ideas about the music, Feintuch's basic concern is with exemplifying a model of folkloric communication. In "A Fiddler's Life" (1984–85) he drops the pseudonym used in the dissertation and presents a brief biography of this performer. In "Examining Musical Motivation: Why Does Sammie Play the Fiddle" (1983a), Feintuch shows a continued interest in the study of performers and a further development of issues well addressed through such study but disappointingly draws very limited conclusions. Robert Swackhammer (1979) has also addressed the relationship of a particular fiddler's life, his self-image, and his repertoire, offering an intimate and detailed glimpse into the musical life of another Newfoundland fiddler, providing more directly comparable information for this investigation. Allen Feldman and Eamonn O'Doherty's *Northern Fiddler* (1979) is a collection that incorporates a good deal of information about fiddlers from Northern Ireland along with selected repertoire. Although somewhat preoccupied with their collecting experience and the decline of this tradition, they provide data suggestive of relationships among personality, repertoire, and style. They are critical of the "revival" in Ireland, which has selectively chosen its models from the variety of local traditions and thus, in their eyes, contributed to the decline of traditional styles they found in this region; they question their own role as collectors in this process. They also provide a rare glimpse of the people behind a tradition through transcriptions of interviews with the performers. What is needed is more such conversations, analyzed in a more systematic fashion and integrated more closely with a musical analysis.

Although stylistic comparison, variation technique, social context, and, to a more limited extent, biographical context have been important parts of the scholarly approach to fiddling traditions, regional collections constitute the bulk of published work. Samuel Bayard's *Dance to the Fiddle, March to the Fife* (1982) provides perhaps the best model for such studies. Following the established format for comparable folk song collections, he publishes multiple versions of each tune, providing data about their sources and comparative notes citing appearances in other major collections. Despite the usefulness of detailed and extensive scholarly apparatus, however, such collections reveal the limitations of even the best of such works. Although it provides an invaluable tool for comparative tune study, it does not offer much beyond a few introductory remarks about the social worlds of the fiddlers and their audiences and the meaning systems that imbue this music with significance for them.

Unfortunately, in addition to their built-in shortcomings, most collections do not live up to the scholarly standards set by Bayard's work. Most tune collections are addressed to a popular audience primarily interested in them as sources for new repertoire. Tunes are given in single versions of presumably heavily edited skeletal notation without accompanying notes, and very little information is provided about the performers or the collectors. This may appear understandable in popular publications, but even collections with scholarly aspirations seem to be influenced by the format of such works, perhaps in the hope of increased sales. Given the lack of publications that meet scholarly standards, however, the student of these traditions should treat such sources with caution.

Although this discussion has by no means provided a complete review of the resources for study of North American fiddling traditions or even of the academic literature addressed to this topic, the studies considered do represent and perhaps best exemplify the major concerns expressed in that literature. Useful bibliographical sources for the large body of fiddling-related publications include Hickerson and Holzberg (1974), Mendelson (1975–77), Miller (1986, 216–22), and for Canada more specifically Hogan and Hogan (1977), Rosenberg (1980), and Lederman (1985).

Creativity, Tradition, and the Folk Performer

Performer-centered studies have a long history in folklore, and recognition of the creative contributions of individual musicians, although not pursued as a topic of investigation to any great degree, can be found quite early. The folk song scholar Phillips Barry, not surprisingly given his attitudes toward folk song creation, noted the importance of this source of variation and cited Patrick W. Joyce's *Ancient Irish Music* (1873) as the earliest statement that "the conscious artistry of individual folk musicians, both instrumentalists and singers," was a factor of equal importance to *zersingen* (Barry 1939, 102). Joyce, noting that the degree of variation among similar tunes ranged from insignificant to great, suggested that some changes were the result of imperfect transmission; others may have been

> made deliberately as improvements by fiddlers, pipers or singers—each change slight in itself—but without any intention of altering the whole into what might be called a different melody. And it is easy to understand, what indeed has now frequently happened, that in this manner, an air might in course of time, be altered gradually and almost insensibly, note by note as it were so as ultimately to become nearly unrecognizable. But I think it will appear clear to any one who studies the subject attentively, that sometimes airs were changed in a totally different way; that occasionally some skilful musician deliberately altered an air all at once, with the direct intention of converting it into a different melody altogether. (Barry 1939, 101 citing Joyce 1873, 22)

He goes on to suggest ways in which such alterations might typically be made. Just how different such compositional processes are from the norms of transmission is a topic addressed elsewhere. I would note here that essential element is intent rather than musical competence.

A few recent, though short, studies have addressed related issues. In "Manco Sneed and the Indians: These Cherokee Don't Make Much Music" Blanton Owen cites Henry Glassie's insistence on the need to study performers to determine "some of the reasons—psychological, social, and cultural—which allow and direct this person to do what he does in the way he does it." An emphasis on studying items, he suggests, tells us at best "something of the normative patterns within a tradition." We need to seek out "the most innovative and creative participants" in order to examine the "limits of acceptable artistic creativity within a tradition" (Owen 1980, 59). My interest lies not only in such limits but also in the generative concepts underlying musical creation in this idiom. Jean-Pierre Joyal's approach to musical creativity in "Le processus de composition dans la musique instrumentale du Québec" (1980) emphasizes variation and transformation. He compares five versions of the same piece and demonstrates how an American hornpipe, the "Democratic Rage Hornpipe," could be transformed into the characteristic "Reel du Québec." This remaking he attributes to "l'inspiration populaire et le genie createur du musicien traditionnel" (1980, 53). Unfortunately, in this brief article he does not pursue the further delineation of these forces.

There are many precedents in scholarly studies of folk song, narrative, and material culture which consider particular performers or producers and their creative processes. These provide alternate analytic models for consideration and suggest hypotheses I have tested here on this somewhat different material.

Interest in the people who produce folklore items has waxed and waned during the history of folkloristics, but there has always been some acknowledgment of the importance of the performers, especially in the work of scholars who engaged in fieldwork. We know, for example, that the Grimms recorded many of their stories from the vivacious Frau Viehmann. We know a few things about eighteenth- and nineteenth-century Scottish ballad singers, such as the large repertoire and unusual performance style of Bell Robertson, who recited her ballads, and how Mrs. Anna Brown acquired her songs. Mrs. Brown in particular has been the subject of much study and debate because of the prominent role she plays in David Buchan's application of Lord's oral formulaic theory of composition to the British ballads (Buchan 1972; Bronson 1969, 64–78; Andersson and Pettit 1979; Gower 1973).

But beyond a few bare biographical facts, we learn little about these performers from those to whom they gave so much material. The scholars' interests lay elsewhere, usually with questions of origin and dissemination, and as a result they were preoccupied with their informants' repertoires as part of a larger data base. Most nineteenth-century scholars acknowledge their informants much as an antiquary might describe a manuscript—as the source from which they gathered a particular item. Scholars were not much interested in the performers themselves or why they performed the items they did in the ways they did.

An exception to this norm, opposed to the general trend in the nineteenth century toward the classification of folklore data, is the work of the Russian folklorists beginning with Gilferding's work on the epic songs known as *byliny* (1877), which established a pattern of individual repertoire study. This work was extended to folktale study by Onchukov (1908), who noted that the personal taste of narrators was crucial in perpetuating certain tales (Azadowski 1974, 1–10). In general the Russian scholars emphasized the performers' biographies, showing how the tales contained traces of their personal experience. Study of the style of narrators was made in conjunction with the changes they made in the traditional subject matter in order to avoid viewing "tradition" mechanistically, as something external to its producers.

Mark Azadowski extended this line of investigation by drawing attention to the importance of the narrator as a creative individual. Given that "the goal of research is to determine those formative forces which govern the generation of the folktale," he notes,

> The importance of the narrator does not lie in the details which insinuate
> themselves from the outside world (that of the narrator). The folktale, like

every other product of art, has at its basis a definite artistic purpose. . . .
[Thus] discovery of this artistic purpose, analysis of the artistic plan is one of
the most important tasks. . . . [This is] inseparably bound up with the study
of the creative individual. Thus the problem of the personality of the narrator
in the creative process of the folktale. . . . Narrowly conceived biographical studies must make way for the study of the artistic physiognomy of the
narrator, repertoire, and style. (1974, 12)

After Azadowski's work, however, the ideological climate in the Soviet Union encouraged an emphasis on collectivity in folklore studies and his recommendations
were not followed by Soviet scholars.

Hungarian folklorists were much influenced by the Russians, however, and
they continued to incorporate investigation of the narrator's personality in their
studies. They published several collections of individual repertoires during the
1940s. These studies proceed from a general anthropological and ethnic overview to
the art and style of the individual. How the community received the narrative and
what part the community itself had in its formation is also considered. Emphasis
is thus primarily on community and shared tradition. In her *Folktales and Society*
(1969), Linda Dégh includes a review of the Russian and Hungarian research and
carries out her own program. She has gone on to systematize the "sociological"
approach, emphasizing the importance of reliable, exact, and repeated recording
of material in the field. The creative "type" of the narrator is only one factor to be
considered in her approach to the study of narrating traditions.

Phillips Barry called attention to the importance of the folk singer in making
Anglo-American balladry (1961, 1933). He was interested in investigating both the
generation of folk songs and their subsequent modification. He saw this process as
one of individual invention and "communal recreation." The latter involved both
unconscious change, which he called *zersingen*, and consciously creative modification. Knowledge of the individual composer and singer was thus important for an
understanding of the process of tradition, which he sought to show could account
for many aspects of ballad style.

The 1970 anthology of articles *Folk Songs and Their Makers* is an important
attempt to study the generation of folk songs in Anglo-American tradition (Glassie,
Ives, and Szwed 1970). In it Henry Glassie proposes what might be called the deviant hypothesis. He contends that the folk song creators he has studied deviate
in important ways from their societal norms and suggests that perhaps such mar-
ginality is necessary for freeing people to engage in the risky business of creation
(Glassie 1970, 49–50). John Szwed studies a song composed by a lifetime bachelor
in a small Newfoundland community, showing how the song reflects his somewhat
marginal position in the society and the composer's view of its norms (1970, 156–
66). Edward Ives attempts to define "creativity" in a way more in harmony with
the generally conservative values of traditional singing than are the term's usual
connotations of extreme originality. He cites three levels of creativity: (1) "the cre-

ativity of the individual performer brought to bear on a particular performance"; (2) that which "occurs when a singer makes changes in a particular song in order to make what he considers a better song out of it"; and (3) that which "occurs when an entirely new song is created" (1970a, 72–73).

Ives has studied song makers in the Northeast throughout his career (1964, 1970b, 1979). His method is to reconstruct subjects' biographies from oral and documentary sources, identify the circumstances in which particular ballads were composed, and examine their subsequent modification, preservation, or disappearance. In his study of Lawrence Doyle (1970b), Ives finds an exception to the deviant model, which was followed more closely by his earlier subject Larry Gorman, a misfit composer of satirical songs (1964). The conclusions in Ives's most recent book, *Joe Scott* (1979), challenge the usual view of tradition as essentially conservative. He notes, for example, the wide acceptance and continued integrity of Joe's somewhat idiosyncratic ballads. It is through acceptance of such new forms, created by individuals with distinctive personal styles, he suggests, that tradition changes and develops (1979, 423). Ives touches briefly on the nature of the creative process, wondering whether Joe Scott's ballads represent reality cast in conventional narrative forms or if the conventions of form have shaped perception itself. This and other questions about the conceptual dimensions of the creative process remain inaccessible, however, because Ives works with historical figures rather than living creators (1979, 406–7). He is better able to examine the subsequent recreative process. In contrast to Barry's formulation, he finds that the individual song maker, not the recreative process of transmission, is the "primary alembic" responsible for the character of the songs (1979, 423).

Probably the most important single study during this century of the creative process in singing—particularly the textual aspects of epic songs—is Albert Lord's *The Singer of Tales* ([1960]/1970). In this now classic work Lord develops the concept of oral formulaic composition to account for the ability of illiterate peasant singers to compose epic songs many thousand lines long. In this genre composition and performance are a single act. The singers realize their idea of the story anew in each performance. Their knowledge of a repertoire of poetic formulas and how to weave these together enables them to do this. Many scholars since Lord have attempted to show the relevance of this model to other genres of oral poetry, including Anglo-American balladry (Buchan 1972). The issue, however, remains controversial (Friedman 1983).

Several authors who have applied this model to the study of musical forms have been primarily concerned with the extension of Lord and Parry's concept of the verbal formula in Yugoslavian epic poetry (Smith 1983; Adler 1980). The concept is problematic because music does not break down quite so easily into units comparable to words.

Other researchers studying Anglo-American ballads have focused their attention on the recreative role of particular singers. Percy Grainger (1908, 1915), like

Phillips Barry, called attention to this role early in the century. But as in the study of folktales and narrators, the singers went largely unnoticed until the general shift of emphasis away from classification and comparative study of texts alone.

Ellen Stekert's "Two Voices of Tradition" (1965) is one of the first studies to examine at length the relationship of personality and, more especially, collecting environment to repertoire. She distinguishes several types of change attributable to the performer: unconscious influence; conscious alteration; and creativity, which weds "to influence and alteration the fashioning hand of individual taste. Creativity involves the developing, changing, or reordering of material by the artist-manipulator to achieve a desired effect on his audience. Whether the product of this creativity is 'good,' 'bad,' 'beautiful,' or even 'art,' depends on the particular group aesthetic of the observer" (12). She finds that creativity in the repertoires of her informants is seen through the changes and interpretations they have made in tune and text, the way they perform their songs, the songs they choose to perform, and the songs they have chosen to learn (22). Stekert "shows clear evidence of the effect of personality upon repertoire and, thereby, upon the oral traditions of which these two men [her informants] were major custodians," finding that "the singer's personality will determine to a greater or lesser extent: how he reacts to, and how he learns from, his tradition; how and why he performs the materials he chooses; to whom he performs it; how he changes it" (40).

I find Stekert's use of standard psychological tests to profile the personalities of her informants less convincing than her reflective examination of the influence of the collecting environment on her data. Robert A. LeVine concludes in a review of such tests that they are inappropriate for use by anthropologists in the field.

> The contemporary anthropologist seeking a method of personality assessment for comparative study finds that: reputable personality psychologists do not agree on which method is best for measuring any particular disposition; different methods measuring the "same" disposition correlate poorly or not at all, yielding differing distributions of results for the same group of individuals; and there is doubt and disagreement about the extent to which the methods tap enduring dispositions of the person or his reactions to the immediate conditions under which the behavior is sampled. (1982, 173).

In my fieldwork for this study I felt that employing such tests would have been awkward and not especially revealing. I opted, rather, for a self-consciously subjective and reflective research strategy attempting to employ what has been called the "orthodox conception of agents," that is, assumptions that allow the interpretation of behavior in everyday life, to understand Emile and his musical behavior (LeVine 1982, 295; Macdonald and Petit 1981, 61–66, 101–4).

John Quincy Wolf (1967) has treated a related subject, identifying a variety of attitudes toward changing songs among traditional singers from the Ozarks. These attitudes ranged from reverence for traditional texts and thoughtful editing of texts to achieve coherent narratives, to rather free variation on the spur of the moment. The resulting effects on traditional repertoire items would fall into Stekert's category of change resulting from conscious alterations.

Roger Abrahams (1970a) has investigated creativity and individuality among a few traditional singers in greater depth. He presents the traditional singer Almeda Riddle's commentary on her repertoire and reminiscences in a book-length study; in another article (1970b), he contrasts her attitudes with those of another Ozark singer, Marybird MacAllester. Like Stekert, Abrahams notes the importance of choice of repertoire as an expression of personality and values, and delves more deeply than Wolf into the nature and causes of different attitudes toward songs which may result in editing or variation.

Eleanor Long (1973) has attempted to summarize and systematize some of the findings of those who have examined the personalities of singers and narrators. She identifies four types of "folk artistry" in a typology similar to those proposed by the Russian narrative scholars previously discussed (Dégh 1969, 173–75). This scheme has been criticized for suggesting that individuals may be so typed, implying a false hierarchy and equating performers of different generic forms (Porter 1980, 21–22), Long did not intend her observations to be taken that way. Her purpose was primarily to relate kinds of variant texts to possible performers' attitudes that could be deduced from documentation in the literature at that time (personal communication from Eleanor Long 1987).

Porter's study of Jeannie Robertson's singing of the ballad "My Son David" suggests just how complicated the relationship of performer and repertoire may be (Porter 1976). He examines performances of this piece over a span of many years, over which important changes occurred in her conception of herself and her singing, finding significant alteration in the text and music of the ballad, both conscious and unconscious. He proposes a model to relate the deep-structural conception of the song to its surface manifestation in performance. In a subsequent article Porter suggests that the study of singers' conceptions of their songs, their singing of them, and especially the "complex of meanings the singer brings to the song in the context of daily life" be referred to as their "epistemics" (Porter 1986, 125). It is just such a composite of "content, structure, texture, aesthetics, and contextual feedback" which I have addressed in this investigation.

The study of objects from this perspective has in general lagged behind the study of narrating and singing. Stories and songs are rather clearly the output of social and conceptual processes, but objects are tangible, thus the need for conceptualization of the subject matter of study as process rather than product has not been so strong. One study of making objects that stands out in this respect is Michael Owen Jones's *The Handmade Object and Its Maker* (1975) and its subsequent revision and further development as *Craftsman of the Cumberlands* (1989), which investigates the chairmaking of a particular individual. In attempting to account for the character of this artisan's products, Jones is forced to take into account the man's motivations, technology, conceptualizations, and relations with others, including his family, suppliers, and clients. His conclusions challenge the relevance of style as a concept that can account for the character of objects, question then current definitions of aesthetics and art, and suggest that his informant's behavior evinces processes basic to human creativity everywhere. In their thoroughgoing processional perspective Jones's studies provide a model for similar studies of other forms of expressive behavior.

Interest in the study of folklore as "performance and communication," which emerged in the late 1960s, brought with it a new perspective on the study of performers' creativity (Ben-Amos and Goldstein 1975, 1). Investigative focus shifted from text to context and a folklore was reconceptualized as the "realization of known traditional material [with an emphasis] upon the constitution of a social event, quite likely with emergent properties. . . . The concern is with performance, not as something mechanical or inferior, as in some linguistic discussion, but with performance as something creative, realized, achieved, even transcendent of the ordinary course of events" (Hymes 1975, 13). Not long after, this approach gained currency in ethnomusicology (Herndon and Brunyate 1975). In their essays on the ethnography of musical performance Herdon and McLeod, for example, have suggested that Richard Bauman's conception of the "emergent quality of performance" provides a means to address the question of creativity in performance. This quality, they observe, "resides in the interplay between communicative resources, individual competence, and the goals of the participants within the context of particular situations" (Herndon and McLeod 1980a, 191).

In general, however, ethnomusicological concern with musicians' creativity has addressed the role of composers in a cross-cultural comparative framework. Dennison Nash, in his comparative survey "The Role of the Composer," noted that inadequate data concerning composers in different cultures and preconceptions derived from modern Western cultures presented major obstacles to a comparative survey (1961, 81–82). Unfortunately, these still remain to a large degree. Alan Merriam has provided a preliminary cross-cultural survey of compositional processes, primarily among African and Native American peoples, identifying these in general terms and emphasizing that composition is the product of individuals, not some collective entity. Most suggestive for my study has been his identification of composition as part of the learning process which is "shaped by public acceptance or rejection, learned by the individuals who practice it," and which contributes to music change and stability (Merriam 1964, 165–84).

Improvisation is another topic of investigation bearing upon issues of creativity in tradition that has been of interest to ethnomusicologists. Improvisation has been defined in a variety of ways which are effectively reviewed by Gregory Smith (1983, 16–34). He argues that there is a lack of terminology to describe the relationship between improvisation and recreative processes in the performance of music transmitted person-to-person and retained through memory, which "reflects the lack of a clear understanding as to how the process differs from improvisation and from the written composition of music" (34–35). He is particularly concerned with improvisation in jazz (1991). Leo Treitler has explored the nature of improvisation in the context of medieval music (1974, 1975, 1981, 1991), arguing that the presence of formulaic units in music termed "centonate" result from oral transmission (1981); an original emphasis on distinguishing traditional formulas and original material in such repertoires has given way to "attention to the principles underlying the music" (Chew 1980, 57). Jack M. Bevil (1984) applies this analytic approach to Anglo-American folk song melody. Jeff Titon has examined improvisational processes in the blues (1978; 1992, 139–40). Several recent publications provide wide-ranging comparative perspectives on this topic: *L'Improvisation dans les musiques de tradition orale* offers an overview together with many particular studies (Lortat-Jacob 1987); the *Yearbook for Traditional Music* 19 (1987) brings together articles on the theme of "creativity, particularly the process of improvisation" (Trimillos 1987, xi); and Bruno Nettl has returned to the topic of improvisation repeatedly (1954, 1974, 1982, 1983), most recently editing a collection titled "New Perspectives on Improvisation" in *The World of Music* (1991).

The few early references to generative processes in folk music scholarship and studies of fiddling traditions which specifically address musicians' creativity were noted previously. They do not reflect dominant scholarly concerns or represent a thorough examination of the subject. Indeed, Western folk music in general has not been widely examined from this viewpoint. Several additional studies, however, have a bearing on the present investigation. Although varied in depth and orientation, they often present useful comparative data and suggest possible models of the composition process for consideration. In his brief comments in "Andrew Jenkins, Folk Composer" (1981), D. K. Wilgus has "begged the question" of what is a folk composer but declines to answer it directly. Rejecting as definitive criteria the entrance of his songs into oral tradition and the presence of "traditional elements and patterns in his work," Wilgus leaves the categorization of Jenkins open for debate, while ably documenting the importance of this creator in relation to American folk song tradition (115). In passing, he comments that Jenkins, "like many—I would say usual folk composers . . . utilized a small number of tunes" (123), suggesting that some generative process based on a few "tune models" may be at work. Thorkild Knudsen's LP disc production treating a Scottish Gaelic poet, *Calum Ruadh: Bard of Skye* (1978), which is accompanied by detailed transcriptions, includes audio documentation of the process of composing one song. Recollections of its creation were elicited and several variants juxtaposed to create "an impression of how different snatches of melody might be circling round in the bard's unconscious memory to be selected by him and used creatively as an effective vehicle for his words" (Cooke 1978). Peter Cooke suggests selection from preexisting melodic units as the generative process in his descriptive commentary to the album. Knudsen does not, however, develop a more thorough analysis of his data in what is primarily an "audio portrait" of the bard. Svend Nielsen's *Stability in Musical Improvisation: A Repertoire of Icelandic Epic Songs* (1982) is a detailed examination of one singer's musical practices. The genre of *rimur* is much more improvisatory than the relatively fixed melodies of Anglo-American folk songs and fiddle tunes. Nevertheless, his discovery of a few alternate melodic models and intonations from which the singer may choose in improvisatory performances is suggestive of possible ways to view Emile's musical cognition. Hugh Sparks's dissertation, "Stylistic Development and Compositional Processes of Selected Solo Singer/Songwriters in Austin, Texas," includes a chapter on the process of composition which is rich in interview data on the attitudes toward composing of his ten informants and suggestive of many comparisons with my own findings (1984, 104–42). The bulk of this study, however, is devoted to developing musical models of style based on melody, harmony, rhythm, and form (5).

There are many more studies that focus on particular performers, but the preceding examples should serve to illustrate the concerns that have led researchers to employ this approach in the past, to suggest some of their conclusions, and to offer models for further development. The relationship of personality and tradition has been a particularly important preoccupation. Although the significance of the relationship has been clearly demonstrated, the several typological schemes proposed as a result reflect the researchers' preoccupation with accounting for observed variation in traditional texts. Studies emphasizing the transmission and expression of worldview in the repertoires of traditional performers explore this relationship further by offering richer portraits of their informants and representing their repertoires more fully. Studies of individual creativity within traditions may incorporate biographical, psychological, and social data to explain innovative behavior in particular forms but in general have investigated the performers' perceptions insufficiently, thus slighting the cognitive dimensions of their topic. This is especially true of folk musical traditions whose practitioners are apparently thought of as musical illiterates. Though perhaps true, this does not mean that they are musically ignorant or without musical concepts that deserve examination.

~ Index

167; kitchen, 9; music, 49; Port au
Port Set, 156, 171
"David's Reel": notation to, 119
"Debbie's Waltz": notation to, 145
Declamando ending, 176
Deep structure, 103
Dégh, Linda, 257
"Delyth's Desire," 73; notation to, 137
Devil, 46–49
"Devil Among the Tailors," 11
"Devil's Reel," 177
"Dianne's Happiness": notation to, 123
Dinn, Noel, 133, 205
Disney Productions film, 191, 205–6
Doherty, John, 223–24 (n. 6)
Dougherty, Johnny, 227 (n. 4)
Dreams, 54–56, 222 (n. 13)
Drinking, 169
Drone, 154

Egalitarian values, 177
Emile as symbol, 205–6
"Emile's Dream," 94; notation to, 122;
rhythm in, 157
Emile's Dream, 191
"Emile's First Tunes": notation to,
110–11
Ensemble performance, 200
Epistemics, 260
Ethnography: method, 216 (n. 1);
writing, 215 (n. 1)
Ethnomusicology, x, xi, 37, 106, 212,
216 (n. 1), 261
Ethnotheory, 107, 211, 225 (n. 4)
Evaluation, 74, 90, 101. See also
Composition
Experimentation, 74, 79. See also
Composition
Extramusical associations, 68, 102, 197,
228 (n. 9)

Faith, 31–32. See also Values

Feintuch, Burt, 221 (n. 3), 223 (n. 16),
253
Feld, Stephen, 222 (n. 10)
Feldman, Allen, 253
Festival, 24–25, 39; performance, 186;
Pinewoods Camp, 186; presenters,
186
"Fiddle concerto," 205
Fiddle tune: collections, 254; form, 84,
87; rhythm, 155–58; structure, 107;
template, 88
Fiddling: North American, 251–53;
styles, 17, 40, 45, 164, 171, 205, 217
(n. 6), 219 (n. 10), 222 (n. 12),
223–24 (n. 6), 251; technique, 10
Figgy Duff, 100, 205
"Fight for Your Rights," 108; bowing
style, 160; bowing notation to, 162;
notation to, 140
Fighting, 170
Film, 191
Fingering, 89; core configurations, 154;
as term for technique, 41, 152–55
Fishing, 3
"Flying Reel," 93; narrative on, 68–70;
notation to, 120
Folk composition, 262
Folklorism, 202
Folkloristics, x, xi, 37, 202, 216 (n. 1),
220–21 (n. 1), 227 (n. 2), 255–61;
performance and communication
and, 261
Folk medicine, 4, 32
Folk revival, 23–24
Fooling, 33, 178, 181–82. See also
Characterization; Gesture
Foot tapping, 151, 172. See also
Rhythm
"Forgotten Reel," 157
Formulaic composition, 84, 211, 258,
262
Framer, Ingrid, 227 (n. 4)

French language, 2, 17, 156
French Newfoundland, 45
French settlement, 1
French shore, 1

Gale, Don, 220 (n. 14)
Garden party, 167, 169
Gardner, Peter, 205
Garrison, Virginia, 217 (n. 6), 253
Generative: heuristics, 68, 74;
    processes, 85, 262–63. *See also*
    Composition: process; Rammages
"Gerald Thomas's Burnt Potato Reel":
    narrative on, 193–95; notation to,
    142
"Gerry Squires' Palette," 171
Gesture, 178, 184, 201; in performance,
    187, 199. *See also* Characterization;
    Fooling; Narration
Glassie, Henry, 255, 257
Goertzen, Chris, 223 (n. 5), 228 (n. 10)
Goldstein, Kenneth, 220 (n. 14)
Gourlay, Kenneth, 216 (n. 1)
Grammaphone, 17
Grand Falls, 31
"Gravel Pond Reel": narrative on, 169;
    notation to, 114
Guinchard, Rufus, 172, 228 (n. 11)
Guntharp, Matthew, 154
Gzowski, Peter, 190

Hall time performance, 171–74
Hall times, 166–70
Halpert, Herbert, 220 (n. 14)
"Hangman's Reel," 51, 177, 227 (n. 4)
Happiness from music, 61. *See also*
    Music: worldview of
"Happiness Reel": notation to, 119
Hardiness, 30, 170. *See also* Values
Hardship, 27–30
Harmonic relationships, 90–91
Heart, 222 (n. 14)

"Hélène's Reel," 93; narrative on, 136;
    notation to, 136
Henssen, Gottfried, 216 (n. 1)
Herndon, Marcia, 222 (n. 7)
Heuristic devices, 68, 74
Hopkins, Pandora, 225 (n. 3), 227
    (n. 4)
Hornby, James, 219 (n. 10), 223
Hospitality, 25. *See also* Values
House time, 14, 174–77; contemporary,
    190; performance, 174, 175, 177–82
Humor, 32–33, 178–80, 193, 198. *See
    also* Fooling; Personality; Values
Hynes, Ron, 133

Ideas about music, 38, 62
Identity, 21, 45; musical, 16, 209–11
Images of wide scope, 213
Improvisation, 65, 84–85, 86, 219
    (n. 8), 223 (nn. 1, 2); vs.
    composition, 224 (n. 9). *See also*
    Composition
Initial idea: in composition, 67, 71. *See
    also* Composition: process
Injury, 28–29. *See also* Hardiness;
    Hardship; Pain; Personality; Values
Innovation, 19, 66, 89, 103; formal, 74;
    in technique, 152; and tradition, 207
Instrumental: airs, 227 (n. 4); music,
    40
Interpersonal context, 216 (n. 1)
Interpretation, 216 (n. 1)
Intersubjectivity, 35
Interview performance, 190
Irish fiddling, 164, 223–24 (n. 6), 253.
    See also Fiddling: styles
"Irish Washer Woman": comparison
    notation, 73; "1" notation, 144; "2"
    notation, 145
"I's the B'y," 189
"It comes from the heart," 56–57,
    59–60

Ives, Edward, 257

Jarrell, Tommy, 220 (n. 13)
Jig, 156
"Jim Hodder's Reel," 93, 99, 157;
  narrative on and notation to, 129
Jones, Michael Owen, 260–61
Joyal, Jean-Pierre, 255

Kelly, Paul, 228 (n. 5)
"Kelly Russell's Reel": notation to, 130
Kibitzer's Club, 187, 205
"Kibitzer's Reel": bowing style, 160;
  bowing notation to, 162; notation to,
  132
Kitchen times, 15
Knudson, Thorkild, 262
Koning, Jos., 225 (n. 3)
Koskoff, Ellen, 209, 221 (nn. 3, 4)

La Grand Terre, 18
Language, 38, 41
L'Anse á Canards, 1
Learning, 218 (nn. 7, 8), 219 (n. 8),
  222 (n. 13); through apprenticeship,
  208; to fiddle, 6–17; musical, 87–88;
  process, 217 (nn. 5, 6)
Lecture-demonstration performance,
  187
Legend, 46–49
"Le Reel de la Pistroli": notation to,
  132, 157
"Les Marionnettes," 50–51, 177
"Les Sabots": narrative on, 114–15;
  notation to, 115
Life history, 186
Life stories, 26–31
"Lightkeeper's Jig": notation to, 118,
  157
Linguistics, 38
Listening tunes, 227 (n. 4)
"Little Beggerman," 57

Long, Eleanor, 260
Lord, Albert, 219 (n. 9), 224 (n. 9),
  258
Lortat-Jacob, Bernard, 222 (n. 13)
Lourdes, 16
"Lovers' Reel," 101; notation to, 118
"Lucien Florent's Anniversaire":
  notation to, 141

"Madeleine's Glass of Lemon Pie," 71;
  bowing notation to, 163;
  composition, 78–79; fingering to,
  153; narrative on, 137–38; notation
  to, 138. See also "Proto-Lemon Pie"
Mainland, 18
"Making the Curve to Black Duck
  Brook," 70, 171; notation to, 116
"Martin White's": notation to, 130
Marriage, 31–32, 44
McCullogh, Larry, 105
McCulloh, Judith, 227 (n. 4)
McDonald, Jerry, 187
McKinnon, Ian, 253
Media, 20; performance and, 190–92.
  See also Radio; Recording;
  Television; Video
Medley, 101, 108, 115, 171
Melodic: formulas, 218 (n. 8); models,
  263; step motion, 88; triadic motion,
  88
Melodizing, 83–84, 89, 212. See also
  Composition process
Memorial University of Newfoundland
  Folklore and Language Archive, xiii,
  251
Metaphor, 222 (n. 10)
Meter, 93, 160; terminology, 156–57.
  See also Music: and cognition
Methodology, 22–26, 65; fieldwork,
  25–26; rapport, 23. See also
  Research: and relationship with
  Emile Benoit

"Michael T. Wall's Breakdown":
narrative on, 121; notation to, 122;
rhythm, 157
Mode, 154–55. *See also* Fingering;
Music: and cognition; Scale
Modification, 74, 98–99. *See also*
Composition: process
Modulation, 90. *See also* Music: and
transformations
Morgan, Pamela, 134
Motivation, 67, 223 (n. 16). *See also*
Music: worldview of; Personality;
Values
"Motorcycle Club Rally Reel": notation
to, 127, 197
Music: and cognition, xi, 43–44, 103–
4, 209; communities, 104; concepts,
106, 225 (n. 3); features, 88–90;
formulas, 103; genres, 40–41; ideas,
71, 106; inspiration for, 60–61, 224
(n. 6); and knowledge, 106; making,
61; power of, 59; sound as, 39; as
talk, 42, 45, 59, 64; terminology, 38,
42, 221–22 (n. 7); and transformations, 105; vocal, 58; wandering style
of, 74; worldview of, 37, 46, 56, 61,
208–9, 220–21 (n. 1)
Musicianship, x–xi, 6
Musicians' role, 166–68; fiddlers and,
18–19
Musicology, x

Narration, 176, 189, 228 (n. 8); and
fiddle tunes, 227 (n. 4); and fiddling,
192–93; with music, 177–78; style,
182. *See also* Characterization;
Gesture
Narrative, 41, 53
Nash, Dennison, 261
Native theory, 107
"Neil Murray's Dinner Jig," 108;
notation to, 126

Newfoundland fiddling, 205, 251. *See
also* Fiddling: styles
Nielsen, Svend, 263
"Noel's Dinn (Noel Dinn's)," 71;
notation to, 133
North American fiddling, 251–53. *See
also* Fiddling: styles
Nostalgia, 34, 60
Notation, 110
Noticing, 74. *See also* Cognition;
Composition: process; Creativity

Objectivity, 215–16 (n. 1)
O'Doherty, Eamonn, 253
"Oil Fields of Newfoundland," 157
"Old Man and Woman, The," 113;
bowing style, 43–44, 160; notation
to, 161, 177
Oral composition, 84
Ornamentation, 52–53, 66–67, 110;
and bowing, 164
Ornstein, Lisa, 252
Owen, Blanton, 219 (n. 11), 255

Pain, 60. *See also* Injury; Values
"Pamela Morgan's Desire," 98, 107–8;
notation to, 134
Participant observation, x, 222 (n. 7).
See also Methodology
"Part Time Fisherman's Reel," 71;
notation to, 124
Pekkila, Erkki, 221 (n. 3)
Pentikainen, Juha, 221 (nn. 1, 5)
Performance, 166; achieving, 190;
audience interaction, 195–96;
contexts, 16, 20–21; distance, 187;
finances, 188; genres, 201; models, 6,
92, 198–201, 201–2; pace, 189;
practice, 10, 63, 172; public, 167;
roles, 176–77; style and setting,
184–85. *See also* Audience
Perkins, D. N., 73

Schemata, 89, 103, 211. *See also* Composition; Formulaic composition

Scottish fiddling, 17, 164, 171. *See also* Fiddling: styles

Seeger, Charles, 62

Self-presentation, 33, 217 (n. 5)

"Set" tunes, 156. *See also* Dance

Shetland fiddling, 222 (n. 12), 223 (n. 6). *See also* Anderson, Tom; Cooke, Peter; Fiddling: styles

Singing, 9, 40, 172

"Skeleton Reel," 193; narrative, 51–53; notation to, 121

"Sleepy fiddler" story, 179, 180

Sloboda, John, x, 65, 224 (n. 9)

Smith, Christina, 220 (n. 14)

Smith, Gregory, 219 (n. 9), 261–62

Smith, Sandra, 225 (n. 4)

Sneed, Manco, 219 (n. 11)

Sound, 39–40, 60–61, 94, 213; environmental, 70, 123; fiddle, 58–59; mechanical, 68–70, 223 (n. 6), musical, 68–74, 106, 153, 172, 214; object, x, 37; that suits overall composition, 90. *See also* Music

Soundscape, 224 (nn. 6, 10)

Speech analogy, 42. *See also* Music: as talk

Spielman, Earl V., 252

Spirituality, 32, 56, 193; and music, 58. *See also* Values

Square dance, 156

Stage performance, 183, 184, 185; persona, 186

Stekert, Ellen, 216 (n. 1), 221 (n. 5), 259

St. John's, 24–25, 34

Such, David, 222 (n. 10)

Sudnow, David, 218 (n. 8)

Supernatural: belief, 46, 55–56; experience, 30–31

Swackhammer, Robert, 253

Swinden, Scott, 99–100

Szwed, John, 257

Taft, Michael, 220 (n. 14)

Talk about music, 38

Talking bow, 42–43, 161, 164. *See also* Bowing

Teaching, 154, 158, 160; bow technique, 226 (n. 7)

Technique, 106; and context, 182; finger, 74; posture, 151–52. *See also* Bowing

Television, 18, 190–91; as performance influence, 198. *See also* Media

Tempo, 157, 158. *See also* Music: concepts

Thede, Marion, 217 (n. 6)

Thomas, Gerald, 37, 136, 176, 191, 192, 193–94, 199, 216 (n. 3), 220 (n. 14); as manager, 188; transcription, 224–25 (n. 12); and tune titling, 139, 142

Times, 61, 166, 227 (n. 1)

Titling, 68, 94–98, 195–96. *See also* Composition: process; Tune title

Titon, Jeff Todd, 86, 224 (nn. 6, 7), 262

Tonality, 90, 92, 153–54; major and minor, 154–55

Tonic, 155. *See also* Fingering; Music: concepts

"Tootsie Wootsie," 171; narrative on, 195–96

"Torbay Jig": notation to, 139

Tradition: as generative system, 212. *See also* Creativity: and tradition; Innovation: and tradition

Traditionalizing process, 88

Transcription, 158, 224–25 (n. 12); difficulty with, 63; methods of, 215 (n. 1), 216 (n. 3); musical, 109; video, 160–63

Treitler, Leo, 262

Tune family, 66, 105, 223 (n. 5)
Tune models, 102–3. *See also* Schemata
Tune title, 224 (n. 11), 228 (n. 10);
complex, 197; and extra-musical
associations, 97; narratives on, 68,
96; use of, in performance, 97–98,
195, 196–97; sources, 95. *See also*
Titling
Tuning, 172

University of California, Los Angeles,
24

Values, 26–33. *See also* Courage;
Hardiness; Hospitality; Humor;
Spirituality
Variation, 66–67, 87, 110
Veilleé, 175–76; performance, 176
"Velvet in the Wind": notation to,
141–42
Vibrato, 153
Video, 226 (n. 7). *See also* Media;
Television; Transcription; Video
Violin: first purchased, 15; handmade,
11; as source of music, 57; toy, 9–10

Wall, Michael T., 121
Waltz, 157–58
Wareham, Wilfred, 170, 227 (n. 3)
"Wayne and the Bear," 54; narrative on,
146–47; notation to, 147
Weddings, 15
"Wedding Waltz" medley, 57–58, 71;
comparison notation, 72; notation to,
143
Wells, Paul, 252
"West Bay Centre," 171; notation to,
115
Widdowson, John, 220 (n. 14)
"Wild fiddler" story, 180–82
Wilgus, D. K., 227 (n. 4), 262
"Willie Laney's Wedding Jig": bowing
style, 160; notation to, 163
Wolf, John Quincy, 259
"Woodchopper's Reel," 93
Workshop performance, 186–87
Worldview, 220–21 (n. 1). *See also*
Music: worldview of

Zemp, Hugo, 221–22 (n. 7)
Zenger, Dixie, 252